MW01221978

I Did What I Had to Do!

James E. Diamond, Ph.D.

To my Dear Friends Bob
and Clem, I Hope you Enjoy Reading about
our adventures in Chad, Africa as
Peace Corps Volunteers. It was
the Toughest job we ever loved.
Enjoy!

VANTAGEPress
New York

Vantage Press and the Vantage Press colophon
are registered trademarks of Vantage Press, Inc.

FIRST EDITION

Copyright © 2010 by James E. Diamond, Ph.D.

Published by Vantage Press, Inc.
419 Park Ave. South, New York, NY 10016

Manufactured in the United States of America
ISBN: 978-0-533-16325-0

Library of Congress Catalog Card No: 2009912856

0 9 8 7 6 5 4 3 2 1

I dedicate the contents of this book to my dearest wife Elizabeth (Betty) R. Diamond because if she would not have agreed to join the Peace Corps, I would not have been able to "Do What I Had To Do!" Thank you, Betty, for believing in me, supporting me, encouraging me and above all, being a loving and caring wife.

Your loving husband and traveling partner
James E. Diamond (Jim), Author

Contents

Acknowledgments	ix
Introduction	xi

Prologue		1
1.	Gotta Have a Dream!	5
2.	Joining Peace Corps	6
3.	Decision Time	10
4.	Getting Ready	11
5.	Language Training	16
6.	Flight to Fort-Lamy, Chad	23
7.	Culture Jolt	26
8.	"Let's Get Going"	31
9.	Whew! We Finally Arrived	40
10.	Red and White Barriers	46
11.	Ritual of Baya	49
12.	Trimming Horse Hooves	53
13.	"What's a Refrigerator?"	57
14.	Needle and Thread	61
15.	"You've Got Mail"	67
16.	First the Chicken, Then the Egg?	69
17.	"May I Borrow Your Paring Knife?"	78
18.	Cholera Epidemic	80
19.	"Uh Oh!"	82
20.	"Ensilage? What's That?"	83
21.	Death in Its Raw Form	100
22.	Tragic Accident	103

23. "She's Going to Get It One of These Days!" 104
24. Friday Night At the Movies 115
25. Un-erasable Moment 120
26. Lake Chad 124
27. Chadian Hunt 132
28. "There Are No Elephants in Africa!" 139
29. Funeral of President Tombalbye's Brother 142
30. Seesaws and Swings 146
31. Making Rope Halters 151
32. Tragedy Strikes 152
33. Worldwide Peace Corps Budget Cuts 155
34. Fulani People and Zebu Cattle 161
35. Vaccinating Cattle 164
36. Castrating Oxen 169
37. Tick, Tick, Scratch, Scratch 174
38. Zakouma National Park (a.k.a. Parc Zakouma) 176
39. Mbandaka, Zaire 181
40. Rubber Trees 183
41. Why Did Two Peace Corps Volunteers Cross
      the Congo River? 184
42. "Just Cruising Along" 188
43. The Only Time Betty Ever Felt Big and Tall 200
44. "Cinva" Ram Press 205
45. Plow Rentals 208
46. Demonstration Cotton Field 212
47. Why Don't You Use a Long-Handled Hoe? 226
48. Giddy-Up," "Whoa-Haw," "Gee," and "Whoa." 230
49. "Madame. Stop!" 235
50. "Jim, How Do You Stand with the Lord?" 237
51. M. Le Président… 240
52. Arbor Day In Chad 244
53. "Mmmmm Good!" 248
54. Corny Story 255
55. October 20th Bulldozer 256

56. "Was Silage Feasible in Mali?"   262
57. A "Hare" Raising Story   279
58. Took the Ginger Out Of My Snap   284
59. Impoverished! Yet a Proud People   287
60. Departing Chad   289
61. Getting Readjusted   294
62. Modus Operandi   305
63. So Do You Want To Do What You Have To Do?   307

Epilogue   315
References   319
Notes   321
Glossary   323

Acknowledgments

The author is indebted to many agencies and people for their confidence in the Peace Corps mission in Chad. The incredible support provided by Peace Corp/Chad during the process of our developing and implementing various Peace Corps projects for the Chadian people led to writing this book to report outcomes. The author especially recognizes **President Lyndon B. Johnson** for his sensitivity to the needs of rural people in the Republic of Chad and accepting the request from Chad's president to send experts to develop both agricultural practices and home economics skills that would expand rural development in Southern Chad; *President François Tombalbaye* for inviting us to transform traditional agricultural practices to modern cost-effective practices in his homeland, the Republic of Chad and the **United States Peace Corps** for its fantastic support and interests in our efforts as Peace Corps Volunteers in the Republic of Chad.

I also wish to thank **Ambassador Terence Todman** for devoting his time to become involved with Peace Corps Volunteer efforts and outcomes that resulted in expressing strong support to legislators in Washington, DC to stabilize the Peace Corps budget; **Ambassador Edward W. Mulcahy** for his confidence, assurance and interests in our various projects that resulted in expressing kind words about Peace Corps Volunteers; **Charles Steedman**, Director, Peace Corps/Chad (1968-71) for his sincere and determined efforts to recruit us to become Peace Corp Volunteers; **John Riggan**, Director, Peace Corps/Chad (1971-72) for inspiring us to accomplish the Peace Corps/Chad goals and **Baudouin**

de Marcken, Director, Peace Corps/Chad (1972-74) for his committed support and encouragement.

Our gratitude also extends to **Dr. David and Ruth Seymour** for their medical advice and willingness to teach us about the culture, traditions and customs of the Sara Madjingaye people; **Jane Diamond Ross** for her time and dedication in sharing her professional expertise in the English language by assisting with editing this book, and last but certainly not least, **Elizabeth R. Diamond** for encouraging, supporting and inspiring me to take on the mission to write this book that documents our unique, one-of-a-kind life experience as Peace Corps Volunteers.

Introduction

"Why me?" I asked myself this question several times. Why would anyone want the task of poring over rough manuscripts, correcting grammar and looking for punctuation errors when there are more interesting ways to utilize my time? I was not even an English major. My degrees are in Music Education!

When my brother Jim described to me how he wanted to write and publish the stories of his Peace Corps adventures in Africa, I offered to edit them for him. Little did I realize then how complicated this project would be and how involved I would become. We live more than four hundred miles apart. How would we manage the logistics of distance and limited time? I had already gotten very busy with several part-time music positions since my retirement from public school teaching and did not have enough spare time, or so I thought! At any rate, I had made the offer, he had accepted and now I felt obligated to follow through. In the end, there were several long drives to each other's homes and twice we met halfway, spending three days at a time working in a hotel. We spent countless hours reading aloud, changing, omitting, adding, revising and rearranging.

During this year-long process, something magical happened! I became re-acquainted with the older brother who went away to college when I was a mere sixth grader. We did not really know each other then; we were too wrapped up in our own growing-up and there was a seven-year difference in our ages. All of a sudden, here we were, talking, laughing, arguing and working together. We bonded in a new, mature way as brother and sister. What a blessing this renewal and time together has been! Although our career paths and life decisions had led us in different directions, Jim and I discovered how alike we are and how much we were shaped and influenced in similar fashion by our parents. We even make our daily "to do" lists, crossing off each chore as it is completed, the same way our father did. I decided that this reconnecting with each other was the answer to "Why me?" Jim could have asked any of his numerous academic friends to edit this book.

In addition, I learned about life in the bush country of Africa. I learned things which, until now, I did not believe I needed to know: how monkeys are prepared and used as food, how to castrate a bull and the horrible rites of passage into adulthood for young men and women. By the same token, I shared the risks and excitement of crossing the Congo River and the thrill of seeing, for the first time, giraffes, elephants and other animals native to Africa in their natural habitats. I learned about the culture and lifestyle of the people who live there. What an enlightening journey this has been for me!

My hope is that, as you read, you will immerse yourself in the lives and experiences which Jim and his wife Betty had as Peace Corps Volunteers in Chad. I hope you will take with you the important message of how the Peace Corps has impacted one little corner of the world for the better. Perhaps you or someone you know will want to reach out in a similar manner and "do what you have to do."

Jane Diamond Ross
Wadsworth, Ohio
September 2009

I Did What I Had to Do!

Prologue

The world, as I now know it, "is but one nation and humankind its citizens" (author unknown). The world is but one nation under God, and it matters not what deity its citizens adore, worship or obey. In the eyes of their respective god(s), there is neither nationality nor national boundaries. The world has always been one nation, and humankind through the eons has established surface boundaries that launched so-called citizen homelands. Homeland leaders who emerged from ancient times to present day have devised rules and laws which govern themselves, "supposedly" in an orderly fashion. After a long history of conflicts, crusades, campaigns, and wars, many homelands have evolved into what are now perceived as great international world powers. In my opinion such armed conflicts are outdated because powerful world nations who are at odds with their neighbor(s) actually tend to destroy themselves as well. They cause immeasurable environmental plights, enormous trade gaps, and agonizing human suffering. Nine years ago we entered into a new millennium. I would hope that we now live in an age wherein conflicts, crusades, campaigns, and wars become antiquated and that nonviolent means of human endeavors dominate diplomatic negotiations intended to bring about peaceful co-existence in a world that is one nation.

"Those who lose their life for my sake, and for the sake of the gospel, will save it." These words of Jesus, from the book of Mark, 8:11 (King James version of the Holy Bible), may to some seem rather harsh. Many Christian people who live in the western

1

world would interpret this to mean that loss of life is a devastating event. According to my personal religious views and beliefs. I do not think Jesus was speaking only of a bodily life. He was speaking of other ways people can lose their lives in the sight of their contemporaries. For example, let's think about the life of Mother Teresa. Born in Europe, she could have chosen the safe and secure life of a nun in a European convent. But she lost that life when she journeyed to India to explain and demonstrate the love of Christ among the poorest of the poor, the most wretched of the forgotten and ignored. She lost a life of ease but gained a life of profound and fulfilling peacefulness.

When my wife Betty and I decided to go to Africa for the first time, my parents just could not understand why I would want to do such a thing. They envisioned us as having a well-paying and stable employment, buying our farm, and having a rather bright and unwavering future. From that point of view, they were correct. However, if financial security, buying a farm and having an unwavering future was what we were destined to seek, that is what we would have found; but for what reason? What "footprint" would we leave on this earth after our Lord called us home? No, there was more to life than just raising sheep on our farm and teaching agriculture to high school students to pay for a farm. I had to follow a strong compelling inner desire to do agricultural work overseas. I honestly cannot say why that feeling existed but I do know it was real and it had to be fulfilled. We left our safe and secure pastoral lifestyle at Cedar Brook Farm in Ottsville, Pennsylvania and journeyed to Chad to live in a remote village for two years with the poorest of the poor. They lacked running water, electricity, paved roads, medical resources, gas stations, restaurants, theaters, public transportation, and a host of other niceties found in Bucks County, Pennsylvania. Yes, we temporarily lost our secure pastoral lifestyle but we gained the toughest job we ever loved. Like Mother Teresa, we gained a life of profound and fulfilling peacefulness in knowing that we had helped impoverished people help themselves. Hopefully this help would contribute toward improving their quality of life.

During the countless hours it took to produce this book, I had an opportunity to look back and reminisce on an amazing and humbling multi-national travel adventure. This adventure was the alpha of an integral part of my agricultural education career that enabled me to have these happy, sad, humorous, dangerous, rewarding, exciting, interesting, educational, intriguing and humbling experiences. As I endeavored to be of assistance to humankind by augmenting rural agrarian lifestyles, helping people to help themselves was the underlying philosophical foundation that infiltrated the objectives of my "reason to be."

Enjoy your journey into Chad, where I worked and traveled. I hope that as a result of sharing my experiences, you will begin to develop a greater understanding and appreciation for other people in spite of their cultures, customs, traditions, religions, governments, skin colors, or languages. We are what others think of us, and I truly yearn and pray that somewhere along the way, I have been able to make a small contribution to the betterment of humanity because the world is but one nation and humankind its citizens. *Bon voyage.*

1

Gotta Have a Dream!

Too many people have uncultivated existences because they dream of their futures and do not make their dreams come true. Keeping hold of a dream without causing it to convert into a reality idles away the present. In spite of this, everyone should have a dream which is accompanied by the aspiration to cause it to come to pass at some point during his or her respective lives. There is a French expression which best expresses my point; it goes like this *"on doit avoir une raison d'être"* (one must have a reason to be). To acquire the fullest enjoyment and fulfillment from life, everyone *"doit avoir une raison d'être."* Dreams, whatever they may be, cause one to have a reason to be.

Time is such a terrible thing to waste. Benjamin Franklin once said, "Dost thou love life? Then do not squander time, for that is the stuff life is made of." To reassure the mind, wishing to do is the first step toward doing something with time that will cause one to love life. One's dream must be complemented by the strength of character to not squander time. My dreams focused on international endeavors that hopefully would leave behind a legacy, which in some way could benefit humankind, and to leave our planet a better place to live for future generations. It is such a wrongdoing to idle away worthy talents, knowledge and time while there is so much to live for and so many humanitarian needs that can and should be done.

2

Joining Peace Corps

At this point in our lives, the only international experience Betty and I had was a day at Niagara Falls, Canada and half a day in a border town in Mexico across from Brownsville, Texas. This was the extent of our international travels. We were very unworldly and inexperienced at traveling abroad. In those days, young people did not travel as they do today. We were truly domestic natives of the USA.

I had a strong, compelling desire to do agricultural work overseas. I cannot say why, but I do know it existed. Nevertheless that driving inner desire had to be fulfilled. Shortly after President John F. Kennedy formed the Peace Corps in 1961, I graduated from Delaware Valley College (DVC) in Doylestown, Pennsylvania and there began my teaching career. At the same time Betty and I were buying a small farm near Ottsville, Pennsylvania where we began our lives together, raising sheep and hogs on the farm. I was teaching agricultural sciences at DVC, and Betty was working part-time as a bookkeeper for Sears, Roebuck and Company. Throughout the 1960s, that compelling desire to work overseas grew stronger. I had not discussed it much with Betty because I knew she was not very excited about selling our livestock, leaving our farm, leaving her parents, and going off to another land for two years. Neither had I discussed it with my parents because I knew they would never understand why I wanted to do this.

In January 1967 I moved on to a position of teaching agricultural sciences at Upper Bucks County Area Vocational Technical School (UBCAVTS). One day, three years later, I went home and said, "Betty, the time has come when I have to do what I have to do!" Just as I expected, Betty did not get very excited about what I had to do. As fate would have it, the next day I learned that the

Peace Corps recruiter for Northeast United States had traveled to Bucks County from Syracuse, New York, to recruit retired farmers and teachers into the Peace Corps. I met him at school and invited him to our home for dinner and an overnight stay at the farm. This gave Betty an opportunity to talk about some of her concerns and feelings. We had a wonderful visit with him and when he left our home the next morning, two Peace Corps applications were left behind.

Betty knew I was serious about joining the Peace Corps and she was torn as to what she should do. She was concerned about her parents' well-being during a two-year period. Our finances and paying the mortgage during our absence were on her mind. She worried about having to learn another language, she was afraid of getting sick overseas and the list went on and on. Many of her concerns were valid and I shared some of her concerns and anxieties. If we were to join, we had many decisions to make before we could leave for two years.

In February 1970, I completed my application and laid it on top of my desk. During that chapter of my life, I was a part-time professional sheep-shearer. Sheep-shearing season normally began the first week of April and lasted until the second week of June. I would routinely shear some 2,000 head of sheep annually throughout Bucks and neighboring counties. During the annual sheep-shearing season, I taught school all day, then sheared sheep in the evenings, on weekends and holidays. When the 1970 shearing season was finished, I said to Betty, "Why don't you fill out your Peace Corps application and let's submit it to see what they have to offer us as a team? We can always say no or reapply some other time." Reluctantly, she filled out her application and toward the end of June we sent them to the Peace Corps/Washington, DC.

By August 1970, we had heard nothing from Peace Corps/Washington. I was getting somewhat unnerved because school was about to start. If we were going to be joining the Peace Corps and temporarily leaving the area, I needed to inform my director and make sure there was ample time for him to search for my replacement before our departure. I asked Betty to telephone Peace Corps/Washington to inquire about the status of our applications.

When Betty called, the person who answered was very accommodating and promptly found our applications. She said, "Because of your age, vast agricultural and home economics experiences, plus Jim's ten years of teaching agriculture, your applications were placed into a special file because they didn't want Peace Corps to stick you into a rice paddy somewhere." She told Betty that our applications were undoubtedly being set aside for a special assignment.

On the following Tuesday, we were preparing to host several dinner guests at our farmhouse when the telephone rang. I took the call in my upstairs study. It was Charley Steedman, Director, Peace Corps/Chad. After a bit of introductory chitchat, Charley asked if Betty and I would be interested in working as Peace Corps Volunteers in Chad, Africa. I had never heard of Chad. Because of my being so unworldly and naive, I thought he said shad, a popular game fish in the nearby Delaware River. That's what I heard when Charley said "Chad." Charley said he was returning to Chad on Thursday of that week and he wanted to meet with Betty and me the next day. Was it possible for us to travel to Washington, DC? I called for Betty to come to the bottom of the stairs and there I told her it was Peace Corps calling and Mr. Steedman wanted us to travel to Washington, DC tomorrow to be interviewed. This really got Betty's attention and she reluctantly said, "Okay." That evening we made our airline arrangements to fly to Washington, DC on Wednesday afternoon.

We arrived at what was then called Washington National Airport. We hailed a taxi and went directly to the Peace Corps Office. When we arrived at 2:30 P.M., Charley Steedman and a delegation of Peace Corps officials were awaiting our arrival. We immediately went into an office and the interview process began. Betty and I were interviewed until 10:00 P.M. A psychologist, an economist, a sociologist, the Peace Corps/Chad Director, and a Peace Corps recruiter interviewed us intensely. We stayed overnight in a hotel and we were interviewed again in the morning beginning with a 7:00 breakfast, until 11:00 A.M. Betty and I assumed that all Peace Corps Volunteers went through such an interview process. We were later told that it was due to the sensitivity of the assignment.

Chad's president, François Tombalbaye, made a state visit to Washington, DC in 1968 and he personally asked President Johnson to send an agricultural specialist and home economist to his home village. President Johnson gave this request to Joe Blantchford, the Director of Peace Corps at the time, to search for qualified, preferably married, volunteers. Peace Corps had searched for one-and-one-half years for a husband-and-wife team with the credentials that Betty and I had. When Charley found our applications, he said, "Where have these applications been? I've been looking for a married couple with these credentials for a long time."

Shortly before we left for the airport, Charley Steedman called us into his office and there he made Betty and me the offer to work in Chad as Peace Corps Volunteers. He wanted us to think it over and let him know.

Wow! We were accepted for a special Peace Corps assignment! How cool was that! But now it was up to Betty and me to make up our minds. As anxious as I was to go and as reluctant as Betty was not to go, we decided to take one month to settle down, think this opportunity through, and then make the decision to go or to not go. We would inform Peace Corps of our decision by 1 October 1970.

3

Decision Time

In September I started my normal teaching schedule at school. Our ongoing decision making process included talking it over with friends and colleagues whom we held in high esteem and those who had experience living abroad. In the meantime, we began to receive word from our references that the FBI had interviewed them asking what they knew about Betty and Jim Diamond. Because of the diplomatic sensitivity of the assignment, Peace Corps required us to have a security background check. Betty was not yet convinced we should go to Chad. However she was beginning to show some interest. She needed some time to be alone to think and reflect about this drastic change in her lifestyle as a homemaker. She would go for long walks along our Rapp Creek. Finally, Betty decided that if she was going to keep her husband and keep him happy, she should accompany him.

If Betty were to make the decision to go to Chad, we would have many logistical decisions to make. We were buying a farm and had mortgage obligations. We had a first-rate flock of sixty registered Suffolk sheep. Betty's parents lived alone in Doylestown. What were we to do with our vehicles? Who would do our income taxes? The list went on and on. The farmhouse with the furniture could be leased. Our personal belongings could be placed in boxes and stored in the farmhouse attic. We hoped that the new tenants would keep Duchess, our Border collie dog, because she was so well-trained in working sheep. We could use the rent money to pay our mortgage, insurance, and upkeep of the house. With the money we could get from selling the sheep, a half-ton pickup truck, a sedan, and a small tractor, we could pay off our other loans. A very dear friend offered to keep our financial records free of charge during our stay in Chad. If we implemented everything we discussed, we would be able to better enjoy our new adventure and not be worrying about our affairs in Ottsville, Pennsylvania. It just seemed that everything might fall into place as if this endeavor were supposed to happen.

4

Getting Ready

After Betty made her decision to go to Chad, we began making decisions to prepare for a two-year absence from our home, known as Cedar Brook Farm. The first week of October I gave a letter to the director at school informing him of our decision and requesting a two-year leave of absence without pay. The school board reluctantly disallowed my request and I had no choice other than to resign. So I tendered my resignation, to be effective 27 January 1971, exactly four years to the day after I began teaching there.

In October 1970 we sold our flock of registered Suffolk sheep to local people. We decided to keep six of our finest Suffolk ewe lambs, sired by the Richard R. Roe ram from St. Ansgar, Iowa. We signed an agreement with the shepherd at nearby Erdenheim Farms, whereby he would have custody of the ewes and have them bred. The lamb crops for 1971–1973 would belong to him as remuneration for keeping the ewes for us. When we returned back from Chad to Cedar Brook Farm in 1973, he was to return the original six ewes. Those six ewes would be seed stock to re-establish our flock of sheep.

Peace Corps wanted Betty and me to begin our French training as soon as possible because it was crucial that we be able to speak French fluently. Each of us was authorized to enroll for thirty one-hour French lessons at the nearest Berlitz School prior to our departure in January. Beginning in early November 1970, Betty and I traveled to Berlitz Language School at Abington, Pennsylvania weekly for our three consecutive one-hour French lessons. We participated in these lessons for ten weeks. We learned vocabulary but the lessons ended just when we were beginning to put words into sentences.

In November we sold our pickup truck and Farmall A tractor. I hated to part with that tractor, but I didn't want any vehicles sitting around the farm for two years. In December we struck a deal with Keystone Motors in Doylestown. We agreed that they would purchase our car and we could use it up until the day we departed for Chad. Our car was only two years old with low mileage and whoever would purchase that car would get a good deal because there was a lot of life left in it. We didn't want any vehicles stored at the farm because in addition to depreciating, the engines would become gummed up and that would ultimately lead to all kinds of repairs. They could also be stolen or, if there were a fire, we would lose them.

We used the money we received from the sale of our sheep and vehicles to pay off loans at Doylestown Federal Savings Bank and Bucks County Bank. It was such a relief to be free of these obligations before our departure.

Two weeks before we were to depart, we still had not rented our farmhouse. We were being very fussy as to whom we would lease it to, while at the same time we were concerned about getting it rented on time. While I was in Plumsteadville for a haircut, I was telling my barber, Dave Nagorski, that I still had not rented our farmhouse. As fate would have it, he was looking for a house and expressed an interest in renting it. I described the conditions to him and spoke about keeping our dog. I knew Dave well and was confident he would be a trustworthy tenant. I told him to let us know soon if he wanted to rent the house. One week before our departure, Dave phoned us and told us he wanted to rent our home and that he would be happy to look after Duchess for us. It was agreed that we would leave our basic furniture in the house for Dave to use, and we would put our personal belongings in boxes and store them in the attic. We were so relieved that we had found an acceptable person to rent our house.

It was agreed that the monthly rent money would be sent to Doylestown Federal Savings Bank to be deposited directly into our account. The bank officials knew us and they agreed to deduct from our account at no charge the monthly mortgage and our real estate and school taxes.

Betty's father agreed to look after our place while we were gone and would do any needed repairs. We gave the bank authorization to allow him to withdraw money from our account for repairs to the house or outbuildings if needed.

Our very dear friend Earl Dieffenbach had taught Betty and me how to keep financial records and do our farm income taxes. Earl generously agreed to keep our records free of charge while we were away in Chad.

It just seemed that everything fell into place as if this adventure were meant to happen. People in our community were so cooperative and supportive of our decision to devote two years as Peace Corps Volunteers in Chad. By this time, as our plans were falling into place, Betty was finally becoming excited about our new adventure.

The week between Christmas 1970 and New Year 1971 my parents traveled more than three hundred miles from Smithfield, Pennsylvania (Fayette County) to visit us at our farm in Bucks County before we departed to serve in the Peace Corps. On Sunday, after we attended the Doylestown United Methodist Church, we invited Betty's parents to come to the farm and have lunch with us. That particular lunch was a very special time, having both sets of parents visit us in our home. This would be the last time we would be together for at least two years. While we were having our lunch the telephone rang. It was Helen Nast, a reporter for the *Delaware Valley News*. She asked if she could come to visit Betty and me for an interview for a story about our forthcoming Peace Corps assignment. I said, "Helen we would be happy to do an interview. Can you come this afternoon? Both Betty's and my parents are here at the farm and perhaps they could be part of the interview." Helen said, "I can be there in half an hour."

When she arrived, we introduced her to our parents and, after some introductory chitchat, she began interviewing Betty and me. As we were being interviewed, both our parents were listening to what was being said with keen interest. After the interview was completed, Helen turned to Betty's mother and father and asked, "What do you think about Betty and Jim going to Chad?" They gave her a brief but supportive statement that was flavored with a tad of reluctance. But overall, they gave us much encouragement and supported our decision. Helen turned to my parents and asked the same question. My father, who was both a coal miner and farmer, had the reputation of speaking his mind with little finesse. He responded with a very bigoted racial comment laced with profanity. Betty and I were absolutely stunned! I was so embarrassed, offended and aghast that my father would even think let alone make such a statement, especially to a newspaper reporter at a time when the civil rights movement across America was at its apex. I asked Helen if she would please ignore that statement and not print it in the newspaper. Helen was a sensitive person and did not print it. Dad just could not bring himself to accept the fact that his elder son was going to Africa to help people. Needless to say that was the last time we asked him his opinion about us going to Africa. A week later the *Delaware Valley News* published a very inspiring article about us going to Chad.

My last day of work at Upper Bucks County Area Vocational-Technical School was 27 January 1971. Both Betty and I had anxieties because the time was very near for our departure. We were to meet other Peace Corps Trainees at the Sylvania Hotel in Philadelphia by mid-afternoon on Saturday, 28 January 1971. For several days Betty's parents helped her pack boxes for storage in the attic, clean the house, install new locks and doorbell, pack our suitcases for traveling, and many other tasks. We very much appreciated their helping Betty get ready for departure.

Finally we loaded our packed suitcases into our car on 28 January 1971, said goodbye to Duchess, and drove our car to Keystone Motors in Doylestown. There Betty's parents met us and we transferred everything into their car. We left our car there as we had previously agreed and the Rohrmans (Betty's parents) drove us to the Sylvania Hotel in Philadelphia. Upon our arrival we unloaded our suitcases, but I suddenly realized I left my briefcase in our car at Keystone Motors in Doylestown. All of our necessary documents were in that briefcase. Betty's father immediately departed for Doylestown. He went to Keystone Motors, got the briefcase out of the car and brought it back to the hotel in Philadelphia that evening. In the briefcase were our passports, dental x-rays, fingerprints, and all of our Peace Corps documents. What a way to begin a two-year saga. Then we said our goodbyes and joined the other Peace Corps trainees by introducing ourselves and becoming part of the group which was headed for St. Thomas, Virgin Islands for our French language training the next day. We mingled and made conversation with our new friends. There were about forty trainees, including Betty and me, traveling to St. Thomas, where we would receive twelve weeks of French language training prior to departing for our respective assigned countries. Some were going to Upper Volta (now known as Burkina Faso), Guinea, Congo, Republic of Zaire (now known as Democratic Republic of Congo) and Republic of Mali. Betty and I were the only two going to Republic of Chad.

At the Sylvania Hotel, we were vaccinated for smallpox, cholera and yellow fever. That evening we were free and didn't particularly want to spend it at the hotel. So we telephoned our dear friends George and Barbara Perry who lived across the Delaware River in nearby Cherry Hill, New Jersey. We asked them if they would like some company. We always liked to play pinochle with George and Barbara, so they drove to Philadelphia and picked us up at the hotel. We went to their home in Cherry Hill and there we visited and played pinochle until nearly midnight for the last time before departing for our two-year adventure. When George took us back to the hotel, the weather was beginning to get ugly.

On Sunday morning, 29 January 1971, there was an ice storm and the conditions outside were rather treacherous. It was windy and the temperature was a little below freezing. The streets and roads were icy and there were some questions as to whether our flight would be delayed. Nevertheless we gathered up our luggage and checked out of the hotel to be transported to the Philadelphia International Airport for departure.

5

Language Training

Our flight was able to depart Philadelphia as scheduled. We flew to San Juan, Puerto Rico where we deplaned and had a two-hour layover before our flight to St. Thomas, Virgin Islands. Before we boarded the plane, we had to be weighed. Now this was a trip! Our luggage had to be taken in another airplane because the aircraft could not carry the weight of twenty passengers plus the luggage! The plane could seat only twenty people, one single row of ten seats on each side of the aisle. As we were taking off, the steward stood in front, in back of the pilot, and over a crackling microphone, gave us our instructions in event of an emergency. He pointed to the emergency exits, said our life jackets were under the seat, and showed us how to get them out and inflate them. He then said, "If you can't get your life jackets out or inflated, do not worry about it because the sharks will get you anyway." That was really encouraging, especially for two greenhorn travelers.

The flight across the Caribbean was absolutely beautiful. The water was crystal-clear and as blue as blue could be. The skies had puffy white clouds, and occasionally tiny green uninhabited islands would appear in the blue Caribbean waters, a sight that will forever be embedded in our minds.

We arrived at the Truman Airport in Charlotte Amalie, St. Thomas one hour later. Neither Betty or I had ever been that far from Ottsville, Pennsylvania. We were really excited but had some anxieties about our luggage. At the airport the Peace Corps Training Director greeted us and told us not to worry about our luggage. It would ultimately arrive at the camp. We all boarded a bus and were transported to the Peace Corps Training Center at Estate Mandahl. Estate Mandahl was once an old Conservation Corps Camp converted into a Peace Corps Training Center.

We were all assigned our living quarters on the side of a steep mountain. Rooms for married couples were in the top row, which meant there were fifty-one steps up to our room. It also meant fifty-one steps down to the ablution block (showers and toilets). Our room had neither windows or electricity, just screened windows since the day and night temperatures were quite comfortable but unpredictable.

We began to feel like pincushions after receiving so many precautionary injections. In addition to the injections we received in Philadelphia, we received a series of rabies shots, tuberculosis, typhoid, tetanus, plague and more. We were very thankful that the Peace Corps officials were taking steps to protect our health while we were in Chad.

While getting acclimated to living in a Training Camp, our schedule for the first couple of days was somewhat loose and we had some free time. So Betty and I walked to Megans Bay Beach for the first time. We walked across the mountain in front of Peace

Corps Training Center to Megans Bay. Wow! When we arrived at the top of the mountain, we looked down onto the blue Caribbean Sea. We saw white sand, a rocky beach and heard a constant crashing of large waves slapping against coral rocks. What a beautiful sight to behold!

On Sunday we were in an ice storm in Philadelphia and on Monday we were swimming and basking in the sun on the sand at Megans Bay Beach. "Life was tough but someone had to do it." It was only a forty-five-minute walk from camp and during the twelve weeks we lived at Estate Mandahl studying French, we visited Megans Bay many times, especially on weekends.

The next day we walked twelve kilometers each way to and from Charlotte Amalie. When one stood on top of the mountain looking down onto the coast at Charlotte Amalie, the town had a unique beauty, with its port crowded with huge tourist ships, the Blue Beard Hotel nestled on the far mountainside, buildings crammed next to each other on narrow streets, and small leisure boats and fishing vessels sprinkled over the blue Caribbean. However, we soon learned that when there was a tourist ship docked in Charlotte Amalie, we would change our minds and not go down the mountain into town. The narrow streets were very crowded with tourists in their straw hats, Bermuda shorts, sunglasses, and flowered shirts. They were so rude, rowdy, and inconsiderate of others. Once I asked a merchant, after observing how a tourist from Europe had treated her very impolitely, "Why do you put up with people like him?" She replied, "Because tourists are our only industry and we need their business."

We began our French classes full-time on Wednesday with a schedule that left little time for exploring the island during the week. Most of our instructors were from French-speaking Africa and spoke only French, so we really had to concentrate. Our daily schedule from Monday through Saturday noon for 12 weeks was as follows:

7:00–7:45 A.M.	French Class #1
8:00–8:45 A.M.	Breakfast (only French)
9:00–9:45 A.M.	French Class #2
10:00–10:45 A.M.	French Class #3
11:00–11:45 A.M.	French Class #4
12:00 noon	Lunch (only French)
1:00–3:00 P.M.	Free time (study French)
3:00–3:45 P.M.	French Class #5
4:00–4:45 P.M.	French Class #6
5:00–5:45 P.M.	French Class #7
6:00–6:45 P.M.	Dinner (only French)
7:00–9:00 P.M.	Cross-Culture Class

There were only three to five people in a class and the focus was on learning how to speak the French language. Each class had a different instructor from a different country because Peace Corps wanted us to learn to hear the different accents. One learned how to read French almost automatically, but writing was another issue. I never did become very proficient in writing French.

One instructor was from Wisconsin and her name was Katie. She was really a beautiful and well-endowed young lady about twenty-four years of age. She was teaching us what to say when one is introduced to someone for the first time. She said to me, "Jim, I'm going to introduce you to my sister, and I want to hear your response." She said, "*M. Diamond, j'ai l'honneur de vous presenter ma soeur, Mlle. Smith.*" (Mr. Diamond, I have the honor of presenting to you my sister Miss Smith.) My response was, "*Je suis tres heureux à faire votre soeur.*" Katie and the others suddenly and uncontrollably laughed while I sat there and watched them howling and not knowing why they were laughing. Finally, after they got control of themselves and wiped the tears from their eyes, Katie asked, "Jim, do you know what you said?" I responded, "Katie, obviously I didn't say the right thing." Katie said, "Jim instead of saying 'I am very happy to make the acquaintance of your sister,' you said, 'I would be happy to make your sister.'" Woe is me!

The trainees who were preparing to travel to the Republic of Mali were known as the Poultry Team. They had two components to their training, language and poultry husbandry. One of the poultry husbandry hands-on activities was to hatch a batch of fertile eggs and raise the chicks to market weight. Nearly none of these trainees had ever been near a live chicken, yet they were going to Mali to teach people how to grow chickens. A retired poultry-husbandry professor from University of California/San Luis Obispo was contracted by Peace Corps to teach these trainees how to raise chickens. Some of these trainees had little interest in learning how to grow chicks, let alone being sent to another country to teach people how to raise them. This is not to say they could not be successful, it just seemed odd that they were selected to teach poultry husbandry with no previous experience. It seemed to me that these trainees had another agenda as to why they joined the Peace Corps. At the time, this was one of the issues I found puzzling, why Peace Corps recruited people who had little or no background in what they were being sent to their country site to teach. The poultry program was just one example.

Toward the end of their program, the chicks had grown to about three kilograms live weight. One of the lessons the trainees had to learn was how to kill a chicken, pluck its feathers, remove the pin feathers, clean the viscera from the carcass, wash it, and cut it into halves. When the half chickens were put into the cooler their task was finished. To promote their poultry training achievements, the next step was to sponsor a chicken barbecue for the entire Peace Corps Training Camp. However there was a problem, no one knew how to barbecue chickens.

Because Betty and I had much experience barbecuing chickens for Barger's Chicken Shop in Doylestown, Pennsylvania, we volunteered to coordinate the barbeque. To barbeque one hundred half-chickens, we needed a double metal frame. To improvise, we found two metal beds with metal springs. To lighten the frame we detached all of the unnecessary parts and used the flat part of the bed frame. Betty showed the Mali trainees how to make the sauce with butter, salt, pepper, and water. We got Peace Corps to purchase a new fly sprayer that was to be used to spray the sauce onto the chickens while over the fire. This event took place on Mandahl Beach. We built a pit using rocks found on the beach that were wide and long enough to hold the frame. We loaded the frame with rows of left chicken halves and rows of right halves. The chicken halves were placed rather tightly because in the cooking process, they tend to shrink a bit, plus, it was easier to turn the frame. We put three bags of charcoal in the pit, and we were ready. After the coals were white, we lifted the loaded frame onto the rocks over the fire. Every four to five minutes we would turn the frame and spray on the sauce. After about an hour, we checked to determine if they were cooked by turning a leg bone; if it was free and loose, the chicken was done. It was time to take the bronze-colored barbecued chickens off the fire, form a queue at the table and let the meal begin. Betty's sauce was a hit because it really gave the chicken a good flavor.

This whole event took place with the sun setting over the Caribbean at Mandahl Beach at the water's edge. What a glorious spectacle. The event was a resounding success and everyone seemed to enjoy the chicken and have a good time.

My agricultural experiences and knowledge base were focused on husbandry practices in the northern temperate zone. I had no tropical agriculture experience. Peace Corps decided to send me to the University of Puerto Rico at San Juan to meet with professors to begin learning a basic understanding of tropical agronomic and animal husbandry practices. Betty and I flew to San Juan and there we met with professors at the University. The first day was very interesting and useful. However, I could only use one of the three days scheduled at the University. The next two days were Puerto Rican holidays and the University was closed. Hence, that was the end of my formal orientation. While touring the sites of Puerto Rico for two days, I did a self-study to observe tropical agriculture in rural areas. What I observed reinforced what I learned at the University the day before. My tropical agriculture orientation was certainly insufficient, but at least it was a starting point that stimulated my interests to learn more.

Learning French was a demanding and challenging task for Betty and me. Language seemed to come easily to some of the younger Peace Corps Trainees, but it did not come easily with us. Even though we both had our frustrations, Betty seemed to grasp parts of the language better than I did. Every free moment we had we studied and practiced speaking our French. We studied at the beach, in our room, in the Peace Corps dining room and at the Bistro. We made up our minds we were going to learn the language because in Chad, our daily communications and activities with the people would hinge on our ability to speak French. We had no choice but to learn it. After twelve weeks of intensive studies, both Betty and I were able to communicate quite well. By this time Betty was much more excited about going to Chad. We also had a good experience with Peace Corps at this point and we were confident that Peace Corps would give us the support we needed. There were still many unknowns such as our project mission, living quarters and in-country transportation that caused us both to have anxieties. We departed St. Thomas, Virgin Islands for Fort-Lamy (a.k.a. N'djamena), Chad via Paris, France on 27 March 1971.

6

Flight to Fort-Lamy, Chad

After completing the three-month intensive French-language-training program at St. Thomas, we were cleared to depart for Chad, to begin our work as Peace Corps Volunteers. Flight connections to other parts of the world from Charlotte Amalie, St. Thomas, Virgin Islands meant first flying to San Juan, Puerto Rico. Because we couldn't get reservations out of San Juan, we were on standby for a flight from San Juan to Philadelphia, Pennsylvania. We traveled to Philadelphia because Betty developed a dental issue that needed attention from her dentist in Doylestown before going to Chad. We were elated when our names were called to board for Philadelphia.

After two days, we departed Philadelphia for JFK International Airport in New York where we were instructed by Peace Corps to pick up our passports with the visas at the airline ticketing counter. It was a Sunday and when we arrived at the airline ticket counter, as fate would have it, no one could find our passports. We could not depart JFK even though we had already checked our six pieces of luggage. The luggage went on to Paris without us. Betty and I found a cheap hotel room near JFK and there we stayed until the airline called us on Monday. Finally, shortly before noon, we got a telephone call from the airline informing us they had found our passports and we could now depart for Paris. When we arrived at the ticket counter, we were told that the passports had been found in a drawer to the right of the attendant at the counter. We departed JFK International Airport with our passports and visas thinking we would never again see our luggage that contained all the "stuff" we needed for two years.

After a delightful flight to Paris, our first trip to Europe, we arrived at the Charles de Gaulle International Airport on 26 April

1971. Being neophyte international travelers, we went through customs just like everyone else. We followed the signs to luggage claim. When we arrived, much to our surprise, stacked in the middle of the floor were all six pieces of our luggage. What a wonderful welcome to Paris! Betty and I were overjoyed that we had found our luggage in the middle of the floor with no security overseeing its safety. Anyone could have walked away with that luggage and no one would have suspected they were stealing it. Now we felt a whole lot better.

We took a taxi from the Charles de Gaulle Airport into Paris nearly to our hotel. However, we did not have an accurate address. So we paid the driver and I went to a policeman standing on a corner of the street to ask directions using my newly learned accented French language. I asked him how to find this particular hotel. Wow! He understood me! What a great feeling, that I was able to communicate with a person with my newly learned French language and he actually understood me! This was for real. There was no one nearby to help me if I got stuck for a word. The policeman gave me directions and I understood his directions. I really felt good about that experience.

After we settled into our hotel, we went to sleep for a few hours after flying all night. We had to adjust from jet lag and the time change. We walked around late that afternoon and because we had no lunch we decided to have an early dinner. That's when we learned our next French lesson. French restaurants do not begin serving food until after 7:00 P.M. and some even later. We finally found a small pizza shop open, so we had a piece of pizza for dinner and then we returned to our hotel room for a good night's rest. That's when we learned French lesson number three. We learned that taking a shower in a French hotel was not like taking a shower in our farmhouse at Ottsville. There was a tiny slot in the corner with a curtain and a showerhead on the end of a metal hose. The water was lukewarm and there was very little space for moving.

The next morning Betty and I got up early to experience

our first day in Paris. We were really excited about this event. A "thumbnail sketch" of our memorable day included *petit dejeuner* (breakfast) with *café au lait* and *beignet* (coffee with milk and deep-fried dough) in the hotel. It was an absolutely glorious cool day as we began our trek on foot across Paris wearing winter apparel. We walked down the Champs-Élysees to *L'Arc de Triomphe* (Arch of Triumph), walked along the Seine River and crossed it to visit *La Tour Eiffel* (Eiffel Tower), on to *Les Invalides* (Tomb of Napoleon). Oh my, what a day! When we were at *L'Arc de Triomphe*, all I could think of was the picture in my mind of Adolph Hitler walking under the *Arc* during World War II and there I stood, at that very spot where that evil person once walked. It was an unimaginable experience! We ended this glorious and extraordinary day by having an evening dinner at a French restaurant at 8:30.

The next morning we checked out of the hotel and departed for Orly International Airport for a nonstop flight to Fort-Lamy, Chad. We had no problems getting a shuttle bus to the airport, obtaining our boarding pass or going through customs. We did have a moment of anxiety when the airline ticket agent told me we were being charged a large sum of money for the excess weight of our luggage. We were authorized by Peace Corps to take an extra eighteen kilograms of excess luggage each to Chad. However the problem evolved in the way the numbers seven and one are written in French. The appearance of seven as written in English is a one in French. The number seven in French has a line drawn across the stem of the number. This event distressed me somewhat because now there was a debate in French over the weight allowed for our luggage. Finally after consulting with a number of supervisors, the ticketing agent allowed our luggage to be checked in. This event was an excellent test of my newly learned French language.

7

Culture Jolt

After we departed Orly International Airport outside Paris, Betty and I settled back for a long night flight to Fort-Lamy, Chad. We now had anxieties as to what our new experiences would entail. We arrived at Fort-Lamy, the capital of Chad, at 4:00 A.M. on 29 April 1971. Just before we landed Betty asked, "What will we do if there is no one there to meet us?" That was a good question, but I said to her, "Just hang loose until we deplane, then we'll see what happens next."

We deplaned wearing winter apparel; it was very hot compared to the cool temperatures of Paris. As we walked across the tarmac, we heard a voice bellow "Diamonds?" from the upper balcony affixed to the outside of the terminal. We looked up, and there stood two people waving at us. Wow, were we delighted to see them! We waved back and continued our trek across the tarmac.

We entered the terminal carrying a camera, a tape recorder and a short-wave radio in addition to our carry-on luggage. Before we got to the window with our passports, this strange man said, "My name is Dr. Morey, I work for the Peace Corps...." He grabbed our gear and handed it to another strange person named Dick Wall. He said, "You won't be able to get these through customs; we'll keep them until you get through." At that moment I wondered if they really did work for the Peace Corps. This all happened so quickly. After waiting for a long time we finally got to a window to show our passports. All the people in front of us had been questioned and searched. This same Dick Wall came to the window and said to the Chadian customs agent, "*Monsieur et Madame Diamond travaillent pour le President Tombalbaye.*" (Mr. and Mrs. Diamond work for President Tombalbaye.) The customs agent took our passports, stamped them and said, "*Bienvenue au Tchad*" (Welcome to Chad), with no questions or searches. We were now in Chad with "nooo" problem.

Dick Wall and Dr. Morey, the Peace Corps doctor, accompanied us to where we claimed our luggage and helped us load it into a Peace Corps Land Rover and together we drove through Fort-Lamy to the Peace Corps Hostel.

Upon our arrival at the hostel, Dick Wall knocked on the door several times until finally the guard unlocked and opened the door. There was a mud brick wall about three meters high surrounding the hostel and stuck fast on top were countless broken bottles sticking up to cut the hands of any thief who attempted to enter. As we entered into the compound, we felt like fugitives in the night, so different from when we were in Paris. We were escorted to a small stuffy room. In it were a bed, a clean sheet, a small lamp, a mosquito net hanging over the bed, a lantern, a flashlight, a small fan and no window. We had no choice but to stack our suitcases in a corner. To get a little air moving I turned on the fan. All Betty and I wanted to do was lie down, stretch out and sleep. We were exhausted from the trip and the stress of experiencing an entirely new environment. Dr. Morey asked if we were feeling all right. He was concerned about our health. He told us to take it easy in the morning and at our leisure, walk over to the Peace Corps office. Dick Wall said, "Do you think you know how to find the Peace Corps office?" From what Dick Wall and Dr. Morey showed us on the way the hostel in the dark, I thought I knew and said, "Sure, we'll find it." Betty and I didn't get out of bed until 9:00 and the temperature was already over 100 degrees Fahrenheit. We lounged a bit in the hostel living room, then Betty made some coffee and we had a snack for our *petit dejeuner*. We felt perfectly safe in our new environment, but we had a sensation that there was a mysterious force pulling us downward. To this day this sensation is still an unexplained phenomenon. We decided to begin our trek to the Peace Corps Office to visit with Charley Steedman, Dick Wall and

Dr. Morey. Betty asked, "Are you sure you know the way?" Why of course I knew the way. Wrong!

As we began our morning walk to the Peace Corps Office, instead of making a left and a right, we made two right turns. We walked and walked, but in the wrong direction. It was hot. Yep, we were lost. Betty reached a point where she could no longer walk in that heat. One of the few taxis in Fort-Lamy approached and I was able to get him to stop. He had never heard of the Peace Corps Office, but he knew where the American Embassy was located. I said, "Okay, take us to the American Embassy." The Peace Corps Office was behind the Embassy. Finally we arrived at the American Embassy and we walked to the Peace Corps Office. What a relief it was to enter the air-conditioned office. Betty's face was fire-engine red. Dr. Morey came by and saw her condition and was quite concerned about her well-being. Once Betty sat down, drank some water and rested a bit, she was okay.

Even though we were lost in Fort-Lamy, we experienced a difference in culture to which we were not accustomed. The people were dressed differently; they wore long creamy white garments and white skullcaps or white turban-like head coverings. Most of the people spoke the Arabic language, which we did not understand. Many children were half-dressed, nearly naked or naked as they played or worked. We observed several beggars begging money to buy food. One's heart was certainly touched when a beggar asked for money. Some were missing a limb, some were blind or crippled by whatever disease. There were lepers who were malformed at birth and there were beggars who just wanted money because they were destitute. However, we were taught that we should not give money to beggars because the local people were not very proud that there were so many beggars and giving them money encouraged them to beg instead of earning their money.

The shops were small mud brick structures with their wares (e.g. pots, pans, clothing, charcoal, lanterns, rope) displayed outside the open door. The dusty streets were dirt and full of potholes. There were several donkeys pulling carts laden with charcoal or dried grass to be sold. Most of the people walked or rode bicycles or motorcycles or in the back of a *Comby* (pickup truck). There were a few who could afford cars. There were huge cargo trucks loaded with heavy cargo, jam-packed with people riding on top for a fee. We were astonished to see men bearing long wooden poles across their shoulders behind their necks with their arms slung over the poles to hold them in place. At each end of a pole there was a short rope attached to a bucket full of water, or bundles of dried grass, or woven baskets full of fruit or other possessions as they slowly trudged along to their destination.

People were everywhere bartering their goods. The vendor's persistent salesmanship was to be admired. Whether they were selling fruit, vegetables or cigarettes, vendors would follow potential customers long distances all the while trying to persuade them to buy their wares. The smell of open sewage in trenches along the street edges was offensive, at least to us. Then there was a fragrance of dried smoked fish smothered with flies intermingled with the sewage odor. The temperature was hot and we had just come off the plane from Paris where temperatures were quite cool. To Betty and me, experiencing the sounds, the smells, the sights and the sensation of being in a new culture so far from home was a humbling event.

At noon Dick Wall took Betty and me to *Hôtel Tchadian* for lunch. Whoa! After a long all night flight to Fort-Lamy and part of the night in the Peace Corps Hostel, going to the *Hôtel Tchadian* was like going from the ridiculous to the sublime. It was an absolutely gorgeous hotel overlooking the Chari River. There we were, sitting in very comfortable white metal chairs at a white table under a broad white umbrella at the edge of a beautiful swimming pool, sipping a cold Gala beer, watching goats walking around eating nibbles of food under the tables. While waiting for our beef shish-ka-bobs to be delivered by a smartly dressed waiter in white garbs, I looked across the Chari River. It was a barren horizon sprinkled with the poorest of the poor. They lived in mud brick huts covered with grass-thatched roofs trying to survive. What a mind-boggling contrast of lifestyles and cultures! Nevertheless, among all of this poverty and destitution, the people seemed to be in high spirits and friendly.

As I sat there looking across the Chari River, Dick Wall talked to Betty. I really was not listening because there were many thoughts going through my mind. Some of them were: How do those poorest of poor people perceive us? Why is it that they had so little and we had so much? I wondered what must go through their minds when they see westerners and Europeans living such a luxurious lifestyle within their midst as they struggle to survive each day? I wondered if they ever wanted to live differently, besides having easier access to food, water, shelter and medicine? These people had been living such a lifestyle for thousands of years; what was good about their lifestyle and what would they want to change? Would they improve or change their lifestyle if they had an opportunity to change it? What could Betty and I do during the next two years that would contribute to improving their quality of life by helping people help themselves? These were some of the initial thoughts that went through my mind as I sat there on the veranda at *Hôtel Tchadian* during my first day in Chad overlooking the Chari River munching on my beef shish-ka-bobs. I concluded that I first had much to learn about the people's culture, religion, customs, traditions, and the administrative structure of the local, regional and national governments before Betty and I could even think of initiating any benevolent efforts that would contribute to the change process within the various societies in the Republic of Chad.

Experiencing this initial cultural jolt and learning to appreciate, understand, value, respect, and cherish the traits of people in cultures different from our American culture regardless of their language, governmental regime, skin color or religion was a lesson in life that contributed much to our professional growth. The ethos we experienced that day was the catalyst that ultimately led me to firmly believe that the world is but one nation and humankind its citizens.

8

"Let's Get Going"

The three weeks that followed our arrival in Fort-Lamy were exciting and humbling. It was a time for Betty and myself to become adjusted to the many differences in the new culture. At the hostel and Peace Corps Office, we met and talked with various Peace Corps Volunteers. We found their unique experiences and exchange of information helpful and interesting.

With Charley Steedman, we met Mr. Ougadjuo, Diplomatic Counselor for President Tombalbaye. He officially welcomed us to Chad and wished us well. He informed us that we would be living in Bessada and the President would provide new furniture and a car with gasoline vouchers for us to use while in Bessada. The government would pay for the gasoline, in principle, although actually Peace Corps paid for it. Mr. Ougadjuo was very cordial and made us feel he was sincere in welcoming us to Chad. He informed us that he was attempting to make an appointment for us to meet the President in the afternoon, but he would have to let us know at what time. He wanted to know where we could be reached. We told him the Peace Corps Office. He apparently was not able to make the appointment because no one informed the Peace Corps Office of the appointment.

We met John Blane, Diplomatic Counselor for the American

Ambassador at the American Embassy. He informed us that when the American Ambassador returned to Fort-Lamy, he wanted to meet Betty and me. The next day we did meet Ambassador Terrence Todman, who was from St. Thomas, Virgin Islands. Ambassador Todman was very pleased that we arrived in Chad to develop the agriculture in President François Tombalbaye's home village. He informed us that anything he could do to assist our work, we were to let him know. Betty and I were very impressed with the sincerity of Ambassador Todman.

During the next week, we devoted much effort to purchasing household goods, lanterns, dishes, silverware, and a host of other goods in Fort-Lamy because much of what we would need was not available in small villages or towns in southern Chad. We purchased used goods from Peace Corps Volunteers who were departing after completing their tenure in Chad. We purchased some used goods from missionaries who were breaking up housekeeping and returning home. Then, of course, we purchased some new paraphernalia as well. We spent most of our settling-in allowance on these items. We packed everything we purchased into boxes and put them in storage at the Peace Corps Office. Charley Steedman agreed to haul the boxes to our site in his Land Rover and he would meet us in Moundou a few days after we departed Fort-Lamy.

It was now time to depart Fort-Lamy and head south where we would be stationed. We were ready to begin the next phase of our Peace Corps saga and I said to Betty, "Let's get going." We were told, and our airline tickets indicated, that we were flying directly to Moundou. However, after we departed Fort-Lamy on *Air Tchad*, we were flying longer than we anticipated. So I asked the steward how much longer to Moundou. He said we were flying first to Am Timam, then to Fort Archambault (a.k.a. Sarh), and then on to Moundou. The pilot reversed our flight plan and didn't tell us. So, we first landed at Am Timan located east-northeast of Fort-Lamy.

Before we landed I looked out the window to see the brown sandy landscape that was punctuated with an occasional tree or bush. I said to myself, "My gosh, what a struggle it must be to survive in such a harsh environment." The airplane first swooped over the dirt landing strip to shoo away the wild animals. As we landed, a man was standing at the edge of the runway with a hand held fire extinguisher. If a fire would have occurred, I was not convinced his fire extinguisher would have been much help. Nevertheless when the airplane taxied down the runway to the front of the terminal, the passengers were welcome to deplane for a short time by climbing down a long ladder to the ground. Betty and I elected to stay on board. We watched new passengers board the plane with a plethora of luggage, live chickens, and baskets of mangos. After a one-hour wait, we departed and headed south for Fort Archambault.

Prior to landing at Fort Archambault I looked out the window and saw hundreds of flamboyant trees lining the streets. They were in full bloom and were absolutely beautiful. The landscape surrounding Fort Archambault was much greener and it was certainly evident that here in the south they had more favorable growing conditions for food crops as compared to the north around Am Timan. Again we were welcome to deplane, but we decided to stay on board because we didn't want to climb down that long ladder. We watched passengers deplane with their chickens, luggage, and mangos. We also watched new passengers board with crates of chickens, goats, luggage, baskets of mangos, bananas, and smoked fish. These flights were certainly not the caliber of Pan American or Trans World Airlines. Finally after one hour we departed Fort Archambault and headed west-southwest for Moundou to our destination.

At Moundou, a Peace Corps Volunteer named either Juanita or Derek was to meet us. When we landed, we deplaned by climbing down the ladder. We walked into the terminal where we picked up our luggage and went outside looking for Juanita or Derek. We had never met either Juanita or Derek and had no idea what they looked like. It appeared to us that neither one was there to meet us. So, we were a bit nervous as to what our next move would be. We decided to wait at the airport for a while in hopes that they would arrive to meet us and take us wherever they had planned for us to reside.

After we had waited for more than an hour, a rather old battered car came speeding down the road to the front of the airport terminal. It was the only car at the airport entrance. We thought perhaps it might be Juanita or Derek. A lady jumped out of the car with her ponytail bobbing up and down and hurriedly came into the terminal. Betty said, "Juanita?" She said, "I'm Juanita, are you the Diamonds?" Betty said, "Yes, we're the Diamonds." Juanita said, "Hell, I was looking for someone young." That's how we met Juanita.

We loaded our luggage into Juanita's car and we departed for her house in Moundou. We arrived at her house and were directed to the rear of her home to a structure called a hanger. It was shelter consisting of four wooden posts planted into the ground with woven *secca* (grass) attached to the sides and slabs of grass placed on the roof to make a shady shelter. On the ground were both a bed and a mat for us to sleep on. This was to be our living quarters until Charley Steedman arrived to take us to the research station. We were quite comfortable. It was surely different from what we were accustomed, but a great experience.

Charley Steedman arrived the next day to take Betty and me to visit a millet and sorghum seed research station north of Moundou. When we arrived, the head researcher greeted us and gave us a tour of the station. We stayed there for the next two days. He was quite cordial to us. I found his research projects to be interesting, enlightening, useful and educational since my previous agricultural experiences did not include either of these two crops. Sorghum and millet were the main staple food crops in all of Chad and were very important to the well-being of Chadians as well as to the local economies.

After the two-day stay at the station, Charley Steedman returned with his driver Brahim to fetch Betty and me. Because Charley was terminating his tenure in Chad, the new Peace Corps Director John Riggan had recently arrived, had flown to Moundou and then accompanied Charley to meet us and to see southern Chad at the same time. Together we traveled back to Moundou. In Moundou Charlie Steedman made his rounds to say goodbye to his many friends and local government officials. At each stop we had to have a drink of Johnnie Walker whiskey. Betty and I did not drink alcoholic beverages other than a social drink to make a toast or simply nurse a drink for the whole evening. After the fourth stop, we all had had enough of Johnnie Walker. However at the fifth stop, Betty asked for just water. She got Johnnie Walker whiskey and water. Betty also had more than enough of the alcoholic beverage so she waited until my glass was nearly empty, then she took a sip from her glass. She sat it down next to mine and very slyly reached over and took my glass.

Finally we began our long voyage east by Land Rover across southern Chad, destined for Koumra. As we were driving along, John Riggan informed Betty that he decided she was going to make it. He said, "Betty, that was pretty slick how you exchanged your glass of whiskey for Jim's nearly empty glass. When I saw that sly maneuver, I said to myself, she's going to make it."

The weather was cloudy, it was drizzling and the anxieties were high. At key points along the dirt roads, usually at the edge of a village along the road, were found "barrières de pluie" (rain barriers). Their purpose was to prevent large trucks and cars from destroying the soft wet road surface during a heavy rain. When it rained, the roads were closed. Vehicles (especially large trucks) sometimes sat idle for two or three days waiting for the rains to stop and the roadway to dry (see Red and White Barriers). It was towards the end of May 1971, the beginning of the annual rainy season, and we feared we might get stopped along the way for a day or more.

After nearly two hours of driving, it was time to stop and get rid of that whiskey (and water). There were neither gas stations or rest areas along the way. We were in Africa and we did what the Africans normally do to answer the call of nature. We stopped and Charley said, "The women to the left, the men to the right and find your bush."

In my mind's eye as it related to first impressions, I found the ride across southern Chad to be most interesting. The environment seemed to be more conducive to agricultural development compared to the northern part of Chad. There were airports for light aircraft, and a main dirt road, but no navigable rivers or railroads or paved roads. There was neither a telephone system nor electricity in rural areas. Electricity was sporadically available in the larger towns. The people seemed to be worn-down and weary from having to live such a difficult lifestyle. Economic development seemed to be minimal at best. Unemployment was rampant. People in general tended to be unproductive because of various health issues. There were no medical services other than dilapidated health clinics in a few villages. There were hospitals in both Moundou and Fort Archambault but they had little to no medicine or medical equipment. It seemed that there was a lot of potential for development but I also realized that there appeared to be many insurmountable obstacles that needed to be addressed.

At long last after five hours of driving on a very rough washboard like road, we arrived at Baptist Mid-Missions located on the edge of Koumra. There we met Dr. Dave and Ruth Seymour, medical missionaries for the Baptist Mid-Mission Hospital. Dr. Dave, as he was known, and Ruth Seymour were two very special people who so graciously accepted us into their home as guests while we made preparations to get settled into our assigned village named Bessada.

Dr. Dave was a medical doctor and Ruth was a nurse. Dr.

Dave and Ruth were truly two incredibly special Christian people. They had devoted their entire lives to doing medical missionary work by building the Baptist Mid-Missions Hospital that had come into being as the most up-to-date, best-equipped hospital in southern Chad. There were other medical missionaries who stayed at the station as well for designated terms and who worked at the hospital.

The philosophical concept that guided Dr. Dave's Christian endeavors pointed toward his being first a medical doctor and then a missionary. He was responsible for developing a five-year medical nurse program for Chadian medical students who were sponsored by their respective home village residents. Each student brought his wife and family to the Baptist Mid-Missions Hospital where they lived for five years. Their curriculum evolved around a holistic approach to education. In addition to their medical studies, religion was an integral component of the curriculum. The wives also attended special classes to learn home economics skills and they too had a religious component to their curriculum. Students were expected to periodically preach a sermon on Sunday mornings and the families were expected to be active in their local church.

Upon successful completion of the program, the students would graduate to become nurses within their respective villages. During the five-year period while the student studied at the Baptist Mid-Missions, the village residents were charged with the responsibility of constructing a new village infirmary for the nurse to practice his/her medical skills after graduation. As a means of supporting the graduated nurses in their respective villages, once a month Dr. Dave would fly via Mission Aviation Fellowship to visit their infirmary, to treat patients with medical care beyond the capability of the nurse. In addition to treating patients, Dr. Seymour would reinforce the nurse's religious training by praying with the patients, nurses, and other people in the village who were in spiritual or medical need.

Dr. Dave Seymour's approach to missionary work truly aligned well with my personal *modus operandi* and blended tolerably with my perception of charitable acts. Dr. Dave and Ruth Seymour were our international mentors who played a very important role in our getting adjusted to living in the bush in southern Chad. Had it not been for the Seymours, I'm not convinced that either Betty or I would have adequately adjusted to life as we experienced in Bessada.

The third day in Koumra, I borrowed a Mobylette from an English teacher, Jonathan Brown, a Peace Corps Volunteer stationed in Koumra. I drove it to Bessada to look around a bit and to begin getting acquainted with some people. Upon my arrival I had introduced myself to a couple of people and that is when I met Nestor. Nestor spoke French quite well and he became my main contact for making arrangements to meet the village chief and other village dignitaries during subsequent visits that week.

Prior to departing Ottsville, Pennsylvania, our job description stated that prior to our arrival a new house would have been constructed in the village, where Betty and I would live during our two-year tenure in Chad. On my third visit to Bessada, I met with the village chief and Sous-Préfet (equivalent to a county commissioner) to discuss our arrival plans in the village and where we would live. They asked me "Where would you like to have your house built?" I sensed at that moment that building a house at this time after our arrival could be a long-drawn-out issue and we would be staying at the Baptist-Mid Mission Station for an extended time. I do believe the chief sensed that I wanted to move into Bessada as soon as possible and didn't want to wait until a house was constructed.

The chief pointed out to me that we could stay in the *case de passage* (guest house) until the house was built. We visited the guest house and it was certainly livable, but was located in the center of the village along a well-traveled road passing through Bessada. I sensed the chief was not too enthusiastic about us moving into the guesthouse for any length of time because it was used extensively for dignitaries, families, and friends passing through the village.

A group of Chinese from Taiwan was living in another house, the only two-story house in all of southern Chad. The company which had built it had constructed the dirt road a few years before. They managed the Chinese Research Farm some twenty kilometers from Bessada. The men had to travel back and forth each day on a rough dirt road to their Research Farm. They had been living there in Bessada for three years but were in the process of building a new house at their Research Farm. According to the Sous-Préfet, they would be moving to that site within the next couple of weeks. I said to the Chief and SousPréfet that we would be willing to wait until that house was vacated if Betty and I could live there. After some discussion between the village chief and Sous-Préfet in their indigenous language, Sara Madjingaye, it was agreed that we would live in the two-story house owned by President Tombalbaye. However, there was one detail to which I had to agree. The President's brother occupied one room in the house and there he would continue living, but he would not interfere with our privacy. I had met "Papa John" and he seemed like a likeable person, so I agreed it was *d'accord* (okay) to have "Papa John" as our next-door neighbor. Once we made this verbal agreement, it was a three-week waiting period before the house was vacated.

9

Whew! We Finally Arrived

Before we left Fort-Lamy, capitol of Chad, I said to Charley Steedman, the Director of Peace Corps/Chad, "You know Charley, our job description is vague; just what is it that we're supposed to do when we get to Bessada?" Charley looked up at Betty and me, puffing on his pipe filled with Granger pipe tobacco and said, "Jim and Betty, just go down there and do your thing!" We traveled by air, car and Land Rover in a southerly direction some 360 miles to Bessada, the home village of Chad's President, François Tombalbaye, to "do our thing."

In May 1971, after living for a month with the Seymours at the Baptist Mid-Mission Compound in Koumra, Betty and I settled into our house in Bessada. We were now ready to begin our work as Peace Corps Volunteers.

Bessada is located in southern Chad, 120 kilometers west of Fort Archambault between the towns of Bedaya and Koumra. We were the newcomers in the village replacing the four Chinese rice production experts who moved to their new living quarters at the Rice Research Station some twenty kilometers south of Bessada along the Chari River. After they moved out of the house in Bessada, Betty and I were able to get possession of their house and we began making preparations to make it livable for us during the next two years.

Our house was a mud brick house plastered with cement. On the first floor there was a small room at the back entrance, which we decided to use for a kitchen. The next small room we used as a dining room and the third room we used as a quasi-living room. To the left of the kitchen, there was a huge storage room from the front to the back of the house. Between the storage room and our dining room was a room where the brother of President Tombalbaye lived. We called him Papa John. The stairs to the second floor were made of cement and each step was a different height. Upstairs there were a bathroom and two bedrooms. We used one bedroom for storage. All of the windows had wooden louvers. Although there were light fixtures, there was no electricity. There were two bathrooms, but no running water.

Betty and I decided the house interior needed a good cleaning. So we hired two Chadian men from the Baptist Mid-Missions Compound in Koumra to clean our house. After they cleaned the house and scrubbed the floors, we traveled to Fort Archambault and purchased some lime and salt to make whitewash. The two men whitewashed the entire interior of our living quarters. White washing the interior did basically two things: it brightened the walls and more importantly, it acted as a sanitizer.

We also purchased the only paint and paintbrushes we could find. We could only purchase a bag of powdered paint and there was only one color, "mustard" yellow. The powdered paint was mixed with water before being used to paint the wooden window frames, louvered windows, doorframes and louvered doors. We hired Nestor and Pierre, two young men from Bessada, to work for us full time. One of their first jobs was to paint the wood inside our house. This was the first time Nestor and Pierre had ever used a paintbrush to paint anything. One day after I explained and demonstrated to the two young men how to paint, I gave them each a brush to begin their painting assignment. After I watched them for about half an hour, they seemed to be doing all right so I thought it best if I would depart and leave them alone to do their job. I had sensed that my presence was making them nervous. When I came back an hour later, the paint job was not what I expected. They were not applying enough paint and there were streaks everywhere. I said to Nestor "Look at these streaks, they're not supposed to be there." Nestor looked at the streaks, then slowly walked across the room, turned, looked back at the streaked window and said, "Patron, if you stand over here you can't see the streaks." To make a longer story of explanation short, Nestor and Pierre finally finished their job two days later. After considering the circumstances, I guess one could say it was an acceptable paint job.

We furnished the house with chairs, a table, an armoire and a bed that President Tombalbaye provided, a kerosene refrigerator, a gas stove and a treadle Singer sewing machine provided by Peace Corps. We purchased dishes and silverware from missionaries. We bought a Petromax lamp, lanterns, pots and pans, glassware and other household items at the market in Koumra, or from departing Peace Corps Volunteers, missionaries or other departing expatriates.

Now that we were settled in a house in the village, we needed to do an assessment as to what type of project(s) Betty and I were going to plan "to do our thing." Our strategy was to keep quiet but keep our eyes and ears open as a means to identify the felt or expressed needs of the people. We had strived to get to know the villagers while at the same time allowing them to get to know us. It was important that they get used to seeing us in and around the village and that we were being perceived as trustworthy. Furthermore whatever we would do for our first project had to indisputably impact some visible aspect of life in the village. This was the reason we kept our opinions, advice, ideas, and suggestions to ourselves.

Note: This news release was published in a column written by the late Lester Trauch entitled "About Town" in *The Intelligencer,* Doylestown, PA, June 1971.

James E. Diamond
Peace Corps Volunteer
(For immediate release)   B.P. 13
Koumra, Chad
AFRICA
28 May 1971

We bring you greetings from the *République du Tchad* (a.k.a. Chad), the heart of Africa, as Betty and I commence our two-year tour of duty with the Peace Corps working in agriculture and home economics in this new and developing African country. We arrived at Fort-Lamy (a.k.a. N'djamena), the capital, on 29 April 1971 after completing a three-month intensive French-language training program at St. Thomas, Virgin Islands.

Chad is truly a developing country with a tremendous economic and agricultural potential. But first, as in every new and developing country, it has many obstacles to overcome and undoubtedly it will take many years for the people of the Republic of Chad to reach their dreams and goals. The chief agricultural products raised are cotton, peanuts, livestock, millet, sorghum, and other grains. Cotton is the main export commodity at the present time; thus a great deal of emphasis is placed on cotton production because France subsidizes it.

Chad is located in the heart of Africa, more than one thousand miles from any coast. It is bounded on the north by Libya, on the east by Sudan, on the south by Republic of Central Africa, and on the west by Nigeria and Cameroon. With an area of more than 500,000 square miles, it is the fifth largest country in Africa. Chad has vast plains, cut by the valleys of the Shari, the Logone, and the Bahr-al Rivers with a low sedimentary basin around Lake Chad.

Chad offers great geographic variety: desert, savanna, forest, mountains, rivers, and plains. Its people are as varied and interesting as its topography: Arabized nomads, Negroid herdsmen, fishermen and villagers, Muslims, Christians, and Animists.

As this new nation emerges into the unknown future, its culture will play a very important role in the rate and degree of development that takes place. Foreign agencies that offer vocational and technical assistance must work into the deeply ingrained cultural characteristics, which have enriched the lives of Chadians for hundreds of years.

During the past ten years (1961–1971), Chad has experienced an agricultural revolution that certainly will be recorded in historical archives. The introduction of oxen by the French ten years ago has revolutionized Chad's agriculture to where production has soared compared to production prior to their use. Now with a pair of oxen, a farmer can plow one-and-one-fourth acres of land per day as compared to at least ten days to prepare the same area of land with a small hand hoe. The oxen are used not only as draft animals, but after they have completed their prime working years at eight years of age, the oxen are then sold for meat. With the onset of the oxen age in Chad, new agricultural production principles can now be slowly introduced.

Life here in Southern Chad is quite different from that in Ottsville, Pennsylvania. Life in Bucks County perhaps could not exist under the conditions found in Southern Chad. The Chadian housewife does not have a car for running downtown to do her daily shopping or to visit a neighbor. Here she walks and often she walks several miles. The *case* (*cah-ze*, rectangular or round mud brick house) does not have running water in the kitchen. The wife sometimes walks two to five miles and draws water from a well and carries it home on her head. Chadian homes and villages do not have electricity. Cooking is done with a charcoal fire and lanterns provide light at night. Mrs. Housewife here in Chad's bush country cannot go to the A&P and purchase a two-kilogram bag of flour. She grinds her own millet flour with a large wooden *pilon* (grain is placed into a hollowed-out log and a rather long and thick wooden pole used to pound the grain into flour). Chadian children do not wait for a school bus; they walk to school. One teacher told me he has a student who walks seven miles to school each day.

Chadian farmers do not have a large modern tractor to plow the land or to plant their crops. If a farmer can afford it, he has two oxen and a small hand plow to till the soil. Children do not have battery-powered car sets for toys; Chadian children use sticks, stones and old cans for toys.

There are no supermarkets where the Chadian women can do their grocery shopping. They must barter at the small open village market each day. There is no Bucks County Rescue Squad to take the sick or injured to the Baptist Mid-Mission Hospital in Koumra. The sick or injured walk if they can to the hospital or they are carried in an ox cart pulled by two oxen. One evening Betty and I were visiting the hospital and we saw a man being brought in by oxcart. His groin had been deeply slashed open after being gored by an ox. There are no township supervisors to complain to about the potholes in the roads. All roads here in Southern Chad are dirt and the people are thankful they have at least dirt roads, even though they are very bumpy.

Even though Chad lacks some of the niceties of Bucks County, it has many advantages. Chad has no landfill problems because Chadians waste practically nothing, and what little wastes they do have, they bury. There are no chemical plants to pollute Chad's soil and water. There are no township zoning issues or development pressures which limit agricultural production. There are no traffic jams because there are few cars in Chad. Here in Chad streams and rivers are not polluted because Chad's rivers are extremely important to the livelihood of thousands of Chadian fishermen. Chad has no problems with the county condemning land for ski resorts. There is no Philadelphia Electric Company attempting to put high-tension power lines through national parks. There is no drug problem with Chad's youth—the only drug problem here is the difficulty of obtaining them for the hospitals and dispensaries.

While life in Southern Chad is so different and perhaps more difficult from that of Bucks County, Chadians are a happy and proud people. Let our labors begin.

10

Red and White Barriers

Each year from mid-September to the beginning of June was the annual dry season in Southern Chad. During this period of time no precipitation came from the clear, cloudless, heat bearing skies. The grasses began to turn brown in October and by early January, they were completely dried and easily burned. From January to early March the people burned much of the bush country. This is done because about two weeks after burning, green grass sprouts emerge from the root systems where stored moisture existed. The green sprouts created minuscule amounts of browse for livestock (cattle and sheep).

In late May we would sit on the veranda with our dear missionary friends Dr. Dave and Ruth Seymour to watch dull eruptions of light illuminating the late evening skies. Lightning far off to the south, in the Republic of Central Africa where the rains had begun caused these. As we neared the first of June, the rains were moving north and the lightning became more spectacular but still no rains. When the first rains arrived, usually around the first week of June, local people rejoiced by singing and dancing accompanied by locally made musical instruments to celebrate the end of the prolonged dry season.

During June it usually rained every other day for short periods of time. Other times it would rain all night or all day. During all-day rains, people would not go into the fields to work. They would stay in their mud brick huts or within the village. I personally found the rainy season to be rather pleasant. The countryside turned green, fields were being tilled for planting crops, the air was fresh-smelling and the mood of the people was more self-assured.

When there were heavy rains, it was not wise to travel on the

A *"barrièr de pluie* (rain barrier) prevented large trucks and cars from destroying the road surface when it rained.

main or back roads. There were three main roads, which were periodically revitalized by the Chadian government. They connected southern Chad with its capitol city, Fort-Lamy. They were made of the natural red laterite soils commonly found in the savannas of Chad. There were no paved roads in all of Chad except for about seventy kilometers (1 kilometer = .6 mile) in and around the Capitol city. When it rained the dirt roads were dangerous to ride on, especially at high speeds. The roads all had "washboard" like surfaces caused by cars and trucks and became slippery when wet. Cars and especially pick-up trucks traveling faster than eighty kilometers per hour (48 miles per hour) would begin to "fishtail" and drivers often would lose control and their vehicles would overturn. Large loaded trucks caused deep ruts and often became stuck on the road, frequently causing the roads to close.

At key points along the dirt roads, usually at the edge of a village, was found a *"barrière de pluie"* (rain barrier) for preventing large trucks and cars from destroying the road surface when it rained. A local villager was paid by the government to be the gatekeeper to enforce the government's rain barrier policies. A barrier was a red and white-striped pipe that reached entirely across the road and rested on a metal post. In the center was a large sign that said *"Arrête, barrièr de pluie"* (Stop, rain barrier). When the rain barrier was across the road, everyone had to stop until the rain ended and the roads were dry enough to drive on. Often there were ten to fifteen vehicles waiting. Sometimes one had to sit at the rain barrier over night or longer.

The purpose of the rain barriers was to protect the roads from being destroyed by large heavily loaded trucks. Where dirt roads passed through low-lying areas, the water often flooded the roads or the road would become squishy from ground water and deep ruts were made in the road. I have seen depressions caused by deep ruts in the road whereby the side of the road was nearly as high as the car and one could not see over the side of the depression as you drove down into it. Heavy trucks made these depressions and they filled with water when it rained. The policy was, if it started to rain while a large loaded truck was traveling on the dirt road, it was mandatory that the driver stop until the rain was over. If the truck continued on while it was raining and arrived at a rain barrier, the gatekeeper in charge would walk back measuring how far back the ruts occurred. Then the driver was fined an established amount of money for each meter of rut. The fine charged to the truck driver was quite expensive. Often times the gatekeeper allowed small cars to pass because they caused little or no damage to the road.

Sometimes people driving small cars (especially the French) were generally impatient when a rain barrier stopped them. While waiting for the gatekeeper to open the gate for allowing them to pass through, they would blow and blow their horns. When they did this, I just cringed because the gatekeeper would get slower and slower, then everybody had to wait. Betty and I never had a problem with the gatekeeper if we were the first to arrive at the rain barrier. We were always allowed to pass through rather promptly. As I passed through, I always drove slowly and waved to thank the gatekeeper. Over a two-year period, all of the gatekeepers grew to know Betty and me. However, if there was a car in front of us and he or she blew the horn excessively, then we all had to wait until the gatekeeper got good and ready to open the gate.

The moral of this story is try not to drive on dirt roads when it's raining and do not tick off the gatekeeper. Be patient when stopped at a rain barrier. When the gatekeeper opens the gate, one should simply say, "Thank you."

11

Ritual of Baya

Chad has more than forty spoken languages. Some are dialects and some are distinct languages. The language which was spoken in the region surrounding Bessada, where Betty and I lived and worked, was Sara Madjingaye. Madjingaye means "good," or "best." Sara Madjingaye dominated the Bessada region and also was the home of the group of people from which Chad's first president, François Tombalbaye, came. Each year when girls in Bessada and surrounding villages reached puberty, they were obligated to go with the elder women of the village(s) into the bush for an extended period of time where the elder women would implement the traditional "rites of baya."

Baya is an ancient traditional ritualistic practice that was denounced by Christian missionaries. However, it is still practiced in many tribes throughout Chad and other African countries today. Traditional westernized missionaries claim baya is linked to local animistic beliefs. In many tribes it is not linked with a religion. It is a cultural rite. Women perform the rite and many Chadian women support this practice.

The rationale for the rite is likened to a garden; the seed is planted and gives fruit. Therefore the woman is impregnated by her husband and has a baby. But she is not to have any sensual enjoyment during the process of sexual intercourse. In some tribes when the woman's genitals are mutilated, it is believed that it purifies her. Since her sexual desire is diminished she supposedly will be more loyal to her husband. This rite takes a girl from childhood into adulthood.

Women elders who are also birth attendants usually do the procedure to girls and young women. They use an unsterilized razor blade or knife, often without anesthesia. This very painful and dangerous procedure involves the surgical removal of the girl's clitoris. An American missionary told us that the girls are sometimes put into a so-called hypnotic state before and during the mutilation process.

While in this so-called state, the village elders supposedly tell them to forget their birth name and when they come out of the hypnotic or drugged state or both several days later, they are given a new name. When those who survive come out of their stupor, the healing process is supposed to have begun and they are given a new name that they will use for the remainder of their lives. Also during this period of healing, the girls are taught the tribal secrets, and women "coach" young girls in the skills, knowledge and societal mores necessary for surviving life within their culture in the bush.

The mutilation process is dangerous and sometimes fatal because of infections. It is thought that a powerful psychosexual effect results in girls who have undergone this rite. Immediate effects are extreme pain, bleeding, infection, tetanus, and hepatitis B. Possible long-term effects include scarring, infections of the bladder and kidneys, infertility, sexual problems and difficulties during childbirth.

During the baya rites, the participants also receive their permanent tribal markings. The Sara Madjingaye people have four long cuts from a level above the ear to the jawbone on each side of the face and four cuts on the forehead to above the eyebrows making a total of twelve long cuts. After being cut, charcoal is rubbed into the bleeding wounds. We were informed that the charcoal contributed toward stopping the bleeding and when healed, the charcoal beneath the skin caused a more pronounced tribal scar. Sara Madjingaye people are very proud of their tribal markings because they make the people feel they are an integral part of a group who will look after each other's well-being. Each tribe or group of people in Chad had some form of distinct tribal marking. Some were tattooed, some scarred, and some had holes in their lips or ears or nose. Whatever method was used, it associated the person with that particular named tribe or group. This component of the rite is also dangerous because there are risks of infection, blood poisoning, tetanus and other health hazards.

Once we observed that portion of the baya rite which takes place after the women elders bring the girls back to Bessada. Each of these girls was adorned with red beads over her face, necklaces of beads around her neck, metal clappers and beads around her waist, bracelets of cocoons around her ankles, and her naked body was glistening with a reddish salve-like substance. This substance appeared to be a fine red powder made from the laterite rock of the region mixed with an animal fat or peanut oil. The beads covering their faces were intended to hide the unhealed scars of their tribal markings and to keep their identity from villagers because they had not yet received their new name. The women elders did not want the girls to be called by their birth names. The girls danced for hours, non-stop. These girls had to be either drugged or placed

51

into a hypnotic state or both to enable them to do traditional dances at such a pace for such a long period of time. Their dance movements seemed to be involuntary; they were unstoppable. Their dancing did not come from the heart or soul.

Young girls are not particularly happy to participate in the unknowns of baya but the mores of their society dictate that they participate. Young boys who reach puberty also experience a circumcision ritual called yondo and receive their permanent tribal markings.

Because of his Christian education at a Baptist Mid-Missions school near Fort Archambault, President Tombalbaye between 1969–1974 denounced the practice of baya and yondo and made both illegal. It was reported that President Tombalbaye had surgery as an attempt to remove the scars he had received when he went through his circumcision rites. His last name, Tombalbaye, was given to him after he came out of his stupor and when he said, "I haven't vomited yet." In the Sara Madjingaye language "Tombalbaye" means "I haven't vomited yet." There was a rather strong force within the tribal elders who disagreed with the president outlawing this practice. When President Tombalbaye began to lose political support from within his own people in southern Chad in late 1974, he yielded to the forces of tribal elders and reversed his stance against such rites. President Tombalbaye ordered all Chadian men and women who did not partake in the rites to go back to their respective villages and be initiated. This action placed a great deal of political pressure upon Chadian Christians such as pastors, church leaders and devoted members who collectively opposed the traditional rites. Many of the Christians who resisted were killed.

12

Trimming Horse Hooves

One day in July 1971, Betty and I were browsing at the small market in Bessada where women had placed their foodstuff and "goods" on the ground to sell. We were just walking around saying to everyone "*lapia, ea-tow carry wah.*" (Hello, how are you). Thus far, those were the only words we knew in the Sara Madjingaye language. The women and children giggled when we said, "Hello" in their native tongue.

Suddenly, I looked over at the edge of the market and there was a horse whose untrimmed hooves were like long upside-down barrel slats at least sixty centimeters in length. The horse could only walk on its heels. A man with a machete was whacking off hunks of the horses hoof. I said to myself, "Oh my God, that poor horse! That's not the way to trim the feet on a horse." I had just completed a horseshoeing course in the autumn of 1970 at Upper Bucks County Area Vocational Technical School and I knew well how to trim a hoof on a horse.

Teaching villagers who owned horses how to trim feet on their horses was my first idea for a project. According to what I observed there in the village market, there was certainly a need for this skill to be taught in the village. This kind of project would get the village people's attention, establish my credibility, help the owners of the horses learn how to maintain the hooves on their steeds and at the same time I would begin teaching a few people how to trim feet on a horse.

The next time Betty and I drove 120 kilometers to Fort Archambault for supplies, I looked around and found what resembled a small hardware store and there I found and purchased a wood rasp, a wood chisel and a pair of nippers. This is all I needed to begin my first project. I actually purchased three sets with the idea that I would ultimately teach two people at a time how to trim feet on a horse and I would have a set for myself to use in the teaching process.

When we returned to the village, I asked my two employees, Nestor and Pierre, to inform the chief of Bessada what I had in mind for my first project and that I was ready to initiate it if it met his approval. If he felt it necessary, I would very much like to discuss the idea with him. The chief of Bessada gave his blessing to the project idea without any further elaboration.

When the village chief gave the town crier instructions to inform the people of Bessada about the hoof-trimming service that was now available, word spread quickly throughout the village the next day and a couple of horses were brought to me. Anyone who would like to have the feet on their horse trimmed could bring the horse(s) to the mango tree in front of our house where I trimmed its feet free of charge. When the horses began to arrive, I looked at the feet on some of those horses and I just shuddered.

Their feet were so bad that I decided not to do a complete trimming job at one time. If I trimmed all the overgrowth on the hooves, the horses would become lame and could become infected. Some of the hooves were so long that they were like barrel slats, some were damaged from a machete having been used to cut off chunks of the long hoof, some had thrush so bad its odor could be smelled three meters away and some were lame from not having their feet trimmed.

It was necessary to trim the feet in phases. I decided to do the first trim myself so the hooves could be reshaped and to get the horses back onto their feet so they could walk more normally. Then I would teach those who were interested in learning the necessary skills to trim and maintain a horse's feet.

I trimmed the hooves to where the blood capillaries began to show and then stopped. It was necessary to explain to the owner that he would have to allow his horse to walk on a hard surface and bring it back in two weeks to continue the trimming process.

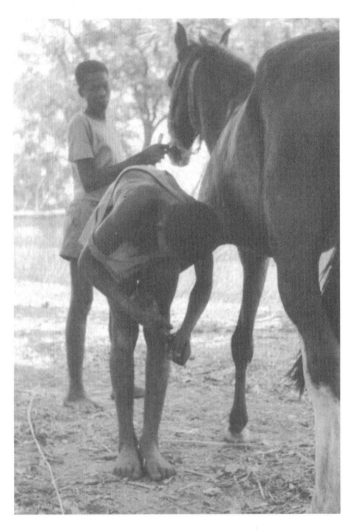

A Chadian farmer learns how to trim hooves on a horse.

This time period would allow the blood capillaries to slowly recede back up into the walls of the hoof and would enable me to take off another layer. I had to do this four or five times before we really got those feet reshaped. The tools I had purchased worked beautifully.

When the hooves were trimmed to where they were supposed to be, the horses did not know how to walk properly. They picked up their feet higher than what was necessary because they were so used to compensating for the long hooves they once had. When I finished trimming their horses' feet the first time, the people were very, very happy. There was a total of thirty-two Arabian-type horses that had their feet trimmed and reshaped. Trimming feet on Arabian-type horses was very hard work.

There were two Chadian men in the village who wanted to learn how to trim horse hooves. I told them that if they followed my instructions and became competent in trimming feet on horses, I would give each of them a set of tools. I began to teach them by explaining the names of each part of the hoof, how to approach a horse, how to properly lift the front leg and how to safely lift the back leg. I also showed them how to control a horse by holding the toe of the front foot when it reared up, how to prevent a horse from kicking and how to use the pick, rasp, chisel and nippers. I emphasized the importance of the hoof's shape by watching the white line in the hoof. I explained how to trim a front hoof, demonstrated how to trim it with the student watching, and then he trimmed the other front foot while I watched. I replicated this process with the back feet. Over a period of six months, both men ultimately became competent in trimming feet on horses and both were given a set of tools and were authorized by me to begin charging a small fee for their farrier services. Darn, I worked myself out of a job.

13

"What's a Refrigerator?"

Generally the destiny of teenage girls in Bessada was to become married after they experienced the baya ritual (see "Ritual of Baya"), become pregnant over and over, cultivate and harvest crops, prepare meals and fulfill other responsibilities as dictated by mores of the village society. Betty discovered a need for these teenage girls when she learned they had less of an opportunity for an education. Even though a few girls were able to attend school (less than twenty percent), generally boys in the village were given priority in receiving an education.

Betty's first official project evolved when she decided to develop a four-week home management educational program for teenage girls from the village who could speak French. The program that she developed focused on teaching practical skills at our home that could be used at both their respective mud brick homes in the village and in homes of missionaries or expatriates working in the area. Enrollment in the program was limited to one girl at a time, because of space restraints, and was scheduled from 9:00 A.M.–noon five days per week for four weeks or a total of sixty hours. Betty relied on Nestor and Pierre (our two employees) to consult with the village chief to determine which girl(s) would receive this practical education program. There were criteria that needed to be satisfied to qualify for the home management program. The participant(s) had to be fourteen to seventeen-year-old females who had the capability to speak French and wanted to expand their home management skills.

When Betty had her first student, she went over the program and explained the skills she intended to teach, such as using a kerosene refrigerator. The girl asked in French, "What's a refrigerator?" This question was not out of the ordinary because people in the village do not own or have access to refrigerators. They are not readily available in rural areas nor could the household head afford to purchase one. The basic skills which were taught included sweeping a floor using a long-handled broom, boiling and filtering water for drinking, making a bed and hanging clothes to dry on a clothesline using clothespins. The girls learned how to wash dishes, use a two-burner bottled gas stove, light a Petromax lamp and candle eggs. They also learned how to follow a recipe, prepare various dishes made from foodstuffs found in the village market, use metal pots and pans, set a table, scrub a floor using a mop and bucket of water, wash leafy foods with Clorox water to prevent cholera and many other skills.

Each day Betty taught the girl how to do one or more household chore(s) and prepare one dish made with food purchased that morning in the village market. At the end of the lesson, the girl was given an eight-by-thirteen centimeter card and she would write the recipe for that particular dish in French. The girl was required to take the recipe home along with a sample of the prepared dish for her family to taste. At the end of the program each girl would have collected twenty different recipes written on eight-by-thirteen centimeter cards for future reference. If the family liked the dish, then they could make it by following the recipe.

We found it interesting that after Betty implemented her program, the first girl who enrolled indicated at the end of the first week that she wanted to be paid, because she perceived her lessons as doing Betty's housework. Yes, Betty was using her kitchen and living room as her classroom and laboratory to teach girls basic domestic skills. What this girl did not realize was that her lessons were focused on her educational needs, not doing Betty's work. In fact preparing for the various lessons was quite an inconvenience for Betty's normal daily work routine but she did not mind as long as the girls would learn the various skills. This issue was resolved by putting a value on the food Betty gave the girl each day to take home for her family to taste. Also, Betty and I met

Betty Diamond teaches a sixteen-year old Chadian girl how to follow a recipe by baking a local vegetable using a gas stove.

Betty Diamond teaches a Chadian girl how to hang clothes on a clothesline using clothespins.

with the village chief to make sure he understood Betty's *modus operandi*. Afterwards there were no more pay issues.

Because girls who enrolled in Betty's Home Management Program had become competent in performing practical household skills, she had no problem getting girls to enroll as the word spread throughout the village of the kind and quality of teaching that was being offered. The girls always came to the house well-dressed in clean traditional dresses. They tended to be a bit timid because they were in the American's home and there were household items that she was not accustomed to seeing or being used in a home. The girls who completed the program became more employable by expatriates and missionaries as cooks and housekeepers because of their competency in performing their newly learned skills. Furthermore, their fathers magnified the bride price for these girls because they had acquired useful skills whereby they had the potential to contribute to the economic well being of their respective household.

John F. Kennedy, President of the United States, who founded Peace Corps once said, "Our progress as a nation can be no swifter than our progress in education." Even though Betty's efforts increased the bride price of the girls, we hope that in some small way Betty contributed to the educational progress of Chad.

14

Needle and Thread

Betty identified a need within the women of Bessada. She noticed that the Chadian women would purchase a piece of brightly colored fabric and wrap it around their torso as a sort of a long dress. The women would have a matching piece of fabric, which they wrapped around their heads in the form of a wrap-around turban-like hat. The women's dress code was rather attractive and everyone dressed in nearly the same style. However, nothing was sewn with a sewing machine or needle and thread.

Peace Corps gave Betty a sewing machine that was operated with a foot treadle. It resembled the sewing machine my mother used to have at the farm at Woodside, Pennsylvania. Papa John, President Tombalbaye's brother, lived in a room in our house and his wife Teresa lived in a hut twenty meters behind our house. She too dressed the same as the other ladies in the village. Betty decided to teach her how to make a dress using a pattern and sewing machine. In retrospect, Betty will always remember this experience because of the frustrations she endured.

The first thing Betty had to do was to teach Teresa how to

hold and use a pair of scissors. She had never used scissors until Betty taught her. Betty showed her how to pin the pattern to the fabric and then cut it according to the directions. After four three-hour sessions, Betty was successful in getting her to finally cut out all the pattern pieces for her new dress.

Now it was time to show her how to use a treadle sewing machine. Betty explained and demonstrated how to thread the needle, put thread in the bobbin, how to put the fabric under the needle, how to clamp the fabric in place, how to pump the treadle with the feet and how to guide the fabric as it was passing under the needle. Teresa could not seem to get coordinated by using her feet and guiding the fabric at the same time. Betty would get down on her knees and put her hands on her ankles to get her feet to move together. A couple times I knelt on my knees and took hold of her ankles and helped her push up and down on the treadle as Betty tried to help her guide the fabric. Whew! What a frustrating experience! This was the first time this lady ever sat down at a sewing machine and everything was a new experience for her. Betty was very, very patient with her and after seven three-hour sessions, her dress was finally finished.

The President's sister-in-law was very proud of her finished dress. It really did look nice on her. One day Teresa went strutting down into the village wearing her new dress. She had accomplished a task that no other person in the village had ever attempted, making a dress from a pattern using a sewing machine.

Betty used a great deal of her time teaching just one person how to make that dress using the treadle powered sewing machine. She concluded that if it took that much time to teach each person how to make a dress, in the long run she would not be able to reach many women. Betty decided she needed to reach more women in the village. She resolved this issue by making plans to teach women in Bessada how to use a needle and thread and how to embroider. Both fabric and brightly colored thread were readily available.

Betty asked Nester and Pierre to put the word out that she would conduct sewing classes at our house once a week for women in Bessada. Betty was anticipating a class size of ten women. She had planned to have the class in our home using an empty living room we did not use. This room was perfect for a class of that size. At the scheduled time, more than fifty women arrived for Betty's sewing class. Her predicament now was that she could not say no to any of the women and the room was much too small for that number of people. So she moved her class outside under a mango tree in front of our house. This is where she held her classes and the women just loved it.

Betty purchased the white "Americana" fabric and colored thread at the market in Koumra or Fort Archambault. She cut the fabric into pieces one meter long. Then she sold the fabric to the ladies at her cost. She gave the thread to the ladies free of charge. The ladies liked the white fabric because the designs were brightly displayed with colored thread. The Baptist Missionaries could not understand how Betty got these ladies to use white "Americana" fabric. Unbeknownst to Betty, the white fabric she purchased and got the ladies to embroider was the fabric the people used to wrap their dead before burying them.

Betty taught the ladies how to make Pennsylvania Dutch designs because they were easy to embroider. She made several Pennsylvania Dutch designs on a piece of cardboard and cut them out for the ladies to trace around. However, she quickly learned that the village ladies could not trace around the design on their fabric because they did not know how to hold or use a pencil. They were never taught how to use a pencil or to write. Furthermore they had no means of purchasing pencil(s) or paper for writing. Betty had to teach them how to hold a pencil and how to use it to trace their designs. Someday an archeologist is going to go into that area and find these pieces of fabric with Pennsylvania Dutch designs on them and will wonder how the Sara Madjingaye people in the hinterlands of southern Chad learned how to embroi-

A Chadian lady learns how to hold a pencil and trace a design onto her fabric to embroider. The box shows how Betty Diamond exhibited the thread and gave it to the ladies.

**Betty Diamond teaches Chadian ladies how to hold a needle,
thread a needle, and embroider Pennsylvania Dutch designs.
Pennsylvania Dutch designs were used because they were
easy to draw.**

der those designs. The French merchants in the capital city, Fort-
Lamy, sold needles but the ladies easily broke them. Betty wrote
home and asked for American needles. My mother and Betty's
mother each sent hundreds of needles for the ladies to use. She
taught them how to thread a needle and to tie a knot at the end of
the thread. The ladies consistently reported that they lost their
needles because they soon learned that Betty would give them
another because she had so many. She suspected the ladies took
the needles home and gave them away to their friends or family
members in the village. Betty felt it was okay to give them new
needles to distribute in the village as long as the ladies taught
someone else how to embroider (that's called the multiplier effect). Generally speaking, one could not purchase a needle in
Chad's rural village, and to them this was a precious commodity.

Perhaps allowing them to steal the needles was a unique way for Betty to distribute the needles.

One tall lady had a question about her embroidery work. Betty walked to her and stood in front of this Chadian lady. The top of Betty's head was at her waist. Everyone started to talk and laugh in Sara Madjingaye. Betty could not understand what they said but she caught on quickly to what they were talking about. Betty used her hands to explain that a 150-centimeter-tall lady was teaching this two-meter-plus lady how to embroider and she laughed with them at their height difference.

Over a period of time the ladies in Bessada became competent in embroidering their fabric. As they became skilled at embroidery, they became rather wasteful in using the colored thread Betty provided free of charge. To end this waste, Betty began charging them a small fee for one meter of thread. The ladies no longer wasted it because they had to pay for it. After six months of teaching, the Bessada ladies embroidery skills improved to the point where all Betty had to do was sell them the fabric and thread, then help them draw their designs on the fabric. Betty then moved her program to the village of Sebe in the same Canton. She taught the women in the village where I worked with the men making silage and pit silos. These women were very, very happy that Betty had come to teach them how to embroider.

In February 1972, the French veterinarian, Dr. Marc Dronne was tragically killed in an automobile accident east of Bedaya (see "Tragedy Strikes"). Since I had worked with livestock and often with Dr. Dronne, the people sometimes called me the "animal doctor." Since there were no local radio stations or newspapers, news traveled around by word of mouth. In the far away villages like Sebe, the people had heard that the "animal doctor" had been killed. They thought I had been killed. A missionary informed us that the village had a day of mourning for the "animal doctor," not knowing that I was very much alive and that it was the French veterinarian who was killed.

Thursday, after Dr. Dronne was killed, Betty was scheduled to work with the ladies in Sebe. When she arrived, there were no ladies waiting for her as they had in previous weeks. The women of Sebe didn't think Betty would be coming because they knew that the "animal doctor" was her husband. They were very surprised and happy to learn that it was not I who was deceased. Betty came again to teach them how to embroider! Her class was a big hit with the women in the villages of Bessada and Sebe even though she was "needled" about her height and "stealing" (losing) her needles.

15

"You've Got Mail"

Our mailing address in Chad was BP (*Boite Postale*) 13. Post Office Box 13 was the address of the Baptist Mid-Missions in Koumra and that is where we received our mail, thanks to Dr. Dave Seymour who allowed us to use their address. Each Wednesday evening we would go into Koumra to the Baptist Mid-Mission to pick up our mail and attend prayer meeting in English with the missionaries. During our tenure in Chad, the mail system for the most part was somewhat reliable. Even though it was certainly slower when compared to the postal service in America or other more advanced countries, it usually took between two to three weeks to receive mail from the United States. From Fort-Lamy, mail would arrive at the large post office in Fort Archambault by air and there it would be sorted, bagged and transported to Koumra. When the mail arrived in Koumra, sometimes it would take two days or longer to get it sorted and placed into BP 13.

Often during the rainy season, the mail would not be transported to Koumra and it would be held in Fort Archambault until the next weekly mail delivery. However if Betty and I or a missionary or other expatriates living in Koumra traveled to Fort Archambault for whatever reason, we had an unofficial verbal agreement that we would stop at the Fort Archambault post office to pick up the Koumra mail bags and deliver them to the Koumra post office. There have been times when we actually helped the Koumra postal workers sort the mail so we could expedite the process of getting our mail in a timely fashion.

I never realized what a thrill it was to receive a letter from someone back home until after we were settled into our village. We always liked to hear the missionaries tell us "you've got mail." Besides our parents, we received much mail from friends. I remember one time in November 1971 I received a letter from a hunting companion back home named Harold Steeley. He had shot a ruffed grouse on the first day of hunting season on our farm and on his letter he taped a feather just to "jerk my chain" a bit because ruffed grouse are difficult to shoot. We always cherished receiving letters from our parents to get updates on our respective families back home.

Betty's parents gave us a subscription to the *Daily Intelligencer*, our local newspaper back in Doylestown. Instead of receiving them bi-weekly or even monthly, every three or four months we would get a box full of *Daily Intelligencer*s. We unwrapped them and sorted each issue by date. Though the national and international news was outdated, we could still keep up with local news back home—who died, who got married and who had a baby. It was "reaaally" important that we got both the funnies and crossword puzzles in chronological order. Although the news was outdated, we read every word in those newspapers.

One should never take for granted how fortunate we are in the United States to have various means of mass communications like the U.S. Postal Service, FedEx, telegrams, televisions, radios and telephones.

16

First the Chicken, Then the Egg?

In Chad's rural bush villages, poultry, namely chickens, was an important food source. Chickens could be purchased directly from the owner or in a village market or from someone passing by with a bunch of chickens tied by their feet to the back of a bicycle, the top of a truck, or on the side of a donkey. There was no electricity for refrigeration in rural villages. People purchased live chickens and at their huts dressed them out (killed and cleaned them) just before preparing the chicken for a meal. Women or teenage girls normally killed and cleaned the chickens. If I visited someone, the Chadian tradition was to purchase a couple of live chickens and give them to my host upon my arrival.

There were no poultry management practices in Chad's rural villages. Traditionally chickens ran free and fended for themselves. No local chicken feed or scratch was available for purchase. Basically it was survival of the fittest. There were no specific breeds of chickens, they were just chickens. However, everyone knew to whom each chicken belonged. The indigenous chickens were hardy, could withstand drought conditions, resist certain parasites and some diseases and were able to tolerate heat and dust.

Even though the chickens were hardy, there was a disease that attacked chickens, usually during the month of April each year. Nearly eighty percent of all native chickens died during that time of the year. I did not have a clue what the disease was called, how to prevent it, how to treat it, or what to do with the dead birds after they died. To be safe, I recommended that they be buried in a hole after being covered with lime or burned or both. I suspected it was a soil-borne disease because the month of April was the middle of the dry season and there was barely enough food for humans to survive let alone chickens. The birds seemed healthy

69

and hardy, then suddenly they would be found dead. Most of the feed village chickens ate during that time of the year was gleaned from the dry soil. Normally, during the dry season, the month of April has had no rain since the end of the previous September and the dry soils were unequivocally bare of herbage.

Because I suspected the disease was caused by a soil-borne organism, I hypothesized that if a modern chicken house were built whereby chickens were totally confined in a chicken house off the ground, the disease would not affect the chickens. I needed to come up with an idea how to build a modern chicken house using indigenous skills, knowledge, resources and introduce modern technology.

Building a structure for raising chickens in confinement and purchasing feed for the chickens was an incredible change process for long-established local traditional poultry husbandry practices. Because Betty and I were new to the village and we needed eggs for our personal livelihood, I decided to build my own modern chicken house as a demonstration unit.

Using a plan, which I found in the VITA Handbook, helped me to be creative and use resources and talents found in the village. In Bessada nails, boards, chicken wire, chicken feeders, waterers, cement blocks, cement and roofing materials did not exist. To adapt the plan we used bamboo in place of boards since bamboo was readily available just outside the village. We used thick layers of dried grass in place of roofing materials, a large gourd cut in half for a chicken feeder and a medium-sized gourd cut in half for a waterer. The locals were experts at attaching building materials with strips of bark in place of nails. The only tools we needed were a saw, an axe and a ruler.

Because of the drastic changes in poultry husbandry management practices I was about to introduce, it was imperative that I build a chicken house for myself and implement these so-called "new" poultry management practices. This would show the villagers that I was "practicing what I preached." The building site had to be within my established concession close to our house so people would not steal the chickens or eggs, yet located in a way so people could easily observe how we were raising our chickens. My mission was to show people how to raise chickens in a chicken house built by using their own talents, resources and "modern" technology. The chicken house-building site was located eight meters directly across from the back door of our house and next to our secca (woven grass) fence.

Termites in Chad were a serious problem with wood products. According to Chadian villagers termites would not eat bamboo or mahogany. Based upon their time-honored wisdom, we went into the bush with an axe and cut six mahogany posts, three meters long. Four of the posts had to have a forked top.

After measuring the building site and putting stakes into the ground to designate the corners, we painted one end of each mahogany post with old used motor oil, dug a hole and set each post into the ground three-fourths of a meter deep and tamped them tightly. We put three mahogany posts on each side, one on each corner and one in the middle. Aligning the mahogany posts was difficult, since they are characteristically crooked.

After the six posts were set, we attached to each side a long bamboo pole one meter off the ground. Then we attached another pole on each end of the structure. The bamboo poles were attached to the mahogany posts with water-soaked strips of bark. When the bark dried, it shrank and tightened the structure. The Chadians were experts at attaching poles to each other with the thin strips of bark. We cut bamboo poles that would fit the width of the bottom frame. Each pole was attached with wet bark and this formed a slatted floor of the structure. The slatted floor was important because the manure and any spilled water would fall through onto the ground below. As a result the hens would always be clean and dry.

We attached to the top of each mahogany post on each side another long whole bamboo pole and one on each end. This formed

Jim Diamond and his Chadian friend Nester cut bamboo poles, which would fit the width of the bottom frame, and attached them with wet bark.

the top frame of the structure. Bamboo lengths were cut to fit the sides of the structure. Using a machete, the bamboo poles were split in half longways (bamboo is easy to split longways). Then each half was split into quarters, hereinafter referred to as slats. Each bamboo slat was attached to the mahogany posts with wet bark leaving a one-half centimeter space between the slats. The slats bore no weight, they simply enclosed the structure to keep the hens confined to a clean, dry space one meter off the ground. The spaces between the slats were important for allowing air circulation within the structure, especially during the dry season.

Three short poles were attached horizontally to one side of the structure. Then each pole was attached to the front of each nest. This framework formed a perch for the hens to fly onto before entering their nests. The perch had to be stiff to withstand the weight and force of hens flying up to it. Short pieces of bamboo

A Chadian poultry farmer gathers fresh eggs, which rolled from the nest into the exterior bamboo trough.

were split several times and attached to the bamboo frame to form the sides of the four nests. The bottom of the nest was made from thin pieces of bamboo split several times. The front of the nest was higher than the back. At the back of the nest two slats were removed to allow an egg to roll out of the sloped nest.

Long strands of thin split bamboo were woven together with bark to form a trough that looked much like a rainspout. The trough collected the unbroken eggs as they rolled out of the nest. These are the reasons eggs should roll from the nest:

1. Eggs cool more quickly.
2. Other chickens entering the nest to lay an egg would not break eggs.
3. Chickens would not be able to eat eggs to satisfy their mineral deficiency cravings.
4. People did not have to enter the interior of the chicken house to gather eggs because entering the structure could contaminate the floor with organisms on their feet.
5. The eggs were readily accessible to gather from the outside.

Bamboo poles were used as rafters to form an A-shaped frame for the roof. Bamboo split in half was attached to the rafters for stability. Thick bundles of dried grass were laid out in rows beginning on the edge of the roof with each preceding layer overlapping the one below it. The layers were attached to the bamboo frame with damp bark. The thick thatched grass roof protected the chickens from both sun and rain and acted as insulation during the cooler winter evenings.

To make the feeder, we obtained from a farmer half of a dried gourd grown near the village edge. I bored three holes an equal distance near the top edge of the gourd. Then I tied three pieces of hemp twine from the roof to the holes and tied the twine to the gourd and hung it there. When I put feed into the gourd feeder, it

Chickens inside their new coop on a slatted floor with slatted sides, hanging feeder, and slanted nests (upper right).

did not take the chickens long to learn that if they got inside the gourd, they could do what comes naturally, scratch out the feed. The feed would fall to the bamboo floor, then fall through the cracks onto the ground. The next morning the village goats would eat the feed from the ground.

To solve this wasting of feed, we took down the feeder from the roof, found a millet stalk and cut it into lengths twenty centimeters long. With the leather bore on my pocketknife, I bored a hole into each end of the twenty-centimeter millet pieces. I tied a knot in the twine ten centimeters above the top edge of the gourd, and put the twine through the holes and alternated the millet pieces until they were five high. Then we hung the feeder from the roof and now the chickens could stick only their heads into the feeder. Mission accomplished! Again we used local materials to make a modern chicken feeder.

There was no running water in the village and we had to be creative in providing water for the chickens. We placed the other half of the dried gourd in a corner of the chicken house. We filled a demijohn (wine bottle that holds four liters) full of water and we turned it upside down and tied it to the side of the chicken house so it would not fall over and spill water onto the floor and ground. The open mouth was placed into the dried gourd. When the water reached its level of equilibrium, it stopped gurgling and the water level remained constant in the gourd until the chickens would drink. When the water level was lowered to below the equilibrium level, the gourd would automatically fill with water by gravity.

It was now time to purchase chickens for the new chicken house. I had learned from a fellow Peace Corps Volunteer that there was a hatchery in Fort Archambault sponsored by the Food and Agriculture Organization of the United Nations. A friendly and very cooperative young man from Switzerland managed it. I purchased twelve layers for our personal use in Bessada. After I transported my twelve newly purchased chickens to Bessada and put them into their new "digs," the President's brother "Papa" John watched and said, *"Elles sont très contentes"* (They're very happy).

While buying the chickens, the young man asked me if I could translate for him a letter written in English. I agreed and when he handed me the letter I immediately recognized the logo on top of the stationary. It was a letter from Moyer's Chicks, Quakertown, Pennsylvania. Ivan Moyer who owned Moyer's Chicks was a dear friend. This incredible letter indicated that fertile eggs had been donated and were shipped to Chad. It described where the fertile eggs were being shipped and the estimated date of arrival. There I was, in the middle of Africa and was handed a letter from a hatchery twelve miles from our farm in Bucks County, Pennsylvania!

There were no major feed mills in Chad because one certainly would not feed good grain to chickens, oxen, sheep or goats. There was a small mill in Fort Archambault that was operated by the Food and Agriculture Organization of the United Nations. People could buy ground millet or take their homegrown sorghum or millet to be ground. The doctrine of the society was that one would certainly not feed good grain to oxen or any animal for that matter, especially when one's family is hungry and food is scarce. I was able to purchase chicken feed made at the FAO Mill. The feed was made from by-products of sorghum or millet or rice or a mixture. It lacked carotene, which caused the yolk of the eggs to be quite pale. Carotene is the precursor to vitamin A and causes the egg yolk to be yellow in color.

During the two dry seasons when we used the improvised "modern, state-of-the-art" chicken house, we had a constant supply of eggs at our home, and not one time did we lose a chicken to any diseases.

People in the village stopped at our home daily to observe the chickens in their new house. They were amazed that they could survive in such a confined space. Furthermore, they were amazed that the eggs would automatically roll out of the nests. People in neighboring villages would walk many kilometers and sit for hours beside the chicken house until a chicken laid an egg and they could watch it roll out of the nest.

One of the Baptist missionaries had a houseboy who became interested in raising chickens and selling eggs to French, American, Italian and Swiss expatriates living in Koumra and the surrounding area. He ultimately quit his job and I helped him build his chicken house. With his saved money he purchased the hens and feed from the FAO Hatchery in Fort Archambault. I assisted him by providing the transportation to bring the hens and feed from Fort Archambault to Koumra. He was very proud of his new chicken house and he was very successful in selling eggs daily to the expatriates.

Terrence Todman, United States Ambassador to the Republic of Chad visited us in Bessada, he was very much interested in the success of our unique chicken house. He had his photographer take pictures of the structure and chickens and he did a feature story in the monthly newsletter published by United States Information Services. This concept of using native knowledge, skills, resources and introduce modern concepts impressed him. This project was a very practical effort, which enabled the village people to achieve.

17
"May I Borrow Your Paring Knife?"

Because native chickens received no balanced diet, they developed vitamin and mineral deficiencies to the extent that a condition known as "cannibalism" evolved. Most of the feed village chickens ate during the dry season was gleaned from the dry soil. Even the chickens that were confined in our new modern chicken house (see "First the Chicken, Then the Egg?" for complete details) lacked proper nutrients because there were no vitamin additives, minerals, or nutrient supplements added to their feed. They were fed a diet made from by-products of grinding sorghum or rice or millet for household use. Their diet needed something their bodies demanded and whatever it was, chickens could find it by pecking at another chicken. The pecking would become severe enough to cause the weaker chickens to bleed and they would become vulnerable for other chickens to peck and finally they became weaker and died. This is called cannibalism.

One way to control cannibalism is to debeak all the birds. To debeak a bird one needs a debeaker. Guess what? There were no debeakers in Chad. So we had to improvise. I asked a missionary if she had a paring knife. She said, "Yes I do. Would you like to borrow it?" I said, "Yes I would like to borrow it for a couple days if you do not mind." She said, "No problem." Now I have part of a debeaker (she didn't ask me how I was going to use it). What I needed next was a piece of wood thick enough so that I could open the chicken's mouth and place the wood between the upper beak and lower beak. Finding an appropriate piece of wood was easy. My next task was to start a charcoal fire to heat the paring knife. When the charcoal got white, I stuck the front half of the paring knife into the fire. While it was heating, Nestor and Pierre started the task of catching the chickens. When the paring knife was red hot, Nestor put the chicken's upper beak on top of the wooden stick, then I placed the red hot knife about one-fourth of the way in from the end of the beak. The red-hot knife burned off the beak's end and cauterized it at the same time. Now the debeaked chicken could not peck another chicken without hampering its capability to eat and drink. Even though we improvised the process, this was a practical and an approved task for chicken growers.

When I returned the paring knife to the missionary, it was still scorched from heating it over and over during the two-day period. She asked me, "What happened to the paring knife?" When I told her I used it to debeak chickens, she was not a happy missionary. She blessed me more than once because she forgot to realize that "necessity was the mother of invention." To keep my missionary friend happy, I purchased her a new paring knife the next time we traveled to Fort Archambault for supplies.

18

Cholera Epidemic

During our first rainy season in Chad (the first week of June to the end of September, 1971) there was a horrible outbreak of cholera throughout Chad. Thousands of people died, especially in the northern semi-desert areas. We received word that entire villages were wiped out by cholera. In some of the outlying villages in the arid regions not yet infected, the chiefs placed sentries around their villages to prevent people who had escaped neighboring infected villages from entering. In many cases the sentries killed the escapees to prevent the disease from spreading. Cholera attacks the gastrointestinal system and spreads rapidly among people.

We were instructed by Dr. Dave Seymour to wash all of our vegetables, especially leafy foodstuffs with water containing bleach. Even though we were inoculated for cholera, we still had to be careful. Betty and I had a difficult time imagining how all the people in a village up north could die from this revolting disease. When we traveled to Lake Chad in December 1971 (see "Lake Chad)" in a Land Rover, we passed by an abandoned village on our voyage to Bol, Lake Chad. It was completely deserted because everyone had died. That's when we were able to comprehend how an entire isolated village could be wiped out. One cannot envision or appreciate the remoteness of those villages at the desert's edge until a visit is paid and the devastation observed. Some of those small villages had no more than one hundred to two hundred people living in mud brick huts and grass thatched roofs. They were eighty-five to one hundred kilometers from another village where they eked out an unstable lifestyle in a very harsh landscape. A cholera outbreak caused people to die while several attempted to escape the disease by leaving their village and trekking to the next village. However, many never made it and died along the way.

Those who were able to reach the next village were met by sentries and were either turned back or killed.

At this time the people of West Germany responded to Chad's plea for assistance and donated enough cholera vaccine for every person in Chad. When the German cargo plane loaded with cholera vaccine landed at the airport in Fort-Lamy, Chad's Minister of Interior at the time demanded that the German government pay a levy on the donated vaccine before allowing it to be off-loaded into the Republic of Chad. The German Ambassador became involved in the debate and said, "Why does the German government have to pay a tax on this vaccine when this was a gift from the people of West Germany to protect the people of Chad?" Meanwhile Chadian villagers were dying by the hundreds each day while the Chadian Minister of Interior debated the issue of taxing the vaccine. Finally at the end of the third day the Ambassador of West Germany directed the German pilots to immediately depart Fort-Lamy for return to West Germany with the vaccine still on board. The vaccine never reached the Chadian people. What a dreadful tragedy! People continued to die until the disease ran its course. So many lives could have been saved had it not been for the greed which was exhibited by the then-Chadian Minister of Interior.

It has been said that greed is the greatest curse of the human race. The Minister of Interior was responsible for the deaths of thousands of people because of his selfishness and greed to glean a tax on a gift from the people of West Germany. The Minister of Interior exhibited neither remorse or concern for Chad's people while they were dying. It makes no difference what God(s) he worshiped or if he worshiped at all, but I always wondered if his God had mercy on his soul when he was called home to meet his maker.

19

"Uh Oh!"

François Tombalbaye was a teacher, trade union activist and head of the Chadian Progressive Party, which ruled the colonial government. On 11 August 1960, when France liberated Chad, he was appointed the first president. After gaining independence, President Tombalbaye formed an autocratic form of government and eliminated opposition within and outside his party by banning all political parties. After he dissolved the National Assembly in 1963, President Tombalbaye nationalized civil services and replaced French administrators with inexperienced Chadians. A sign of liberalization came in 1971 when President Tombalbaye admitted to the Congress that he had made mistakes and steps began to take place to reform the government.

Order seemed to be unfolding throughout Chad in 1971 and France withdrew its troops from the Republic. In August we were informed that there was an attempt to assassinate President Tombalbaye near Fort Archambault. The details that we heard indicated that a small disgruntled group with links to Libyan leader Muammar al-Gaddafi attempted to shoot him, but were thwarted by bodyguards. The perpetrators were immediately shot as punishment. President Tombalbaye was quickly driven away and kept out of sight for a number of days. In the meantime, he severed all diplomatic relations with Libya. This event was kept very quiet and clandestine. It was not reported in the news media but rumors were rapidly disseminated throughout the villages.

Betty and I had been saving a portion of our meager Peace Corps living allowance to take a vacation in March, 1972. We had a sum of money saved in the bank in Fort Archambault. If there should ever be a coup, the first institution affected would be the banks. All funds are normally frozen and often lost. Betty and I decided we needed to get our money out of the bank pronto. In a nonchalant way we traveled two hours to Fort Archambault on our normal monthly trip to purchase supplies. One of our tasks was to visit the bank to make our usual monthly withdrawal. But this time we requested a large sum in American dollars. We were told that we could only withdraw US$600.00 for Betty and US$600.00 for me. We withdrew US$1,200.00 in cash but there was still a sum of CFAs that remained. I asked the clerk if he would give the remainder in French franc Travelers Cheques. We were asked why we were withdrawing our money. We told the teller we were going on a vacation. That response was usually acceptable because that was when expatriates withdrew larger sums of money. We drew down most of our money and took it quietly back to Bessada and stowed it inside our mattress. God forbid but if for some reason that we had to be evacuated, we now had our money and travel documents ready to grab at a moment's notice.

20
"Ensilage? What's That?"

When we arrived in Chad on 28 April 1971, it was the height of the annual dry season. The annual dry season begins to evolve beginning at the end of September and ends in late May or early June. During that time, not one drop of rain fell. In early May there were gratifying evening breezes and far-off lightning but no rains. There was no hay, silage, grass or feed for cattle to eat. I wondered how these cattle survived during the dry season. Having a livestock background, I set out to study this scenario and explored options as to how oxen can safely be fed during the annual dry seasons.

I learned that French "*Animation Rurale*" (Rural Training) personnel introduced the use of oxen to Chadian farmers in 1960. Up to that time, one hundred percent of the cultivated agricultural land was tilled by hand using a short-handled hoe. The French introduced oxen to Chadian farmers and they were taught how to train oxen, how to hitch a team to an ox cart and how to plow. Chadian farmers were not taught how to feed their newly purchased oxen or how to acquire proper feedstuffs to keep them healthy and strong during the dry season. During the dry season, the only thing the farmers could do was turn their oxen loose into the bush and let them fend for themselves with hope that they would survive until rains arrived in late May or early June.

Many of the oxen died from starvation and thirst. Often they were so hungry that they would browse on certain plants that would not normally be eaten because they were toxic to animals. In May of each year, farmers would send children into the bush to look for their oxen. Often they would find dried carcasses or skeletons. When the owner of an animal learned of the death of his oxen, he became angry and blamed it on someone he considered being his enemy. The fact was the animal, in its desperation to find food, ate poisonous plants, accumulated toxins internally and this was what ultimately killed it. There have been reported cases where farmers would murder their enemies in revenge for killing their oxen. Sometimes they said their enemy paid the witch doctor to put a spell on the animal to cause it to die. The truth was no feed or water for the animals were readily available during the annual dry season.

During October, November and December, the matured indigenous grasses became very dry. Traditionally villagers cut the dried grass and wove it into a "*secca*" fence to surround their mud brick homes. It was also used as a roofing material to cover their homes. Oxen and goats would nibble through it but little if any nutritional value were obtained from the dried mature grass. Beginning in mid-January, even though the government discouraged it, the dried grass was set afire and thousands of square miles of land would be burned. The grass was burned for these reasons:

a. Two weeks after burning the bush, small green sprouts of grass began to grow to about eight centimeters high. This resulted in small amounts of grass for cattle and sheep to browse.
b. It was a way farmers controlled insects, which were detrimental to field crops.
c. It was a way farmers controlled weeds affecting their vegetable gardens and field crops.
d. Burned land was easier to plow with an ox-drawn hand plow or by tilling the soil by hand with a short-handled hoe.
e. The ash from the burned grass tended to raise the pH of acidic laterite soils.
f. Fire was used to hunt animals by chasing them toward waiting hunters.

The historical practice of burning the bush is a management practice that had its merits, especially in a society where there was little to no development. At this stage of development, burning the bush was probably a more practical and economic means of increasing yields without using expensive inputs.

When the rains arrived in June, the grass grew with gusto. During the last week of June 1971, I drove through the bush and looked out across a wide-open grass covered plain, I observed that the native grasses were plentiful and readily available. I asked myself, "I wonder why these people do not make grass silage to feed their oxen during the dry season? Grass silage is a nutritious feedstuff for ruminants and would be a way to keep the oxen strong and healthy during the dry season."

Two days later I asked a farmer in Bessada, "Why do not farmers here in the village make grass silage?" The farmer responded, "*Qu'est-ce que c'est* (What's that)?" I explained to him what silage was and how we fed it to cattle in America, but it seemed to me he didn't quite understand the concept. Then I asked another farmer, and he responded "*Qu'est-cd que c'est?*" After I got the same response the third time, I realized these villagers had never heard of silage.

Here we were in the height of the rainy season, grasses readily available everywhere, oxen starving in the dry season and farmers had never heard of silage. I perceived this as a rural development opportunity but there were many questions which needed to be answered.

The first question was, "How was I going to make a silo to store grass silage?" There were no modern tractor-powered forage choppers or large diesel tractors or cement or glass-lined silos or long plastic bags. These are pieces of equipment that were common to American cattle farmers. Cement was not readily available and when it was, the cost was prohibitive. I concluded that if a farmer could afford a bag of cement, he would rightfully build a home for his family with cement bricks as opposed to mud bricks.

For a period of three weeks I kept thinking, "How am I going to build a silo?" One day Betty and I were having lunch and suddenly I slammed my hand onto the table and said, "That's it!" Betty asked, "That's what?" I replied, "I just figured out how I'm going to build a silo." Betty replied by saying, "I thought you were thinking about something." All this time I was thinking I had to build a silo upward like the traditional silos on American livestock farms. What I really needed was a cylinder. By digging a round hole into the ground, I would have my cylinder. The silo would work on the same principle as the trench silo my father once had on his farm. The Chadian people were genuine experts at digging holes in the ground. They had shovels and all I had to do was show them how to determine its diameter and how deep to dig the hole.

The more I thought about this idea, the more I knew it just had to work. My only concern was termites. They were everywhere. My limited knowledge of termites evolved from an entomology class in college and my observations in Chad. It seemed that the termites would prefer to munch on dry rather than moist materials. Since properly fermented silage would be moist and have an acidic pH of approximately 2.8, I hypothesized, based on these two variables, that the termites might not attack the silage mass. I was willing to take the chance to prove my hypothesis. Because of the time of the year, it was time to make plans to implement the concept.

The village chief and I worked together on a strategy to get people to try this new idea. Through my interpreters, we scheduled a meeting with the *chef de village* and the *chefs de quartier* (villages are divided into quarters, and each quarter has a chief). One-and-one-half hours after the scheduled time, under a big tree, sitting on logs, (meetings never start on time), we began the meeting with local protocol formalities. They hoped that both my wife and I were in good health, they were honored to have us live in their village and have me meet with them, they appreciated my willingness to help the village and other official niceties were offered. Finally, I began to speak. I too had to go through an expected formality. I thanked them for their time to meet with me, expressed my appreciation for their willingness to listen to a new idea, *et cetera*. Then I began to explain to them the concept of making silage. None of them had ever heard of silage. So trying to explain a concept that was completely foreign to these gentlemen was very difficult. I made every attempt to keep it simple. I used my father as an example and explained how he stored silage in a trench silo for his cattle to eat during the winter months. I used the following simple outline to teach village leaders how to make silage:

A. Define silage.
B. Demonstrate the following:
    1. Make a circle three meters in diameter using a

Farmers cooperatively dig holes called "pit silos" three meters in diameter and two meters deep. A pit silo this size had the capacity to store seven to eight tons of silage.

      piece of handmade rope one and one-half meters long for measuring.
2. Dig a hole.
3. Cut the grass.
4. Chop the grass.
5. Fill the pit silo with chopped grass.
6. Cover the pit silo with unchopped grass and soil.

G. Describe when to open the pit silo.
H. Describe how the silage should look, feel, smell and taste.
I. Answer questions.
J. Ask the group if anyone would like to volunteer to make silage and store it in a pit silo.
K. Announce to those who volunteered that I will agree to work with them the first year.

Farmers sit at logs with hands full of grass chopping it into pieces ten centimeters long with machetes. The chopped grass falls directly into the pit silo.

A thick layer of grass is placed over the chopped grass because it would ultimately rot and form a seal for the silage mass.

Using this plan, I went to seven different bush villages and was able to get 19 volunteer farmers to make silage. This was a milestone for the Village of Bessada and surrounding villages.

Beginning in early September 1971, we began to dig holes. We called them "pit silos." We dug round holes three meters in diameter and two meters deep. The soil was piled one meter away from the edge of the pit. A pit silo this size had the capacity to store seven to eight tons of silage, enough to feed two oxen for four months. I had encouraged farmers to work together to help each other with the digging of their respective pits. Once a pit was dug, it could be used for several years with minor maintenance.

The farmers selected sites for their pits far into the bush away from the village, although I tried to urge them to dig their pits closer to the village. This was important because they would have had to transport their silage from the bush to the village on a daily basis. The farmers insisted that they place the pits closer to the grass so they wouldn't have to carry it very far to be chopped. That was what they told me. It took me a year to find out the real reason. I will explain the real reason for placing their pit silos in the bush later. At this point the location of the pit was not vital, it was more important for the farmers to make silage and a pit silo for the first time. Pit location was a detail farmers would sort out themselves as they became more experienced at making silage.

When the hole was dug and cleaned, it was time to begin cutting the grasses from the local area. We used various kinds of herbage to make silage. A local grass known as *hiya* was to be had everywhere. Other local grasses we used included young bamboo, millet leaves, partially dried rice straw and peanut vines. Grass was usually cut with locally made machetes. The grass was gathered into bundles about forty centimeters thick and tied with bark stripped from a young sapling. Strips of bark were used because there was no available hemp twine. The grass was carried to the pit on one's head or, if we were fortunate enough to have a team of oxen with an oxcart, the grass was loaded and hauled to the hole in the cart. There it was unloaded on top of the piled soil alongside the pit.

Since there were no tractor powered forage choppers or diesel tractors in Chad, we used machetes to cut and chop the grass. We went into the bush to find a couple of logs and carried them to the pit. The logs were placed between the pit and the piled soil. Farmers would sit alongside the log, grab a hand full of grass, lay it on the log and with a machete chopped it into pieces about ten centimeters long. The chopped grass fell directly into the pit.

Periodically someone would jump into the pit and tramp the pit's edge, pushing the chopped grass down and forcing out the air. It was not necessary to trample the middle of the grass mass because it would settle by itself. The earthen sides of the pit would cause resistance to chopped grass sliding downward forming air pockets that caused spoilage. By tramping the edges air was forced out so the silage mass would properly ferment.

After the pit was filled with chopped grass, it was piled high in the middle and sloped to the edges. A twenty-centimeter-layer of un-chopped grass was piled on top of the chopped grass. The stems of the un-chopped grass were placed in the middle and the heads toward the edge, giving the silage mass an upside-down cone shape. The thick layer of grass would ultimately rot. This is the reason it is not chopped. The rotted grass would form the seal for the silage mass.

After the silage mass was covered with a thick layer of un-chopped grass, the entire mass was covered with sixty to seventy centimeters of soil from around the silo's edge. When the grass is covered with soil the fermentation process begins. Aerobic bacteria is found naturally on grass and works in the presence of oxygen. It goes to work to begin the process of converting sugars in the grass to acetic acid using the entrapped oxygen. When all of the oxygen is depleted within the silage mass, the anaerobic bacteria which works in the absence of oxygen and is found naturally on the grass, kicks in and continues the process of converting the sugars to acetic acid. When all the sugars in the grass have been converted into acetic acid, the pH is lowered to an approximate pH of 2.8 to 3.2. The lowered acidity of the mass then arrests the action of the anaerobic bacteria and the silage is then preserved. It is possible to keep silage in an unopened pit silo for more than one year. During the ensiling process, the silage mass would settle forty to fifty centimeters. The weight of the soil pushing down prevents the fermented silage from being exposed to oxygen.

The first silo to be opened was done by necessity. On the last Sunday in January 1972, Nestor came to our home and clapped his hands outside our house (Chadians are accustomed to clapping their hands instead of knocking since they have no doors on their mud brick huts). I went to the door and Nestor said to me, "*Patron, nous avons une problème*" (Boss, we have a problem). I said, "What's the problem?" Nestor informed me that "...one of the farmers in the village opened his silo and all of the grass rotted." I was pretty sure I knew why the silage he observed was rotten; it was supposed to be rotten. It was the long un-chopped grass we used to cover the chopped grass. This rotted grass formed the seal between the soil and chopped grass. I said to Nestor, "Would you please inform the village chief that we are going to open that particular silo at three o'clock this afternoon and that all of the villagers are invited to observe this event." The chief sent the village crier into each quarter of the village to loudly inform the people that the first silo was going to be opened and that they were invited to watch. This was the first silo to be opened and my reputation was about to be tested! The hypothesis of the silage concept was about to be proved or disproved.

When I arrived at the pit silo at 1:15 the farmer had indeed dug a small hole in the middle of the pit. When he got to the silage mass, he observed only the top rotted un-chopped grass. By 3:30 more than 300 people had gathered around the pit silo which was about to be opened. We began to shovel the soil off the top of the

After digging through the rotted grass, we reached the chopped grass. It was the greenest, sweetest smelling, best tasting grass silage one could ever find anywhere.

With three hundred people watching I placed the silage on the ground in front of two oxen for the first time. Those two oxen took one whiff of that silage and devoured it like they had never eaten.

silage mass. It took three of us about two hours to uncover the silage mass. When we finally uncovered the entire mass, it all appeared to be rotten. The village chief stood at the edge of the hole with his arms crossed and a non-verbal look on his face which said, "I tried to tell that American that it would rot." I explained to the people that the rotted portion of the silage mass was the unchopped grass we used to cover the chopped silage. I knew it was going to rot, which was the reason we did not chop it. At this point I did not know for sure if the chopped silage under the rotted grass was good or not.

I got down on my knees and with my hands dug through the rotted grass. When I reached the chopped grass, I found the greenest, sweetest smelling, best tasting grass silage one could ever find anywhere. I was absolutely elated. I shouted, "Madjingaye, Madjingaye (good, good)!" I took a hand full of chopped silage and held it up for the people to see and passed it around to allow people to feel and smell it.

The people were not convinced their oxen would eat this "weird" smelling grass. I asked Nestor if he would send for a pair of oxen so we could determine if the oxen would eat the silage. It was important for the people to see with their own eyes the oxen eating the silage. A short time later, a farmer brought before all the people two oxen. I filled a homemade basket full of silage and was about to feed two oxen their first mouthful of silage in front of more than three hundred people. I said to myself, "Ox, if you have never eaten before, now is your chance." When I put that basket filled with silage in front of those two oxen, they devoured it like they had never eaten before. The people reacted by saying, "*Ki, ki, ki* (wow, fantastic)!"

Now that the people knew that the grass did not rot and that the oxen would eat it, it was now time to teach farmers how to feed it. Since there were no scales available for farmers to use, it was necessary to figure out how to teach farmers to feed their oxen the proper amount of silage. A French extension officer had a portable twenty-five-kilo scale that he lent me. Because older men and women in the village made baskets, containers were available. I asked the farmer, "Show me a basket that would be used to carry the silage to the oxen." Then I asked the farmer to fill the basket with silage and I weighed it with my borrowed scale. Depending upon the size of the basket, I explained to the farmer that he needed to feed three baskets of silage to each ox every day during the dry season. Because farmers had no scales, they had no way to measure a kilo. However, they understood very well how to feed two or three baskets of silage per ox per day.

That first year we made silage and stored it in pit silos at seven different bush villages with nineteen volunteer farmers bold enough to try making silage. When each silo was opened, we had the same results that we had in Bessada. The farmers were very pleased. They had a success that used their indigenous skills of digging a pit, cutting grass with a machete and carrying grass on their heads. They also used their own resources of grass, oxen and ox carts and implemented the modern concept of silage.

When we started this project the French Extension officers were very skeptical. They predicted that the farmers would not try it. The silage would rot and termites would eat it. The grass would not make proper silage and the nutritional value would not justify the effort. Their skepticism certainly made me think seriously about these issues, because the French had lived in Chad longer than I but it seemed there was always a practical explanation for their concerns.

When I met with village chiefs and farmers and began my plan, the French were astonished by the fact that I had nineteen farmers who volunteered to try it. They had told me they knew these farmers and that they say they will do something but usually did not follow through. Then when the farmers began digging their pits, the French would drive by in their pickup trucks to observe what was happening. They were flabbergasted that a Peace Corps Volunteer could pull this project off with virtually no financial support. I often felt like I was being spied upon and they were waiting for me to fail.

When we opened the silos and experienced such success, I filled a plastic bag full of silage and drove fifteen kilometers to Koumra to where the French Extension Central Office was. M. Depeux, Director of *Animation Rurale* (French Extension System) was one of the people who was a skeptic. He and I were aligned colleagues and amiable friends. I walked into his office, sat the plastic bag full of silage on his desk in front of him and said, "*Voilà, mon ami* (there my friend)." He carefully examined the silage and was very impressed and congratulated me. From that point on the French were no longer skeptics, but very cooperative colleagues.

The second year of the project, we had forty-two pit silos dug and filled with silage in the same seven villages. The farmers had expressed the need of being able to find a practical and inexpensive way to feed their animals during the dry seasons. A team of oxen was a major investment for village farmers and usually if their oxen survived the dry season, they were gaunt and too weak to pull a plow at a time when their land should be tilled. The concept of this project assisted them in successfully addressing the issue.

The farmers who made silage this time, dug new pits closer to the village. The real reason they dug the pits in the bush one or two kilometers from the village the first year was that they had a need to protect their self-esteem just in case this project failed the first year. If it failed, the silage and pit were hidden away in the bush from the village people and it would quietly dissipate. People would not see a failure or chastise the farmer. After we had success story after success story of making silage, the word rapidly spread among the villagers that this was a practical way to store local grasses to feed oxen.

I filled a plastic bag with silage and sent it to President François Tombalbaye in Fort-Lamy so he could see it and to share in its success. I wrote a report for the Minister of Agriculture describing the concept of making silage and pit silos. He took excerpts from my report and made large yellow posters and distributed them to be posted in public places such as post offices, veterinary clinics, government buildings and even road signs. The posters urged people to make silage and described how to do it.

I was asked to teach how to make silage and pit silos within various rural development programs in Chad. These programs were sponsored by French, Swiss, Italian and American agencies. My feeling was that we were all in Chad for the same reason, and that was to help Chadians. It made no difference who received the credit for these efforts. The important thing was that Chadian farmers learned to make silage to feed their oxen during the dry season. Among those who requested that I teach silage making at their own institutions were missionaries from the American

Baptist Mid-Missions, Italian Catholic Agricultural School, volunteers from the French *La Maison Familiale*, Swiss Farm School and American Peace Corps Volunteers.

Meanwhile the *Director de l'Élevage* (Director of Livestock) for the Republic of Mali was in Washington, D.C. in July 1972, where he had learned about a Peace Corps Volunteer in Chad who had developed a practical method for making silage to feed oxen during the dry season. When he returned to his capitol city of Bamako, he approached the Director of Peace Corps/Mali Jack Burch. He inquired about the silage project in Chad. The Peace Corps/Mali Director began to send a series of telegrams to the Peace Corps/Chad Director, Boudouin de Marcken. The Chad Director summoned all Peace Corps Volunteers to Fort-Lamy in December 1972, for routine group and individual meetings. When Betty and I met with the Director, he asked us if we would be willing to travel to Mali to do a feasibility study for Peace Corps/Mali to determine if the pit silo and a silage project could be done there. We said, "…why not!" On 3 January 1973, Betty and I departed Fort-Lamy, Chad for Bamako, Mali via Abidjan, Ivory Coast (see "Was Silage Feasible in Mali?").

When we arrived in Bamako there was no one there to meet us. By coincidence, and to our good fortune, we met the Peace Corps/Mali nurse and she took us to the Peace Corps office. We settled in the Peace Corps hostel and rested until our evening meal.

The next day a series of meetings with Peace Corps/Mali Director, *Director de l'Élevage,*" and Peace Corps Volunteers was conducted. After two days of meetings we used the third day to prepare for a nine-day trip. On 7 January 1973, Peace Corps Volunteer Leslie Temanson, Betty and I left Bamako and toured Mali to collect data for the feasibility study. We traveled north to San, Mopti, Bandiagara and south to Sikasso and back to Bamako. On this trip we talked with farmers and veterinarians, checked the depth of the water table by looking into water wells, checked stoniness of the soil, examined the types of available grasses, determined what types of crop residue could be used to make silage and we talked with people to determine if they were nomadic or sedentary.

The trip was very educational and eventful. We were able to purchase gasoline along the way in towns. We could not do that in Chad. One has to carry all needed gasoline in jerry cans. We stayed in motels each night. There were no motels along the dirt roads or in Chadian villages. We had running water in the motels while we did not have it in Bessada, Chad. We climbed down the Bandiagara Fault and visited the cliff dwellers. There we saw how the cliff dwellers grow onions on top of a rocky mountain. When the onions were harvested, they were pounded into a mush and formed into round balls about the size of a softball. The onions were dried and stored for selling at a later time. We visited the oldest mosque in West Africa, the famous mosque at Djenné.

While in Mopti, we studied the delta where the Niger River flows north, then makes a huge "horseshoe" turn and flows south. A large acreage of rice was grown there on the delta. When rice was harvested, the straw is generally still green and a possible resource for silage. We had to study the dates when the delta was flooded and the dates when the rice was harvested.

After we returned to Bamako, we scheduled a series of training sessions for Leslie Temanson to learn how to make pit silos and silage. Following his training, Leslie decided to extend his Peace Corps Volunteer stay in Mali for an additional year to take the leadership in introducing silage and pit silos in Mali. Leslie's silage project was very successful and it continued on as a Peace Corps Project for a period of eight years.

The United States Agency for International Development (USAID) provided funding for the project to give farmers seed to grow forages for pit silos. Farmers received free seed from USAID for three years until funding was phased down. Then Peace Corps Volunteers found it difficult to get farmers to again make silage from local grasses because there were no funds to purchase seed.

They did not want to use forages after getting free seed. It took volunteers two years to convince farmers to make grass silage again. Peace Corps/Mali ultimately phased down their successful silage project in 1981.

Creativity is a necessity in developing countries. One should never "pooh-pooh" an idea that can possibly help people to help themselves. We were able to introduce a modern concept of feeding oxen quality grass silage by using the people's own knowledge, skills, and resources.

21

Death in Its Raw Form

With Nestor, Pierre and Papa John (President Tombalbaye's brother), we left Bessada at 6:15 A.M. on 15 October 1971. It was a glorious morning, the sky was clear and blue, the sun was up and people were beginning their daily walk to the fields to toil at their chores. Our mission was to drive to the village of Sebe to work with farmers who were filling their pit silos with grass. Sebe was located in the southern part of the Canton of Bessada.

We arrived at Sebe at 6:50 and saw that several people were gathered around one particular hut. One young man spotted us and came running out to the road to flag us down. I stopped and excitedly he told us someone was very sick. So we got out of the car, went over to the front of the hut among all the people and lying on the ground was a young man about twenty-two years old who was dying.

We just stood there helplessly and watched this man die. There was not a thing we could do for him. I never felt so amateurish in all my life. I knew this fellow well! He was one of the cooperating farmers who was in the process of filling a pit silo. In fact, it was his silo we were planning to visit and help him until noon that day.

That morning at about 5:30 he drank some *bili-bili* (a form of local beer) before going out to his silo. Unknown to him, the bottle that he had filled with *bili-bili* had been used the previous day in the cotton field to measure a pesticide. This pesticide was being distributed to farmers by the government to be used for preventing weevils from invading their cotton. Filling that bottle and pouring it into a knapsack sprayer filled with water according to mixing instructions was how the farmers measured this pesticide. The pesticide was stirred into the water before spraying it. The sprayer is attached to a man's back and he pumps it as he walks along each row and sprays pesticide onto the cotton. This pesticide is deadly poisonous to humans if ingested. Apparently the bottle had not been washed or rinsed with water before putting *bili-bili* into it that morning. It was suspected that residue from the pesticide was in the bottle and he drank it mixed with the *bili-bili.*

After he drank the *bili-bili*, he walked about two kilometers to his pit silo to begin chopping grass silage. After he arrived, he began to feel sick so he walked back to the village. By the time we drove in, at 6:50 A.M., he was almost dead. He was soaking wet from sweating and his lungs were full of fluid. As I listened to him breathing, there was much gurgling. He went into convulsions and one man on each side held his arms down. Everyone gathered around and watched him die. All I had to say was that "It was a heck of a way to die."

I was in a very awkward situation. Two young men pleaded with me to take him to the hospital in Koumra, some forty kilometers away on a narrow, deep sandy road. Koumra was at least an hour's drive from Sebe. My better sense told me not to get involved. It was rather obvious that this man was almost dead by the time the two young men pleaded with me to take him to the hospital and I knew I would not have enough time to get him to

Koumra alive. When one takes on the responsibility of taking a sick person from his or her village and that person should die in route, the driver of the car (in this case me) would be responsible for his/her death. This was an unwritten tribal law. Fortunately the President's brother was with me and he knew there would not be enough time to get him to the hospital alive, so he said, "No" to the two fellows who were pleading with me.

According to this unwritten tribal law, if an expatriate or anyone for that matter transports a sick person to the hospital who dies en route to the hospital, there are serious ramifications of which one must be aware. If the family does not know the driver, the driver will most likely be killed if he/she does not have some form of police protection. We were instructed by the Peace Corps Director that if this ever happened, we were to drive immediately to the nearest large town and report it to the police. They in turn would give you some form of protection and deal with the issue.

While we were standing there, an old woman came toward us and began to wail. Two younger women walked over, placed their arms around her and locked hands to keep her under control. She then went over to the dying man, knelt down beside him and stayed there until he was dead. I had assumed it was his mother or close kin.

With a death in the village, no one works that day or the next. Sometimes no one goes out to the fields for three or four days, depending upon the level of importance the deceased had in the village. Generally the elder women from the village washed the body, then wrapped it in a white cotton Americana cloth. While this was taking place, the men went to the burial grounds and dug a grave.

If the family of the deceased was not Christian, they would wail and beat tom-toms all night. If they were Christian, they usually sang hymns, prayed, gave short sermons, or just sat with the family and said nothing. The people sat around the body all day and night. Early the next morning the deceased was buried. Immediate family members of the deceased were responsible for feeding all those who came to pay their respects. People, especially family members, came from surrounding villages and far away towns. This could be a costly event because many people stayed in the village for several days to mourn after the burial.

After the gentleman died we went about our work at another silo site in the next village like nothing had happened that morning. After the burial, life went on and the people eventually got back to their daily lives and routines. That morning we experienced an inevitable part of life that's the destiny of all humans. Observing it first hand left an indelible image in my mind that will be forever remembered.

22

Tragic Accident

One Wednesday evening Betty, Nestor and I were driving to Koumra from Bessada to prayer meeting and to get our mail when we came upon a tragic fatal accident. We looked up ahead and a large truck was stopped on the road with people standing around a dead man lying on the road. When the truck hit a bump on the road he had fallen from the back. The truck was hauling lumber and several passengers. When the truck hit the bump, a board began to fall and the deceased apparently reached for it, lost his balance and fell off the moving vehicle.

I stopped to see if there was anything we could do and was informed that they were waiting for family members of the deceased and the police to arrive. We went on our way to the prayer meeting in Koumra. We had dropped Nestor off in Koumra to visit his friends while we went to the Mission Station. Two hours later (9:15 P.M.) we picked him up and while we drove back to Bessada, we saw the same truck still stopped at the same spot and the dead man was still lying on the road. The people were still waiting for the family and police to arrive. We stopped again and Nestor spoke to someone in the Sara Madjingaye language and we were asked if we could take the truck driver to the police station in Koumra. Since Nestor was with us as an interpreter, we agreed to turn around and take the driver to the Koumra police station. He wanted to be put in jail before family members arrived at the scene of the accident. Often the driver in a fatal accident was killed on the spot, especially if the driver was at fault. He wanted to be put in jail for his own protection. We dropped him off at the police station and resumed our drive back to Bessada. As we again arrived at the accident scene we did not stop because we had been advised that there was no further need to get involved.

23

"She's Going To Get It One of These Days!"

Important Note: Except for the names of Dr. Dave and Ruth Seymour, President François Tombalbaye, Ambassador Terence Todman, Mary Baker, John Riggan, Betty and myself, the other names listed in this story are fictitious to protect those involved in this regrettable saga.

John Riggan, Peace Corps Director/Chad was touring southern Chad to visit several Peace Corps Volunteers to assess their well-being and project(s) progress. He visited us on 17 and 18 November 1971, and stayed overnight. During his visit we featured farmers with pit silos, Betty's sewing class, and trimming horses' hooves. We took John to visit Dr. Dave Seymour at Baptist Mid-Missions in Koumra because he wanted to express his thanks for supporting Peace Corps/Chad. John said his goodbyes to Betty and me at mid-morning when he departed Bessada for Doba, a town two hours west of Bessada via a dirt road. We knew he would be in Doba for at least three days. We were pleased that the Peace Corps/Chad Director visited us in Bessada to discuss our program.

Late that afternoon, seven Peace Corps Volunteers arrived at our house in Bessada. Four volunteers were on the Peace Corps well-drilling team stationed at Fort Archambault and the other three were English teachers in Koumra. We had a wonderful visit with everyone. The mood was festive with much laughter; we exchanged information and briefed each other on our respective projects. The well team needed to head back to Fort Archambault and I said, "I'll take the three teachers back to Koumra." Shortly after the well team departed Bessada, Betty and I left to return the three teachers to their houses in Koumra. We took Joe and Peter to their respective houses then we took Helen home last at 7:00 P.M.

Helen had asked us to take her to the house of a fellow teacher from Dahomey because he had the key to her house. As she walked down the lane in front of our car to his house it was obvious that Helen had no underclothes on and her dress was rather snug. I said to Betty, "She's going to get it one of these days." We waited until she was there before we departed for Bessada. When she got to his house we drove away thinking she was safe.

Betty and I were sleeping soundly when suddenly we heard someone from outside yell, "Jim! Jim!" I jumped out of bed and went to the window. There was Dr. Seymour's truck and Ruth Seymour was standing below our window. She said, "Helen's been hurt and Dr. Dave wants you to come in." We hurriedly got dressed, gathered our travel papers and money. We then dashed outside to get more details from Ruth. She said Helen had been beaten up and Dr. Dave was working on her and he wanted me to go after John Riggan in Doba. I went back into the house, got two jerry cans of gasoline and put them in the back of my vehicle. There were no gas stations anywhere on the road that I would be driving.

Betty and I followed Ruth to Koumra and there we found Helen in critical condition. Her jaw was broken and sewn shut, cuts everywhere, a black eye, and she was in a stupor-like condition. Dr. Dave told me she had to be medically evacuated. He patched her up enough to stand the trip to Fort-Lamy and on to Germany. He was going to immediately take her to Fort Archambault and put her in bed at Mary Baker's house (another Baptist Missionary) until morning. Then he said, "We will put her on an airplane for Fort-Lamy." We put two mattresses in the back of Dr. Dave's pickup truck and lifted Helen onto the mattresses. One of Dr. Dave's male nurses volunteered to accompany her in back of the truck.

Before they left, Dr. Dave assigned his houseboy to accompany me to Doba. He did not want me traveling on that road alone in the middle of the night. I was to find John Riggan and together we would meet Dr. Dave in Fort Archambault in the morning. Betty stayed with Ruth Seymour at the Baptist Mid-Mission Station. Dr. Dave would get Mary Baker to radio the Peace Corps Office the first thing in the morning to inform the Peace Corps nurse to meet Helen at the airport in Fort-Lamy. Mary would also purchase Helen's plane ticket in the morning.

At 1:00 A.M. we left Bessada for Doba. I was really on a roll, traveling no less than eighty kilometers per hour. About halfway to Doba I spotted a wild rabbit on the road and I hit it with the car. That was the one and only wild rabbit I saw while living for two years in Chad, and I killed it. Someone would have surely picked it up in the morning and eaten it, because no food is wasted.

I arrived in Doba at 3:00. I knew where the house was and

went directly there. I first knocked on the door and got no response. Then I went into the house and yelled for John. Finally he woke up. John was sleeping soundly and was groggy. I sat at his bedside and told him that Helen was seriously injured and she had to be evacuated. Dr. Seymour was on the way to Fort Archambault with Helen and he wanted us both to meet him there early in the morning. John's driver Brahim woke up when I yelled for John. He knew something was wrong, so he quickly began preparations to leave. Finally John dressed and sat down and said to me, "Jim, now that I'm awake, tell me one more time. What happened?"

Brahim was instructed by John to drive on to Moundou to inform the Peace Corps Volunteers that the Director had to delay his scheduled visit, make an attempt to radio the Peace Corps Office in Fort-Lamy then return to Koumra and await John's arrival. At 3:45 John climbed into my Renault and we left for Fort Archambault, at least a four-hour drive in the middle of the night. If there were no problems we could arrive in Fort Archambault by 8:00 A.M.

After John realized what happened, he wanted to see Helen before she left Fort Archambault to get additional details and information directly from her. She would undoubtedly be on the next plane out of Fort-Lamy for Frankfurt, Germany, bound for the U.S. Military Hospital before John could return to Fort-Lamy. On our journey to Fort Archambault, driving at eighty kilometers per hour, we had to be on the lookout for elephants, antelope, hippopotami, Cape buffalo, domestic cows, donkeys, or other animals on the road, especially when we neared *Parc Mandal*.

Fortunately we had no driving problems and John and I arrived at Fort Archambault a little after 8:00 in the morning. We went directly to Mary Baker's house where we found some additional complications. Helen was still rather out of it, and her mouth was sewn shut and she could not verbally communicate with us. So John got very little information as to what had happened to her in Koumra.

Mary Baker learned that the only Saturday flight from Fort Archambault to Fort-Lamy was canceled. When Mary radioed Peace Corps/Chad in Fort-Lamy to inform them that the flight was canceled, she asked them to charter an airplane and send it directly to Fort Archambault. When the American Embassy informed President Tombalbaye of the crisis which unfolded at Fort Archambault, he immediately dispatched his official plane to evacuate Helen.

We waited at Mary Baker's house until we heard the plane circling over Fort Archambault as it prepared to land. As soon as we heard the plane, we placed Helen onto the same two mattresses in the back of Dr. Dave's pickup truck and drove her to the airport. The plane had landed and we drove directly onto the tarmac toward it. We backed the pickup truck to the plane's rear-side door and the three of us lifted Helen's stretcher into the plane. An American Peace Corps Volunteer who was a nurse assigned to the hospital in Fort Archambault had assisted Dr. Dave in caring for Helen. At the plane I asked her if she would travel to Fort-Lamy with Helen. She agreed but she had not expected to travel and did not have her travel documents or money. The plane was ready to depart and she did not have time to fetch them. I gave her some money so she could accompany Helen. John, Dr. Dave and I stood and watched the plane taxi down the runway and fly off to Fort-Lamy.

We all went back to the mission station and Mary Baker radioed the Peace Corps Office in Fort-Lamy to inform the duty officer that Helen and a Peace Corps Volunteer nurse were on their way. By this time it was 11:00 and none of us had had any sleep. We were all very tired so Mary Baker decided that we should all go to bed there at the mission station and sleep for a couple hours. We all took good "ole" Mary's advice; she was such a gracious person.

At 2:30 John and I awoke from our siesta and prepared to travel back to Koumra to begin an investigation to determine what really happened and to obtain as many facts as possible. We thanked Mary Baker for her hospitality and assistance in allowing Peace Corps to use her mission as a staging point for getting Helen evacuated to Fort-Lamy and then on to Frankfurt, Germany.

When John Riggan and I arrived in Koumra, we first went to the *Sous-Préfet*'s Office to report the crisis that occurred in Koumra the day before and to describe what we knew thus far. Even though he had already heard about the incident, it was best if he heard it from us. We asked the *Sous-Préfet* to accompany us to Helen's house to oversee our actions as we went through Helen's personal belongings in a government house. Along with the *Sous-Préfet* and a *gendarme* guard, John Riggan and I drove to Helen's house in our respective vehicles. Since it was a government house, the *SousPréfet* had a key to open the door.

When we entered the house we couldn't believe what we saw. The inside of that house indicated that a tremendous degree of turmoil had taken place. The contents of the house were strewn everywhere! There were broken glasses, dishes, ripped curtains, broken chairs, the kitchen table was upside down, papers scattered, clothes strewn about the whole house and blood was splattered everywhere. We suspected that some form of drugs was involved to cause that much chaos.

As each of us examined Helen's personal belongings, I found a silver colored pipe in Helen's bedroom that appeared to be well-used for smoking marijuana. Unseen by the others I put it into my pocket. The only thing we could do at the moment was to leave everything as we found it. While John and I followed the *Sous-Préfet* to the prison in my car, I showed him the pipe I found. He said, " Keep it in your pocket."

We had asked the *Sous-Préfet* if we could interview the teacher from Dahomey who was an imprisoned suspect. He agreed to accompany us to the prison. He took us inside the prison and asked the prison guard to open the cell door and allow us to interview the teacher suspect in his cell.

The teacher, dressed in a pair of shorts and a shirt, was sitting on a cot in his prison cell when we arrived. He stood up and greeted us and said he was glad we came to see him. His behavior pattern and speaking ability seemed to us to be normal. However his physical well-being was obviously stressed or fatigued and he was badly cut on his hand, leg and thigh.

The *Sous-Préfet* left John Riggan and me alone with the prisoner while we questioned him. We asked the teacher his name, where he worked, where he lived, if he knew Helen and what had happened. He told us that Helen and he were colleagues at the school where they both taught and that they were very good friends. Helen had come to his house to get her house keys and she invited him to her house for something to eat. He accepted her invitation and went there with her.

During his visit, Helen lit a pipe full of marijuana and while smoking it she offered him a puff. He told us he refused. I took the pipe out of my pocket and showed it to him. He immediately said, "That's it!" Helen apparently made up her mind that she was going to turn him on to marijuana and made cookies. In the cookie mix she allegedly added marijuana. After the cookies were baked, she asked the teacher to try them and he ate several. A short time later he apparently went berserk. He said he did not remember anything soon after he ate the cookies.

After our interview with the prisoner we were escorted from the cell. By this time it was dark and we were both exhausted. John and I went to pick up Betty at Ruth Seymour's home at the Baptist Mid-Mission in Koumra. We left Koumra and went to our house in Bessada where John stayed for the night.

The next day we continued on with our investigation by re-visiting Helen's house. John took some of Helen's personal belongings with him to ship back to her home in United States. After seeing her injuries and physical condition, he was reasonably sure Helen would not be returning to Chad.

From the evidence we found in Helen's house, data from the

prisoner interview and information we got from Dr. Dave Seymour, we concluded that Helen was probably the person who attempted to get her teacher friend to use marijuana. He apparently refused to smoke the lit marijuana in the pipe, but ate homemade cookies not knowing they were laced with marijuana. It was when the effects of marijuana kicked in and caused him to go berserk and assault Helen that caused her serious bodily harm. John and I were rather confident that this was what probably had occurred. John put together his report for the *Sous-Préfet* and *Préfet*.

That afternoon John and I again traveled to Fort Archambault to meet with the *Préfet* to give an official report. When we arrived we went directly to the *Préfet*'s Office Building to make an appointment. While we waited two hours to see the *Préfet*, John and I went to a restaurant and had a late lunch.

We went back to the *Préfet*'s Office and I waited in the car while John met him. John was the official spokesperson for the Peace Corps and it was not appropriate for me to be with him during the presentation of his report. I was very curious as to how the *Préfet* would react to John's report.

When John finally returned, he seemed to feel that the *Préfet* accepted the report with dignity and the incident would not jeopardize the work of other Peace Corps Volunteers within the region of his jurisdiction. John then returned to Fort-Lamy by Air Chad to give his report to the American Ambassador.

When he returned to Fort-Lamy, the Peace Corps Nurse had already evacuated Helen out of Chad to Germany where she was ultimately transferred to a hospital near Washington, D.C. for surgery and treatment. The American Ambassador considered this incident to be an embarrassment to the people of the United States of America.

Ambassador Todman met with President François Tombalbaye and described the incident to him as reported by John Riggan. He profusely thanked the President for sending his official airplane to Fort Archambault to evacuate Helen. The Ambassador apologized to President Tombalbaye and the Chadian people for this deplorable and unconscionable incident. He assured the President that he would personally address this issue with the Peace Corps Volunteers living and working in the region.

On Thanksgiving Day 1972, several of the Peace Corps Volunteers agreed to meet in Fort Archambault and have Thanksgiving Dinner together. One of the volunteers found an old turkey somewhere and that was going to be featured at the dinner. *"Sooo"* we got together in the morning and the mood was rather festive. Betty had made a squash pie and everyone was to bring something. There was much laughter while we were making preparations with the meager household items such as dishes, cups, glasses, pots, and other kitchen items found in Peace Corps Volunteer houses. Suddenly there was a knock at the door. One of the volunteers answered the door and there was a messenger from the *Préfet*'s residence. He informed us that we would have Thanksgiving Dinner at the *Préfet*'s residence with the American Ambassador at 2:00. Whoa! Now this was serious business. All the plans we had made to have Thanksgiving dinner together were put on hold.

We knew right away why we were to have dinner with the American Ambassador. The group's mood became more somber and we began to get ready to go to the *Préfet*'s residence. None of us was dressed for such an occasion. Joe had a long beard, which was not appropriate to the Chadian authorities. Against his better judgment we sat him down on a chair and trimmed his beard. Betty borrowed a dress from Mary Baker, the Baptist Mid-Mission missionary. All the men borrowed dress shirts from Jean-Paul Marteau. Two of the girls borrowed dresses from Jean-Paul's wife. I desperately needed a haircut, so Betty gave me a trim. After a while we all began to laugh about getting dressed up for this special occasion with the *Préfet* and the American Ambassador.

When we all arrived at the *Préfet*'s residence, we didn't look too bad. At least we had looked better than we did three hours earlier. The *Préfet* was very cordial and warmly welcomed us. The American Ambassador Terence Todman also warmly greeted us and actually called some of us by name. We socialized for nearly an hour before the festivities began. The *Préfet* gave us an official welcome to his residence and told us how he was privileged to have the American Ambassador with him on this important American holiday. He then introduced Terence Todman, Ambassador to Chad from United States of America.

In front of the *Préfet*, Ambassador Todman talked to us in French about how tragic it had been that Helen had to be evacuated from Chad. He told us that this incident jeopardized the image of Peace Corps and the United States of America. He went on to say that because of this repulsive event the Government of Chad was considering asking all Peace Corps Volunteers to leave. He assured the *Préfet* and the President that this kind of behavior was unacceptable to the American people and that he expected all Peace Corps Volunteers to represent America with dignity and integrity. The event that caused Helen to be evacuated was unacceptable and he assured the *Préfet* this would not happen again with this group of volunteers. With this all being said, we began the festivities and had an enjoyable Thanksgiving dinner with the *Préfet* and Ambassador Todman. The Ambassador's talk to us in front of the *Préfet* was the proper diplomatic expression that in all likelihood prevented Peace Corps from being asked to leave Chad. The *Préfet* seemed to be satisfied and one can be assured the President knew what the American Ambassador said within a short period of time. It was obvious the volunteers took Ambassador Todman's comments to heart and we had no more problems.

The teacher from Dahomey who assaulted Helen had taken a turn for the worse, and had to be taken from prison in Koumra and transported to a large hospital in Fort Archambault. His mental capability was damaged from the allegedly drug-laced cookies and resulted in his being out of control. After two days in the hospital at Fort Archambault, Dr. Dave Seymour was making his rounds to see him and other patients. Ironically, as Dr. Dave was walking down the hall he saw the teacher making an attempt to escape from the hospital while nurses and orderlies attempted to restrain him. When Dr. Seymour saw what was happening, he literally tackled the teacher to restrain him from doing harm to the hospital attendants. Dr. Seymour was slightly injured from this episode but was successful in keeping him restrained.

To make diplomatic matters worse, the teacher who was now mentally incapacitated was the son of the President of Dahomey. This caused President Tombalbaye to be in an awkward state of affairs because this teacher was also a volunteer teaching Chadian students. The last bit of information we heard about this teacher was that his mental condition required institutional confinement and he was sent back to his village in Dahomey to be cared for by his immediate family.

In the final letter Peace Corps received from Helen, she indicated she wanted to return to Chad. John Riggan, Director of Peace Corps/Chad promptly responded. He told her that Chadian government authorities had informed his office that if Helen ever again set foot into the Republic of Chad, she would immediately be arrested at the airport and imprisoned for improper behavior for causing permanent mental damage to an international volunteer teacher. As far as we know at this writing thirty-seven years later, Helen never again returned to Chad. Also I have never heard from her nor do we know her whereabouts. The last time I saw Helen was when we lifted her into the airplane at Fort Archambault.

Helen was a bright young lady, very talented, with a sincere benevolent desire to help people, was personable and had much potential for a successful career. We have often wondered how her injuries healed, if she too was permanently disfigured, how she coped with her emotional well-being as she reflected on what happened to her in Chad, if she had ever learned that her teacher friend became mentally incapacitated, what she was now doing, where she was living, if she ever got married and if she ever had any remorseful feelings for her behavior.

The title of this saga was "She's Going to Get It One Of These Days." Well, she did get it that day and her shenanigans resulted in an international incident between Chad, United States of America and Dahomey. Why did Helen do what she did? What possessed her to give a drug to another teacher? Why was this evil deed important to her? Why would an intelligent person like Helen not know at the time what she was doing was wrong? Answers to these questions and many others will forever be mysteries.

24

Friday Night At The Movies

Living in Bessada was exciting, but much more tame in the evenings than to what we were accustomed in Pennsylvania. Living without electricity or running water for two years was a humbling experience. For light in our house we used Petromax lamps and kerosene lanterns. We carried in buckets of water from the village well for bathing each night and to flush the toilet. We had no telephone, no air conditioner, no television, no medical facilities other than the Baptist Mid-Mission Hospital some twenty-five kilometers away and our only contact with the outside world was our short-wave radio. We usually listened to the BBC world news while eating breakfast and dinner. After dinner each night, Betty and I carried two chairs outside and sat them down at the bottom of the steps. It was cooler there and we listened to the sounds in the village while I smoked my pipe. It was so interesting. Sometimes we would hear the drone of people talking, arguing, shouting, laughing, wailing, crying, moaning, dogs barking, donkeys braying, cows bawling, sick people coughing, the village crier yelling out messages issued by the village chief and a rare car or truck passing through the village. Other times the village was rather quiet. At 8:00 we listened to Voice of America programs on the battery-powered short-wave radio as we watched stars and satellites cross the crystal clear skies above. Sometimes for variety we listened to British Broadcasting Corporation (BBC). We sat outside until one of us fell asleep, then we carried our chairs and radio back into the house and went to bed. This was a typical evening for us in Bessada, Chad.

Each year in mid-December at the beckoning call of the Peace Corps Director, Peace Corps Volunteers journeyed to Fort-Lamy for the annual all volunteer meetings. After the conclusion of group and individual meetings, most of the volunteers stayed in the capital for the Christmas holiday and returned to their respective posts after New Year's Day.

One evening after Christmas in December 1971, at a gathering in the American Ambassador's residence, I met, for the first time, the U.S. Embassy warehouse manager. He invited me to the Embassy warehouse to look at a motor he wanted to have removed because he didn't know what kind of motor it was or what it was used for. He wanted to know if I could use it in Bessada. I accepted his invitation and the next day I visited the warehouse. He showed me the motor that was taking up space and needed to be removed. I said to myself, "Oh my gosh, if that engine works, I certainly can use it." It was a Wisconsin air-cooled engine attached to a small generator. I told him, "Yes, I'll take it as is." The engine was brand new, still in its crate and had never been used. However it was covered with dust and dirt.

We loaded the motor and generator onto the Peace Corps Land Rover and hauled it to the Peace Corps workshop. There we unpacked it from the crate and found the generator was covered with layered dust. There was no operator's manual. In spite of this

I knew the Wisconsin engine well because my father had one on his hay pick-up baler and I was quite familiar with it. We pulled out the air hose and blew off the dust, cleaned the spark plug, blew air through the gas line, changed the oil, put gasoline into the tank, cleaned the points and cleaned the sediment bowl. Then we held our breath to see if the engine would start. During the second pull on the rope, it fired. On the third pull the air-cooled Wisconsin engine started and it ran like a new engine. We let it run for nearly thirty minutes and then we flipped the switch for turning on the generator. Again we held our breath because if a generator is not used for a long period of time, the brushes become corroded and foil its performance. After about five minutes, the gauge dial moved from red to yellow and finally into the green. We knew it was working properly. Wow! What a find! The total cost to Peace Corps for a new Wisconsin air-cooled engine and one generator was $0.00.

In the Peace Corps warehouse there was a 16mm movie projector that could be used with the newly acquired engine and generator. I asked the Peace Corps Director for permission to take the projector south to Bessada for several months until our next trip back to Fort-Lamy. He said it was not being used and I could keep it as long as we needed it. The only drawback was the generator was 110 volts and the movie projector was 220 volts. I knew where I could borrow a transformer in Fort Archambault, so that wasn't a problem.

There was a United States Information Service (USIS) in Fort-Lamy that was an integral part of the American Embassy. I visited the USIS office and learned that they had 16mm films in French available for Chadians to view. I asked if I could check out films to show in southern Chad. The person who was in charge was glad that she could make these films available for people living in remote areas of Chad. I checked out three films: *President François Tombalbaye's Visit to United States, NASA Flight to the Moon* and *American Wrestling*. I was not sure when these films could be returned but they would eventually be returned to USIS. The lady had said there was no rush to return them.

Now that I had collected all the paraphernalia I needed, it was time to return to Bessada. We drove the Peace Corps Land Rover, loaded with luggage, supplies, spare parts, gasoline, equipment and all the paraphernalia we needed to show a movie in our village. Betty and I drove for sixteen hours on a dirt road all the way from Fort-Lamy to Bessada without incident. It was a long and dangerous trip. If one breaks down in the bush, there are no gas stations, garages and mechanics or nearby villages for help. Sometimes one can be stranded for two days before another vehicle comes along to flag down for assistance. Nevertheless we arrived back in Bessada safely. On the way to Bessada, we stopped in Fort Archambault to rest and visit other Peace Corps Volunteers. One volunteer and her French husband Jean-Paul Marteau had a transformer I could borrow for the generator and movie projector. They willingly lent it to me.

When we returned to Bessada the people were happy to see that we had arrived safely. Betty and I were tired after such a long hot journey, bouncing in a Land Rover for more than six hundred kilometers of rough and dusty dirt roads. We rested all the next day.

About two weeks later I was able to find some time to see if all the paraphernalia that I had accumulated would work. I started the Wisconsin engine, turned on the generator and plugged in the transformer to see if it worked. All the gauges functioned normally. The only thing I had to do next was to determine if the projector would work off the transformer. I plugged the projector cord into the socket box on the transformer and it worked beautifully. Now that I knew everything worked, I was ready to see a movie that evening.

For the first time, we *thought* we would have a private showing with special guests. I had asked the two young men who worked for me, Nestor and Pierre, to invite the *Chef de village,*

118

Chef de canton, secretaire de canton and the President's brother to our home after dark and we would try to show a movie on the side of our house. We lined up chairs facing the wall on the backside of our house. Shortly after dark our guests arrived and I gave each of them a Gala beer to sip while they watched the movie. Prior to their arrival, I had set up all of the equipment, including threading the film on the 16mm projector. I started the engine, flipped the switch to the generator, plugged in the transformer, plugged in the projector and then turned on the projector. I held my breath, hoping nothing would go wrong, but everything worked like a charm.

For the first time in Bessada's history a movie was shown. The movie could be heard and seen all over the village. Within fifteen minutes, more than three hundred people from the village literally ran to our house and surrounded our guests to watch the movie. There were so many people they broke down our grass fence around our concession. The movie was about President Tombalbaye's visit to the United States. The villagers were really excited to see a movie for the first time. Their reactions were very interesting. When President Tombalbaye laughed, they laughed. When the people in the movie clapped their hands, the villagers clapped their hands. When the President waved his hand, the Chadians waved back to him. When the thirty-five-minute movie was over, the people wanted to see it again. I said, "No, that was all for tonight."

The next day I asked Nestor and Pierre to let the village chief know that we would show a movie each Friday night at about 7:30 P.M. It would then be the chief's responsibility to announce to the villagers that a movie would be shown on Friday nights. Usually the chief gave such announcements to the village crier. On Friday night we took a sheet off our bed, thumb-tacked it to a bamboo pole and hung it from a tree branch in the center of the village. That was our screen. It worked quite well except when there was a slight breeze. I had set up the projector and transformer on the back of the Land Rover. That night the movie was titled *American*

Wrestlers. Wow! The people really enjoyed this movie, especially when one wrestler would slam the other down onto the mat. They enjoyed it so much that they wanted to see it again. This time I said, "Okay, I'll show it to you again."

Every Friday night Betty and I showed a film. We only had three films but that was all right; we just showed them over and over again. Because this was the first time in Bessada's history that the villagers had ever seen a movie, I often wondered what was going through their minds. What did they think when they saw their President Tombalbaye waving at them, heard him talking, saw him shaking hands with President Johnson and so many other scenes and actions? That must have been one awesome experience for the Sara Madjingaye people. We Americans take too much for granted!

25

Un-erasable Moment

A teacher from a remote village some forty kilometers north of Bessada and his students dug a pit silo and filled it with chopped grass to ferment into silage for their goats during the dry season. He summoned me to his village to inspect their work before covering it with soil. Betty and I decided to visit his village. To reach that remote village, we had to drive our Land Rover north on a narrow ox-cart pathway through the bush and deep sand, and zigzag around tree stumps. We had established three goals for this long risky trip: build a seesaw at their school, inspect the silo and silage and show a movie.

Along the way, nine kilometers north of Bessada, there was

a small village of people whose hand-dug water well had collapsed. They had no water! The younger village women, seventeen to twenty years of age, would walk to Bessada each day to fill their earthenware pots with water. Before they lifted the filled pots to their heads, they would put mango leaves on top of the water to keep it cool and prevent the water from splashing out. They would then begin their nine-kilometer trek back to their village laden with earthen pots full of water on their heads. When I knew I would be passing through that village, I would place a 55-gallon drum in the back of the Land Rover, fill it with water from the well in Bessada and haul it to the village. When I reached the village I would stop, off-load the barrel and then drive on to where I was going. The villagers would empty the water from the barrel into their containers and on the return trip I would stop to pick up the empty barrel. The people were so appreciative of that small act of courtesy.

Back in Doylestown, Pennsylvania, at the United Methodist Church where Betty and I are members, we had a friend named Clara Stock who was an elementary school teacher at Doylestown Township Elementary School (now known as Kutz Elementary School). Because of our friendship, she wanted her students who were studying about the continent of Africa to do a project for elementary school students in Chad. Clara had her students go into their respective neighborhoods to rake leaves, do odd jobs, clean garages, pull weeds, and many other tasks to raise $50.00 to pay for materials to build a seesaw at an elementary school in Chad. The students brought their hard-earned money to school, and Clara showed the students where Chad is on a map of Africa and how she was going to send it to us. After we received the money, we drove to Fort Archambault and purchased the boards, u-bolts, eight-centimeter pipe, elbows and cement and kept it in storage at our home in Bessada until we were ready to use it.

It took us two hours to drive to the remote village due north of Bessada. We arrived at mid-morning, around 10:30. Most of the day was consumed building the seesaw at the elementary school. These children had never seen a seesaw or knew that children used them to have fun. Betty and I had to teach the students how to use a seesaw because they didn't have a clue how to use it. For whatever reason, they didn't like sitting on it face to face. We couldn't seem to get them interested in facing each other the way children do in the USA. They would always sit on the seesaw back to back with up to ten students on each side. What a fantastic gift Mrs. Stock's students gave to those children in that village deep in the bowels of Chad. Thanks to the financial aid of those students back home, children in that isolated school in Chad now had a seesaw.

For the second task of our visit we inspected the filled pit silo. I had taught the schoolteacher how to make silage in Bessada. He felt that grass silage would be good to feed the children's goats during the dry season. He went back to his school and explained to his students how to make grass silage and a pit silo. They did everything exactly as the teacher taught them and I was very pleased with their progress. I helped them do the final step and that was to cover the chopped grass with a cap of un-chopped grass and then covered with sixty centimeters of soil.

By this time it was almost evening and the sun was setting. We decided it was time to set up the equipment for the movie phase of our visit while there was still daylight. The people were really excited that we were going to show them a movie. People in nearby villages apparently had heard about this special event and they had walked several kilometers in the bush to see it. We hung a bed-sheet screen, thumb-tacked to a bamboo pole, to an overhanging branch on a tree in the center of the village. On the ground I set a motor, generator and transformer. At the back of the Land Rover I placed a 16mm projector. After I threaded the film we waited until it was almost dark before we began to show the movie. It was a full-length movie of President François Tombalbaye during his 1968 visit with President Lyndon B. Johnson in the United States. When I started the engine-powered generator and flipped the switch on the 16mm projector, suddenly movement and sound were on the bed-sheet screen. The people all clapped! They were amazed, astonished, and bewildered that they could hear their president talking and actually see him moving on the bed-sheet screen. Some feared he was real. Their reactions were incredible. They all seemed to drift toward the center in the shaft of light from the projector blocking the image. Like they did in Bessada, when the president clapped, they clapped. When President Tombalbaye waved, the people waved back at him. When he talked, some of the people talked to him. The people's mood was very festive, and for the first time in their history, these people living so far away from western civilization saw their first movie. I showed a second film featuring American wrestlers and they really enjoyed watching wrestlers slam each other down onto the mat.

After we showed the two films, we loaded all our parapher-nalia onto the Land Rover. At 9:00, we began our long lonesome two-hour trip down that narrow ox-cart pathway with its deep sand, zigzagging in the dark around tree stumps on our way back to Bessada. The darkness made it even more difficult and danger-ous for driving. Betty and I had to be on the lookout for wild ani-mals, especially elephants and Cape buffalo. We were back home in Bessada at 11:00 P.M., dead tired.

We decided to unload the equipment in the morning because we were hungry and so tired after working all day in the sun and driving for two hours each way on that terrible road. I decided to light a lantern and take my usual bucket bath while Betty lit the Petromax lamp, turned on the gas stove and made each of us fried egg sandwiches. She called me when the sandwiches were ready. We sat down at the table, gave thanks to our Lord for a good day and traveling mercies, then turned on the short-wave radio and tuned in Voice of America. We were astonished as we listened to a live broadcast, from the other side of the earth, of the U.S. Navy on the Pacific Ocean picking up astronauts who had just returned from the moon. It was hard to believe that in Chad's hinterland, we had just returned from showing a movie to people in a tiny remote village for the first time in their history while simultaneously the United States Navy was picking up astronauts who had just returned from the moon! **What an un-erasable moment of contrasting and memorable events!**

26

Lake Chad

Betty and I loaded our luggage into the back of a Peace Corps Land Rover for a grueling 250-kilometer trip to Lake Chad, north of Fort-Lamy, on 31 December 1971. We rode with two Peace Corps Volunteers who were assigned to live in a village known as Bol. This was a once-in-a-lifetime opportunity. Betty and I were fortunate to be able to see the life style of people living in a desert village plus observe the flora and fauna in the Sahara Desert. What an intriguing experience this promised to be!

The first thirty-five kilometers from Fort-Lamy were a rather smooth drive on a tar road. When the pavement ended the road quickly turned into a rough, dusty dirt track for several kilometers. The road became narrower and incredibly sandy the farther north-northwest we traveled. This particular area was the edge of the Sahara Desert. Finally the last 135 kilometers were a trace of previous truck tracks in the sand, that often vanished. Only four-wheel drive vehicles were able to travel this type of terrain. Previous trucks or Land Rovers following old tracks made new ones. Sand blown by dry desert winds covered the tracks and they simply evaporated. When the track disappeared the driver would drive in large concentric circles in the sand until a semblance of a track again reappeared. Sometimes the driver knew the general direction he should be driving and just drove in the direction of Bol. Bol was located on the edge of Lake Chad in barren, harsh, hot, dry, sandy environs.

During the last three hours of the trip, the terrain of the Sahara Desert was nothing but one high sand dune after another. The driver had shifted the Land Rover into four-wheel drive and he drove as fast as he could down one side of a dune to get enough speed and momentum to climb the next one. Going upward, nearing the top of a dune, the speed and momentum would diminish and all four of his wheels would begin spinning in the sand. The driver would then turn the steering wheel abruptly to the right then to the left, to the right and to the left until we got to the top of the dune. The abrupt turning gave the Land Rover little traction yet it was enough to get us to the top. Then the whole process would be repeated over and over as we crossed many kilometers of sand dunes. One should always travel in the desert in the early morning because the sand is firmer. When the hot afternoon sun heats the sand, air within the sand particles expands and causes it to be more fluid.

Before we reached the dunes we occasionally would see small thorn bushes or date palms growing in areas which were not as sandy. Also we would see an occasional wild donkey among the thorn bushes. The dunes exhibited no flora, at least none that we could observe at that time of the year. During the entire trip, Betty and Bill Kanapel rode in the cab with the driver and I rode in the back with the two other two volunteers. Needless to say we were exposed to all the elements such as dust, blowing sand, hot dry air blowing in our faces and hot sun with no shade. After nine hours of riding in the back of a Land Rover, we arrived tired and thirsty at the village of Bol.

Our first impressions of Bol were interesting. We observed that the people who lived there were mostly Arabs and we found them to be very friendly toward us. They appeared to have had a hard life as a result of working to survive each day in a harsh arid environment. While looking at the small village from a holistic viewpoint, it resembled houses that one would have seen during Biblical times. These Biblical visions were embedded in our minds from artists' renditions of scenes during the times of Christ. These mental Biblical pictures evolved from our reading the Bible and through Sunday school handouts when we were young. Betty and I stayed in a mud brick house, which we thought resembled life during Bible times.

To compliment the Biblical visions we saw portrayed in Bol, we observed many camels and donkeys tethered at or near mud brick houses. In the desert there were caravans of camels and donkeys laden with goods being transported to Bol or traveling across the desert toward similar villages.

Once all of North Africa was an ocean of water. What's left of that ocean is now known as Lake Chad. The Lake has hundreds of small islands and some of them float. The floating islands are made up of dense plant growth which seals off the oxygen and cannot rot, causing them to float.

The source of water for the lake comes from fresh water flowing northward in the Chari River. Lake Chad is a large shallow natural inland lake of fresh water with numerous fingers, or inlets, jutting into the desert. Water recedes from the desert inlets during the annual dry season and during the rainy season it again rises and flows back into the inlets.

When the water receded from the desert inlets during the dry season, the French government had provided funds to build earthen dams to prevent water from reentering the dried and parched inlets during the rainy seasons. These dried inlets were called "polders." As a result, there were hundreds of hectares of deep fertile lake bottom soil that had the potential to be a "horn of plenty," enabling this poor country to become self-sufficient in food production.

In addition to the fresh water in Lake Chad, ground water

was readily available. If a hole two to three meters deep was dug into the ground, one would find a water table which had ample water for irrigating food crops.

Bill Kanapel from the State of Washington was the Peace Corps Volunteer assigned to Bol. He was a retired farmer who had much experience irrigating crops on the eastern side of the Olympia Mountains in Washington. The first thing he taught the Chadian farmers was how to level the land to effectively irrigate crops. He made a broad, camel-drawn "V"-shaped drag and properly leveled the land so water could flow and be absorbed uniformly across the polders.

Using Peace Corps funds, Bill purchased a camel, and with a jerry-rigged camel-powered water pump, he was able to pump irrigation water effectively. The pump itself was funded and designed by engineers of the New Holland-Sperry Rand Company in New Holland, Pennsylvania. It was shaped like a waterwheel using the detached rear end of an old Land Rover. Holes were drilled into a large steel plate to align it with the lug bolts on one wheel. Then it was placed in an upright position, resting vertically on its rim, firmly supported by the steel plate. On the other wheel rim was attached a long pipe which was hitched to the camel. When the camel walked in circles around the well with the long pipe attached, the turning wheel caused the universal joint in the chassis to turn. To the universal joint was fastened a sprocket which turned a long chain affixed to half-gallon juice cans. As the camel-powered sprocket rotated, the chain with its half-gallon cans simultaneously lowered empty cans into the water while lifting full ones. As the full cans reached the top of the sprocket they automatically emptied water into a wooden water trough. The water flowed by gravity along the entire side of the polder. From the wooden channel, short hoses were used to siphon water into irrigation ditches between the rows of vegetables growing in rich lake bottom soil.

The camel-driven irrigation pump worked very successfully. Water was easily found. Soils were rich. There was a 365-day growing season. People seemed to be very optimistic that this project was going to revolutionize Bol's economy and that particular region of desert in Chad. However, there was a problem. As described earlier, all of North Africa was once a large ocean of water and what is left is now Lake Chad. Remnants of the old ocean still existed in the underground water table. Along the wooden channel for irrigation water from the well, one could easily observe a white line on each side at the waters edge. This white line of salt was caused by evaporated salt water being lifted from the hand-dug well. The water could be used effectively on the rich soil for year one. During year two, salty water again irrigated into the soil again caused food crops to grow but the plants were not as robust or productive as in the previous year. During year three nothing would grew, not even weeds. The salt water applied during the first two years caused the soil to become sterile. This irrigation practice resulted in reducing what was once rich, productive lake bottom land behind those expensive dams to be nothing but idle, barren and unproductive sterile polders. Salt water forced this successful water pump project to stop.

If vegetable crops were to grow, fresh water had to be pumped out of the lake. Pumping fresh water from the lake required a diesel engine to power a pump because it had to be pumped up and over the dam into the polder. Farmers could not afford to purchase expensive pumps or diesel fuel to operate them.

If fresh water from Lake Chad had been irrigated into a polder, the vegetable production yields would have been phenomenal. Due to the desert terrain and high dunes, there were no suitable roads, railroads or navigable rivers to transport perishable vegetable crops in a timely manner to Chad's populated centers. Furthermore the high cost of irrigation and transportation by trucks of perishable food crops to the populated areas would have inflated the price of each food commodity. Most Chadian people would

128

not be able to afford to purchase Lake Chad food crops. The following lessons were learned from this Irrigation Project/Chad:

1. The camel-powered irrigation pump sponsored by New Holland Sperry Rand Company worked very successfully and could be used where there was a shallow well with "fresh" water.
2. Camels could be used effectively as animal traction to power a waterwheel-type pump.
3. Prolonged use of salt water for irrigation caused soil to become sterile within two to three years.
4. The cost of transportation of perishable food crops across a harsh desert to populated areas was too high.
5. There were no available funds from local or national governments to operate a diesel-powered irrigation pump for pumping "fresh" water from Lake Chad into the polders for irrigating food crops.
6. Lessons learned from other foreign national projects need to be studied before establishing an innovative project.

Conversely, life is full of lessons. It is okay to make a mistake as long as a lesson was learned. It is not too smart to make the same mistakes again. The French agronomists and Chadian farmers knew that the well water was salt water and that it sterilized the soil but they didn't tell anyone. Peace Corps personnel spent much money, time and effort to learn a lesson that was already known by others.

Betty and I had our first and only camel ride at Bol, Chad on 2 January 1972. What an extraordinary experience! The camel we rode belonged to the Peace Corps and was used to pump water for irrigation. This particular camel was not a friendly beast. Nevertheless the camel was made to lie down so I could mount it and sit on a wooden saddle. When the camel rose, first its back legs went up causing me to look nearly straight down. Then suddenly the front legs went up and I was thrust backward looking into the sky. The beast was steered only with a halter that had a rope tied to it. To turn its head to go into the desired general direction, one would pull the head either to the left or right. Usually the camel went in the direction it wanted to go whether one wanted to go that way or not. The camel started to trot into the desert and I thought I was headed for Egypt. After a long ride in the direction the camel wanted to go, I finally was able to get it turned around and head back toward the water well.

When we got the camel to lie down so I could dismount, it first bent the front legs down causing me to look nearly straight down and then suddenly the back legs went down thrusting me backward looking into the sky as the camel lay down.

Betty then mounted the camel but the Chadian camel herder was not pleased, since women in that culture are not supposed to ride camels. He feared she might be injured because the camel was mean. When the camel stood up, Betty experienced the same sensations that I had. She was not a happy camel rider. Betty was terrified! After the camel stood up, it took a few steps, and then we made it lie down so Betty could dismount.

Bill Kanapel then mounted the camel and took it for a ride. When he returned, the camel started to lie down and the rope which went around the base of its tail to hold and support the saddle broke and the saddle with Bill on it slid onto the camel's side. When the camel lay down, Bill's leg and the saddle were under the camel. The camel tried to get comfortable and began to act like it was trying to injure Bill. The Chadian began beating the camel with a spade because they feared it was trying to kill Bill. I took out my pocket knife and cut the rope to free Bill's leg and then dragged him out from under the camel. He was not injured but he could have broken a leg. I was elated that this unfortunate event did not happen when Betty was on the camel. We persuaded the camel boy to stop beating the camel. Bill was okay, the saddle was not broken, the rope I cut could be easily replaced, the camel had a cut lip from being hit by the spade but otherwise it was okay. So ended our camel rides.

On New Year's Eve in Bol there were no celebrations, fireworks, or parties in this remote desert village. It was quiet except for the braying donkeys. We slept on a bed made of alternating tree branches, each one about two centimeters in diameter. They were attached with tree bark and wrapped around the branches to form a bed frame. The bed was actually quite solid and comfortable even though there was not much of a mattress. Nevertheless we slept in a sleeping bag because during the night the air became chilly. The temperature dropped from 85° F during daylight hours to 50° F at night. That thirty-five-degree drop in temperature made our sleeping bag feel very, very good!

New Year's Day was much like any other day except for the children. They came to us and said *"Bonne année, bonne année"* (Happy new year! Happy new year!). They expected a small gift from us and then they would move on. We gave each of them a *bon-bon* (candy) as their traditional gift. The children were very happy to receive a piece of candy because they seldom got to eat a *bon-bon*. Also on New Year's Day we picked fresh peas, cabbage, radishes, peppers and leeks for supper.

We flew from Bol back to Fort-Lamy in a small six-seat airplane the following Wednesday, 4 January 1972. When we flew over Lake Chad, my last view of Bol and the lake branded an image into my mind which was forever beautiful. What a sight to behold and an experience to cherish!

27

Chadian Hunt

It was the dry season and nearly a year had gone by since Betty and I had arrived in Chad. It was February 1972, and by this time we were pretty well settled into our work routine as Peace Corps Volunteers in Bessada and as such we were starting to feel that the people there and surrounding villages were beginning to accept our being in their midst on a daily basis. They showed several signs of having confidence in our work and were cooperative.

During the times when I was traveling in my vehicle with the President's brother "Papa John (jah-on)," I had expressed to him much interest in the regional fauna surrounding Bessada. I asked questions such as: "What kinds of animals were common to the area?" "What kinds of damage do animals do to crops?" "Does anyone in the village go hunting?" "Were there established hunting seasons like there are in Pennsylvania?" "How did the people hunt?" "What kinds of weapons do the people use?" "What kinds of dangerous animals are in the region?" I described to Papa John the kinds of small and large game found in Pennsylvania, our hunting seasons, kinds of weapons we used, how we hunt, kinds of crop damage caused by wild animals and told him that I too was a hunter back in Pennsylvania.

Much to my astonishment, one evening we heard Papa John clap his hands outside our door. I greeted him and invited him into our home. I asked him to take a seat and offered him the customary drink of water. The purpose for his visit was to ask me if I would like to *"faire la chasse"* (go hunting) with him, the chief of the village, the *Sous-Préfet*, and the Secretary of the Canton (township) the next day. Whoa! What an opportunity! What a stroke of luck to experience how the Chadian people hunt! I accepted his invitation with gusto and it was agreed that we would depart at 4:00 A.M. (ugh). The *Sous-Préfet* would provide me with a gun.

As a Peace Corps Volunteer, it was illegal for me to possess a gun, much less shoot one while hunting. It was illegal for any of us to go hunting because none of us had a government permit. Given the caliber of people with whom I would be hunting, I decided that if we got caught, I was sure they would have taken care of things.

My clock went off at 3:30 A.M. and I jumped out of bed, got dressed, filled my canteens with water and met Papa John at 4:00 as planned. Together we drove to the Chari River. There we cautiously drove my car onto a ferry consisting of a platform of wooden planks attached to the sides of eight empty 55-gallon drums. After my vehicle was on the platform, I had to sign a release document in the event the ferry sank in crocodile-infested waters. A Chadian moved the ferry forward with a long bamboo pole. He put the pole on the bottom of the river and pushed, moved the pole forward and down and pushed again. He repeated these actions over and over until the ferry slowly crossed the river. Then I drove my car off the ferry onto land. Whew! What a relief! The kicker was that I had to repeat that process to get back across the river to return home.

The ferry crossed the river empty to pick up the *Sous-Préfet* and his Land Rover. His vehicle was heavier than mine but they too made it across safely. From that point on, there was no road, just a narrow footpath.

I drove in an easterly direction by straddling the path, knocking down tall dry grass with the bumper. Twice I had to stop to clean the front of my car's radiator because seeds and chaff from the dry grass plugged it, causing the engine to overheat. Finally after a seven-kilometer drive on that footpath along the winding river, we arrived at a small fishing village. Some 120 people lived there in small mud brick huts with grass-thatched roofs, eking out a livelihood mostly from fishing and selling fish.

Papa John hired a man who appeared to be in his late twenties to accompany me into the bush on foot. The *Sous-Préfet* gave me a double-barreled 12-gauge shotgun with a handful of shells containing slugs. We agreed to meet back at the village at noon. I pointed straight up to where the sun would be at that time of the day.

By this time the sun was on the horizon and off we went, the guide and myself headed toward the river while the others got into the Land Rover and went in the opposite direction. My guide and I walked to the river's edge and climbed into a *pirogue*, a hand-hewn log made into a canoe-like boat. He paddled it across the river to the other side. He got out there and pulled the boat onto the shore. Then I climbed out.

Now the hunt began. The bush was freshly burned and one could see a long distance. We walked and walked, looking for tracks, scat and movements. We finally spotted six kob antelope standing at the edge of a dried water hole. They were out of my shooting range. In a stealthy manner we began our approach to get closer. I got onto my knees and elbows with my gun in front of me and crawled toward a cluster of unburned grass. Black from the soot, I quietly hunkered down in the tall dry grass. I was still a bit too far away to shoot. I lay there on the ground for a short while so as not to disturb the antelope. By this time the sun was at about 10:00 and starting to get hot. My guide's hand motioned to me to move in a little closer. When I finally got within shooting distance, the antelope winded me and off they ran. That bunch got away.

We started to walk in a different direction and ended up in some tall, unburned grass. While walking in the tall grass, I looked down and spotted fresh piles of Cape buffalo droppings. They looked just like cow manure. One rule of the bush is you never find yourself in tall grass with Cape buffalo nearby. Cape buffalo is considered one of the most dangerous animals in Africa.

A Cape buffalo, especially a rogue bull will attack unprovoked. Hunting guides will always tell you before the hunt, "When aiming at a Cape buffalo, always shoot to kill." If the animal is wounded the guide has a very serious problem on his hands. A wounded Cape buffalo is an extremely dangerous animal. They will actually stalk the hunter and/or guide as they follow his trail of blood. When I spotted the Cape buffalo droppings I said to my guide, "Let's get out of here." My gun was not large enough a caliber to gun down a cape buffalo. Besides, the sun was high and becoming very hot and my canteens were out of water. We walked more than an hour back to the river's edge to the *pirogue*.

We crawled back into the *pirogue* and the guide paddled it across the Chari River to the fishing village where we were to meet for lunch. By this time of the day it was hot! I was *sooo* thirsty, but I knew I could not drink the water from the village well without making myself ill. So I had to go without quenching that overpowering thirst. The others arrived in the village shortly after we arrived. They had shot four antelope during their time in the bush but they were not hunting on foot like I was. I will describe their hunting method later.

When Papa John and his group shot their first antelope, they brought it to the village and gave it to the villagers. The women in the village were very kind and prepared a Chadian meal for us. They had pounded millet into flour and boiled it for an hour or longer, then poured it into a calabash to cool slightly. While the flour boiled they made a sauce using parts of the antelope (liver, heart, intestines, and lungs). After we washed our hands, we all sat in a circle around a small table (men only, according to Chadian custom), and with our fingers we broke off a piece of the *"boule"* (cooked millet) and dipped it into the sauce. The boule and sauce were quite tasty, but still I still had nothing to drink and was becoming even thirstier.

After we ate our meal, a huge watermelon was brought out and cut into chunks. It was yellow on the inside as opposed to the traditional red. When I ate that watermelon, I thought I had died and gone to heaven. I finally had something to begin quenching my enslaving thirst. I ate three large pieces of that watermelon to quench my thirst. Today, thirty-seven years later, when I eat a piece of watermelon, I remember eating pieces of yellow watermelon in that fishing village along the Chari River in Chad.

Papa John said to me, "...this afternoon you will go hunting with us and we'll get some antelope." After we rested for about an hour we all climbed into the Land Rover for the afternoon hunt. This hunting experience had a different *modus operandi*. The Land Rover driver had riding on the passenger side in the cab a person called a "runner." In the back, a "spotter" stood behind the cab, which had the back window open. Two of us sat on each side of the bed of the Land Rover. The spotter sighted several antelope and he reached through the open rear window to tap the left or right shoulder of the driver to indicate in which direction to drive. When the antelope ran in a different direction, the runner would jump out and attempt to chase the antelope in the direction of the Land Rover. The antelope ran into high grass in a ravine. The runner set fire to the grass and we waited until the fire drove out the antelope. We moved ahead of the burning ravine and waited for the antelope to come running ahead of the fire. "Here they come!" yelled Papa John.

The driver began the chase. He chased the animals at nearly fifty kilometers an hour. As we got within shooting distance we all stood up and each picked out an antelope. I had my safety off, was aiming and about to shoot. Suddenly all four of us were all airborne some sixty centimeters off the rear floor of the Land Rover. Fortunately no guns discharged. Wow! Were we lucky! Needless to say those antelope got away safely. The driver of the Land Rover stopped to make sure no one was injured and allowed us to settle down and get organized to continue the hunt. What happened?

During the annual rainy season the soil is very soggy and poorly drained. When elephants, weighing five to seven tons each, walk through these low wet soggy areas, they make tracks about 150 centimeters deep and thirty to forty centimeters wide. When the rainy season is over the soil dries and large holes remain from dried elephant tracks. The Land Rover hit a bunch of these dried elephant tracks which is what threw us into the air. We were *sooo* fortunate that no one was injured. What an experience!

After riding through the bush for an hour, with our spotter looking intently across the dried, burned savannas, he spotted antelopes again. The back window of the cab was open and the spotter reached through to tap the driver's left or right shoulder. The spotter and the driver maneuvered the antelope in front of the truck and two of us shot and bagged two antelopes. The runner and spotter threw the un-gutted antelopes into the back of the Land Rover with us and the driver began the long drive across the open savanna bush country back to the fishing village. The hunt was essentially over.

Upon arrival in the fishing village, we gave the spotter, driver and runner some money for their help with the hunt. They were very tired but appreciative of the money we gave them. Papa John and I climbed into my car and we began our journey back to the ferry, once again straddling the footpath. The *Sous-Préfet* and the others loaded three harvested antelope into his Land Rover to be taken back to Bessada.

We arrived at the Chari River and loaded my car onto the ferry the same way we did early in the morning. The Chadian again moved it forward by putting his bamboo pole on the bottom of the river and pushing, moving the pole forward and down and pushing, repeating these motions over and over until the ferry slowly crossed the river. I then drove my car off the ferry onto land. Once again we safely crossed the river and it was an easy dirt road drive back to Bessada. I was dreadfully dirty, thirsty, hungry and tired when I got back to Bessada late that afternoon. Betty was waiting for me as usual and was happy when she heard my vehicle pull up to our *secca* fence gate.

A short time later two boys brought one antelope to the back of our house to be skinned, gutted, and butchered. Papa John also arrived and said to me, "You do not need to do anything, these two boys will clean the antelope." They placed the antelope on its back and with a knife handmade by the village blacksmith they began skinning it. When skinning was completed, the carcass laid on the ground atop the stretched out skin. They carefully removed the viscera from the carcass. The men insisted that I take as much meat from the antelope that I wanted. I told them, "We could use only a small piece of meat." I took a small hunk of the rump and they insisted I take a piece of the liver. We had more than enough. I said to Papa John, "You take what you want and divide the remainder among the other hunters."

When those two boys finished cutting the carcass into pieces of meat, there were six equally divided piles. Every part of the carcass was used as food. This included the stomach, intestines, lungs, legs and head. The skin, hooves and horns were used to make tools, bags and other items. The only thing that remained on the ground was the contents of the stomach and by the next morning the free-running village goats had eaten that. Excluding me, each person on the hunt, including the driver, runner and spotter got their share of the meat. Each took their cornucopia of antelope parts to his respective hut and there he would re-divide it so that members of his immediate family, extended families and friends would have a piece of meat for their evening meal.

Because of the hot temperatures, it was important that the meat soon be consumed because there was no refrigeration in the village for preserving the meat. At this point the hunt ended.

What an extraordinary adventure! This hunt caused within me feelings of happiness, enthusiasm, anxieties, mystery and tension. After this hunting adventure it was then that I knew that I had earned the Chadians' trust. The local authorities who had asked me to go hunting with them told me by way of their hunting invitation, that they were sure that I could be trusted and that I was now one of their confidants. From that point on my work in Bessada and surrounding villages was readily accepted because the people trusted me. Because of this trust, I made many wonderful friends. Making friends was a heartfelt achievement.

28

"There Are No Elephants in Africa!"

During our first year in Chad, we yearned to see an elephant in the wild. Seeing pictures of elephants in *National Geographic Magazine* just did not cut it. Up to that time we had heard about nearby elephant sightings but the only thing that we would occasionally observe were their huge droppings on the road. Each time we went into the bush or drive past Mandel Park on our way to Fort Archambault, we strained our eyes looking for elephants. Jokingly I always said to the Baptist missionaries, "There are no elephants in Africa." They assured me there were elephants but Betty and I were not yet convinced.

Parc (Park) Mandel was a wildlife park thirty-five kilometers west of Fort Archambault. It covered a vast remote area of approximately 1,300 square kilometers with a tributary of the Chari River running through it. The national wildlife parks in Chad were not as well developed as in other African countries. They usually consisted only of a few pistes (two-wheel tracks) to enable one to drive a vehicle in and through the bush country. The vast plains seemed to never end or have been touched by human hands. There were no buildings, hotels or motels, gas stations, restrooms, souvenir shops, snack bars, coffee shops or bus stops. The purpose of *Parc* Mandel was to set aside a vast area of untouched land to preserve Chad's flora and fauna.

It was mid-winter on 19 February 1972, when we made our monthly, sometimes bimonthly two-day trip to Fort Archambault to shop, purchase supplies, visit other Peace Corps Volunteers, and missionaries and have a Capitaine fish dinner at our favorite Lebanese restaurant. Capitaine, also known as Nile perch, is a fresh water fish that's plentiful in the nearby Chari River. Some of these fish are huge and weigh as much as 150 kilograms. We did most of our shopping and business in the morning and we decided to visit *Parc* Mandel in the afternoon on our way back to Bessada.

We entered the park from the main road onto a *piste* with tall grass on both sides of the car. It was late afternoon, nearing the time to observe wildlife. The best times to see wildlife are from sunrise to 9:00 A.M. and from 3:00 P.M. to dusk. We had just two hours left before the park closed and we would have to begin our trip back to Bessada. We drove about fifteen kilometers into the park. To see wildlife one should drive at a speed of only ten to fifteen kilometers per hour. The first animal we observed was a huge male waterbuck along the road where we were driving. I snapped a really good picture of that waterbuck standing only twenty meters from where we stopped the car. As we drove deeper into the park, we saw a herd of twenty-five waterbuck. We observed two warthogs before arriving at a tributary of the Chari River and there we saw several huge hippopotamuses.

All too soon it was time to begin driving back to the gate before it closed at 6:00. About half way to the gate, I spotted a large flock of helmeted guinea fowl on the ground. I stopped for a minute or two to look at these birds. Then as we looked straight ahead and, only forty meters in front of us, emerged a colossal gray elephant stepping out of the wooded bush onto the two-wheeled *piste*, paying no attention to us! Then another and another until twenty elephants in all crossed right in front of us with an occasional glance at our vehicle. WOW! Was this exciting! It was the first time we had ever seen elephants in the wild. Several stood in the road watching us. We sat there for fifteen minutes waiting for them to move off the road and out of the way so we could safely pass by. Those elephants were in no hurry. We had been advised not to honk the horn and to keep the engine running. We were told that honking the horn can frighten an elephant and cause it to be defensive and it may charge if its young were among them. Keeping the car engine running does not attract their attention. However, turning it off causes a difference in the sounds around them and they may begin to investigate. The car overheated and I had to turn it off. Before I did I backed up away from them around a slight turn out of their sight. Finally they all meandered off into the bush and we decided this was our chance to get by them without causing them too much concern. I restarted the engine and we successfully went by them. As we drove by we looked at them one more time. They were intimidating and their size was enormous!

We drove a short distance and there in front of us we spotted another bull elephant with two females to our right. We had to stop again. After waiting for a short time, they moved off the *piste* and we passed these three elephants and drove another kilometer. Unbelievably, there in front of us we came upon another herd of seventeen elephants! This time when we stopped, we had elephants in front of us and in back of us. I had to watch the herd in front of us and continually looked in my rear view mirrors for the elephants behind us. After a while, this group of elephants moved quickly off the *piste* and we were able to drive on and make it to the gate right at 6:00. Betty was so scared her mouth was dry. She was literally petrified because she had heard a lot of exaggerated stories about elephants attacking people and cars. This was also her first experience at seeing free-roaming elephants in the wild.

We never realized how overwhelmingly impressive these animals really were. I've read that a mature bull elephant can weigh up to seven tons. I had waited a long time for that exciting moment! Seeing elephants in the wild for the first time was something far beyond the wildest expectations of a farm boy from rural Woodside, Pennsylvania. After having that extraordinary experience, I informed the missionaries, "There really were elephants in Africa."

29

Funeral of President Tombalbye's Brother

President François Tombalbaye had three brothers and one sister that we knew and had befriended. His sister and one brother both lived in Bessada; a brother lived in Fort Archambault and a brother who lived in Koumra. We knew them rather well and found the President's family to be good-natured and friendly. The brother who lived in Fort Archambault was quite a politician and well known. He liked to throw parties for his political friends and this was how he networked with special people of importance. He was quite popular throughout the *Préfecture* (state).

One day in February 1972, we received word from our employee Nestor that the President's brother had suddenly died. We were saddened to learn of his fate; we had been at his home just a week earlier. We learned later from Dr. Dave Seymour that the cause of his death was a strangulated hernia. We learned that according to tradition within the Sara Madjingaye society, that when one dies, it is imperative that the deceased be taken to his or her home village for burial. The funeral would take place in Bessada. Hundreds upon hundreds of people were expected to participate in both the wake and funeral. This event caused much activity in Bessada.

The preparations included putting up shelters for protecting people from the hot sun. Various types of temporary sleeping accommodations were built. Gifts of cows, sheep, chickens and sacks of grain began to arrive. For the throngs of people who were beginning to arrive, no fewer than twenty-five cows, forty sheep and hundreds of chickens were slaughtered. Gifts of sorghum by the hundreds of kilos were hauled to the village. Paid wailers began to arrive. Military trucks hauled people from the faraway hinterlands of Chad to Bessada to pay their homage to the family.

Men played tom-toms and wooden xylophones throughout the village as hundreds of people arrived in the small village of Bessada.

When one attends a wake tradition dictates that one sits with the family. No one needs to speak to the bereaved. Just knowing that a visitor was there satisfied the family. Women in various quarters of the immeasurable crowd wailed on and on as men played tom-toms and xylophones. Some of the women danced while they wailed and then threw themselves onto the ground.

Betty and I had been informed that the President was to arrive at 11:00 P.M. and that we should be prepared to stay with the President. We were to remain in our house until the officials came for us. We dressed up and waited and waited until finally at 1:30 A.M., we were summoned to be with the President. We were escorted in the dark through the huge crowd to where President François Tombalbaye was sitting with his legs crossed on a large maroon oriental rug. There were two other men with him sitting on chairs. As we stepped onto the rug, Betty and I were asked where we were going to be. We said we would be over there standing with the crowd. One man said, "No, Patron, you will sit here with us." With that he said something in their Sara Madjingaye language and almost immediately we had two chairs. Now there were five of us on the rug: the Minister of Interior, the Consular Diplomatic, and Jim and Betty Diamond sitting together beside the President. We sat there for nearly two-and-one-half hours listening to women wail, tom-toms playing and all kinds of interesting sounds among hundreds and hundreds of people in the middle of the night. For lighting there were Petromax lamps everywhere and people quietly milling around. As we looked around, Betty and I were the only white people in attendance. There were no French, Swiss, American or Chinese expatriates living in the area attending the wake at this time. At 4:00 A.M. it had seemed as if Betty and I had been there long enough and up to this point we had said nothing to the President. He knew we were there with him. We were advised to just sit there and say nothing. Finally

I decided we had been there long enough and I leaned over and whispered to Betty, "Well, how are we going to get out of this situation? We surely can't sneak out."

We rose up from our chairs and respectfully walked to the President, and, for the first time, he stood up to greet us. My first words to him were *"M. le President, je regret!"* (Mr. President, I'm sorry) His response was *"Merci beacoup."* (Thank you very much). The President asked us how we liked living in Bessada. We told him we were very happy living in Bessada and we hoped that our work would help improve the quality of life for the people living here. We invited the President to visit us the next time he was in Bessada or the area. He told us, "The next time I come to Bessada I will stay with you." We said, "Mr. President, you are always welcome in our home." With that we turned and slowly departed the rug and into the crowd as the President again sat down on the rug. The mass of people showed their respect toward us by opening a walkway for us to walk through as we went toward our house. We finally went to bed for a couple hours.

The next day we again dressed up and joined the masses of people who came to show the President their respect for both him and his brother. There were ambassadors, *préfects* (governors), missionaries, all of the expatriates who lived in the area, dignitaries from Fort-Lamy, immediate and extended family members, chiefs from all of Southern Chad, and the list goes on of those in attendance, A Chadian Baptist minister gave the eulogy followed by two other people whom I did not know. There was what looked like a 1920 model black hearse with two shovels tied to the top of the roof. The body was put into a wooden casket and placed into the hearse and all of his wives (no fewer than five) jammed themselves into that hearse as well. The procession began to slowly move toward the burial site. Betty and I walked along with the people past my cotton field to his final resting place. Before the body was lowered into the pre-dug hole, there were women who did much wailing, followed by the singing of a number of Chris-

144

tian hymns and a short sermon. As the casket was lowered into the hole, close friends and acquaintances, (including myself) walked by, picked up a hand full of soil and threw it onto the casket.

After the burial everyone walked back to the village to celebrate the life of the departed. For the next four days hundreds of people in the village mourned the passing of an important person while singing, dancing, visiting family and friends, and doing business before the military trucks began to load the people to take them back to their own villages.

According to tradition, the spirit of the deceased hangs around the village for one year before it departs for the happy hunting grounds. During this time all of the deceased's business must be resolved and settled. When all of the business affairs have been concluded, the spirit will be happy and will leave the area. The person who determines if the spirit is happy or unhappy is the village shaman. At the end of one year, he has a unique way to determine if the spirit is happy or unhappy. According to what one of the villagers told me, the shaman cuts the head off a chicken to see if it flops around or not. If it does not flop around the spirit is happy. If it does flop around then the spirit is unhappy. An unhappy spirit will not leave the village. It is believed by animists that the spirit in collaboration with the shaman can cast a spell on those who have not yet settled their affairs with the family. Only the shaman can lift a spell—for a considerable sum of additional money of course. To prevent a spell from being cast upon someone who hasn't settled their accounts with the deceased's family, they can pay the shaman to appease the spirit. This process may take several sessions and at each session a fee is charged. When the shaman decides the spirit is happy, it is announced to all the people followed by a huge village festival to celebrate the anticipated journey of the spirit to the happy hunting grounds. This festival lasts three days. Cattle, sheep, goats and chickens are killed and sacks of grain arrive to feed the multitudes of people who come to partake in this festive occasion, according to cultural customs and traditions.

30

Seesaws and Swings

Diagonally behind our house at Bessada was an elementary school which served more than 250 children. Like most Chadian schools, there were few girls enrolled; boys dominated the school population. It was perceived by the parents that if a boy received an education, he could possibly get a good job in the urbanized areas like Moundou, Fort Archambault or Fort-Lamy. He would be able to support not only his immediate family, but his extended family and parents as well. It was expected that sons would care for their parent's financial needs, especially during their twilight years. Girls on the other hand, were expected to get married and leave their villages to care for their husband, produce and raise children and do most of the agricultural chores to sustain her family. Women as a rule had little financial capability to support their parents.

One day Betty and I were watching the children play in front of the school and we noticed there were neither seesaws or swings for the children. We decided that what the school needed was some playground equipment. After I discussed this idea with the village chief, he gave us his approval to proceed with what we had planned.

We needed a small sum of money to purchase supplies for building seesaws and swings. I was able to determine which supplies were needed and how much they would cost. We needed US$200.00 to purchase materials for building the seesaws and swings. Our church back home was a potential source of funding for this project. We sent a letter to the Doylestown United Methodist Church (DUMC) via Betty's mother and father, Bill and Mary Rohrman. The letter contained a proposal for building a set of swings and seesaws along with funding them. The DUMC Missions Committee responded and we received a generous amount, enough to complete the project. We were able to purchase eight steel pipes nine meters long from the Peace Corps Volunteer Well Drilling Team. They lived near Fort Archambault where their headquarters was located. Since they had a Land Rover truck, they delivered the pipe to our village and lent us their pipe cutter and threader. Their pay for delivering the pipe and lending us their equipment was Betty's home cooked-lunch, which was much appreciated.

The next time we went to Fort Archambault, we went to what resembled a hardware store and purchased elbow joints, T-joints, bolts, chains, eyebolts and U-clamps. At a building supply store we were fortunate to be able to purchase two bags of expensive cement and three mahogany planks. We hauled these materials to Bessada using the back of our enclosed Renault 204. One day when there was no school, Nestor, Pierre and I accumulated all of the supplies and transported them to the site where we decided to build the seesaws and swings.

Our first task was to prepare the pipe for the swing assembly. We cut one pipe into sixty-two-centimeter sections and threaded each of the ends. On one end of each section we attached a ninety-degree elbow joint. We attached a 3.7 meter pipe to each elbow. On the other end of each section we attached a T-joint. These steps were repeated for the other side of the swing set. To attach the two sides, the 3.7-meter pipe, threaded on both ends, was attached to each T. This formed the frame for the swings. The frame was lifted upright and the end of each pipe was placed one meter into the ground. After the frame was leveled and straightened to align with the school building, concrete was mixed and we filled each hole to secure the pipe and make the swing safe, solid and secure. No one was going to walk away with those pipes once they were set in concrete.

On the cross pipe, we drilled two holes sixty centimeters apart for each of two swings. We pushed an eyebolt with a ring on the end through each hole. We tightened the bolt down with a flat

Chadian children learn how to swing on their newly constructed swing set. Note the swings frame as described
above.

Chadian teacher teaches the school children how to use a
seesaw. These children had never seen a seesaw and were
fearful during their first try.

washer and lock washer between the nut and pipe. We attached a section of chain to the two rings. The ends of the chain were bolted to a piece of mahogany wood seventy-seven centimeters long and thirty centimeters wide. We did this to both sides so there would be two independent swings. After a week of allowing the cement to set and dry, we allowed the children to begin using the swings.

The children did not have a clue how to use the swings. We demonstrated how to use it by asking Betty to get onto the swing and I pushed her. Betty showed much happiness as I pushed her on the swing. Then we asked for a volunteer to sit on the swing. Gosh! We had a whole bunch who wanted to try it. Taking turns, we would allow one child on each swing at a time. Betty pushed them on swing number one and I pushed swing number two. The children had a wonderful time! After they understood how to use the swing, Betty and I stepped back and allowed the children to push each other. From that moment on the swings never stopped!

The following week on a Saturday when there was no school, Nestor, Pierre and I accumulated all of the supplies and transported them to the site where we decided to build the seesaws, near the swings. Our first task was to prepare a pipe by cutting it into two 1.85-meter sections, and threaded one end. To the threaded end of each six-foot section we attached a 90-degree elbow joint. Another 3.7-meter pipe was threaded on each end and was attached to the elbow on each of the two ends. This formed the seesaw frame. Lying on the ground, the seesaw frame was lifted upright and the ends of each pipe were placed into one-meter deep holes. After the frame was leveled and straightened to align with the previously built swing set, we filled each hole with concrete to secure the pipe and make the seesaws safe and solid.

We had four U-bolts made to fit around the pipe. Through four holes which we drilled into the middle of a five-meter-long by thirty-centimeter-wide and eight-centimeter-thick mahogany plank, we placed two U-bolts from under the pipe and up through the plank. We tightened the U-bolts down with a flat washer and lock washer between the nut and planks. When we finished we had two seesaws on the pipe frame. After a week of allowing the cement to set and dry, we allowed the children to begin using the seesaws.

The children did not know how to use the seesaws and were actually frightened by them. We demonstrated how to use the seesaw. Betty got on one end and I climbed onto the other end. We both smiled and laughed as we went up and down on the seesaw. Then we asked for two volunteers to sit on the seesaw. We didn't get as many volunteers as we did when we invited them to try the swings. We soon learned the reason they were reluctant to try the seesaw. They did not like to sit on the seesaw the way Betty and I did by facing each other. After we got a few of the children to try using the seesaw, they quickly learned it was more fun if they would not face each other and sit on the plank back to back. They really enjoyed that method of using the seesaw. Betty and I stepped back and allowed the children to seesaw their way. From that moment on the seesaws never stopped, as long as they could sit back to back. A little while later the children learned that more than one person could ride on each side of the seesaw. The next day during recess, there were as many as eight children sitting on each of the two sides, going up and down, and truly enjoying themselves.

Thanks to the financial support of Doylestown United Methodist Church, the children enrolled in Bessada Elementary School, along with other children in the village, had a new seesaw and swings on which to play. In a land where people had so little to look forward to, so much poverty, no control of their destiny, so much anguish, so much despair, so little money to live on, so many health complications and so little health care, it was heartwarming to see children playing, laughing and having fun in the midst of so much strife. After school, children would stay to play on the seesaws and swings and their parents would have to go looking for them when they were needed for chores.

Six days after we installed the swings and seesaws, we looked out our window at recess time and there at the swings was a good old-fashioned fistfight between two boys who were deciding which one of them was getting on the swing next. Children are basically the same the world over! They all like to play and have fun.

31

Making Rope Halters

In villages of Southern Chad, including Bessada, the older men who could no longer work in the fields sat under a shade tree and made rope. At the close of the rainy season village children went into the bush and collected a specific grass, which was suitable for making strong rope, and brought it to the old men. The name of the grass was always described to me in their native tongue and I was not able to translate it into its Latin genus or species name. The men would dry the grass and store it near their huts until it was needed.

When the men were ready to weave the grass into rope, they first placed the dried grass into water to soften it a bit for weaving. A small cluster of men sat on a log hour after hour swapping life stories and weaving the moistened grass into strong rope. When it dried, the grass would pull together, making it tighter and even stronger.

Usually the children led the oxen with a rope attached to a metal nose ring. This ring had been punched through the septum tissue which separates the oxen's nostrils. The lead rope was tied to the ring to control the oxen by their noses. Because the young boys showed no fear of the oxen, they were able to better handle them without getting injured. Grown men often showed some fear when handling oxen and the oxen knew when they were feared. Once I got knocked down and run over by an ox, not because I was afraid, but because I was careless and did not pay attention to the ox.

Using the rope the old men made in the village, I taught farmers how to make a rope halter. The rope was strong and made great halters. The halter was not meant to replace the nose leads. With a halter on the ox and a rope attached to the nose ring, the handler had more control of the oxen team making them easier to lead.

In addition to leading an ox with a halter and nose lead, the halter alone was used to lead horses as well. Soon farmers made halters for their oxen and horses. Sometimes it is the simple things in life that make a difference.

32

Tragedy Strikes

On Sunday, 13 February 1972, we had a very tragic event that temporarily affected our work in southern Chad. The red laterite soils of Chad formed the base for three main roads throughout the country. Once a year the government's *Bureau de Transport* scraped and rolled the roads to make them smooth. After a time, large trucks laden with heavy cargo and people caused the road to transform into what the locals called *toll*. The road surface resembled an old-fashioned washboard. When it rained the road surface became soft and slippery and all traffic stopped at rain barriers (see "Red and White Barriers").

When driving a pickup truck, car or station wagon on such a road, it was safer to drive at eighty kilometers per hour. If the vehicle were driven more slowly, the wheels would go up and down into each rut causing a very noisy and uncomfortable, rough, vibrating ride. If the vehicle were driven faster than eighty kilometers per hour, the ride would be much smoother because the wheels would ride only on the tops of the ruts. However, the back end of the vehicle would have a tendency to fishtail, often causing the driver to lose control of the vehicle.

On Saturday, 12 February 1972, I received a note from a traveler passing through Bessada. Since there was no mail delivery to Chadian villages, people gave letters to drivers who would deliver them. This was standard procedure when traveling anywhere in Chad. Drivers were generally trustworthy and would make sure the letters were delivered to the appropriate people. Even I carried mail or notes when I traveled to various villages in southern Chad.

A Chadian driver had stopped at our home in Bessada and said, "I have a note for you from the Doctor (Dr. Marc Dronne, the French veterinarian, was known as "The Doctor)." The letter was from Dr. Dronne and it was sent from Fort Archambault. The note said he was bringing a visiting French veterinarian, a German agronomist and Chad's Director of Animal Services from Fort-Lamy to Bedaya. Bedaya was a village twenty kilometers east of Bessada.

Dr. Marc Dronne wanted to tour the Bedaya Veterinarian Center with his guests and show them the oxen, goats and sheep management practices being introduced to farmers in the area. Then he would travel to Bessada to observe my Peace Corps pit silos and silage project. He wanted me to join them at the Bedaya Veterinarian Center the next morning (Sunday) at about 8:30.

A Chadian para-veterinarian arrived at about the time as I did the next morning; his first name was also Marc. Together we waited for Dr. Dronne's arrival. We waited and waited because he was always late. At 10:30 a young Chadian boy excitedly came running toward us and frantically said, "There was an accident about ten kilometers east and they were Europeans."

Immediately Marc and I went to the accident scene. When we arrived we were horrified to find Dr. Dronne and Dr. Godit lying on the road, dead. The other two and a Chadian driver were very seriously injured. A Nigerian had already taken them to Koumra to Dr. Seymour. Marc and I covered the bodies of Dr. Dronne and Dr. Godit. We covered Dr. Godit with shrubbery branches and I had found a sleeping bag in the overturned station wagon to cover Dr. Dronne.

The next thing we had to do was to inform my good friend M. Depeux, Director of the French BDPA (*Bureau pour le Développement et Production de le Agriculture*), but someone had already told him about the accident and a half hour later he, the authorities and police were at the scene of the accident. After preliminary data had been recorded, we put the bodies into the back of a pickup truck and Dr. Dronne's French colleagues took them to Fort Archambault to prepare the bodies for the flight to Paris, France.

Three days later Dr. Ox from Germany died, making a total of three fatalities. Dr. Ox was a German agronomist who worked for the World Bank. All of the victims had head injuries. The back of Dr. Dronne's head was seriously injured.

The following Tuesday, we went to the Catholic Church in Koumra for a memorial service celebrating the lives of Drs. Dronne, Godit and Ox. Chad and France had lost two hard working veterinarians and Germany lost a very capable agronomist, all whom enjoyed working with the Chadian people. This was a tragic experience for me personally and one that I'll never forget. Dr. Dronne and I were good friends and we often worked together as a team. He was very supportive of my pit silo and silage project and I supported his livestock vaccination program. We had vaccinated hundreds of cattle owned by the nomadic Fulani people. He often had dinner with us at our home in Bessada. Once in awhile, late in the afternoon on his way back to Koumra, he would stop at our house as he passed through Bessada just to sit, have a bottle of Gala beer and talk about the day's events. We were blessed to have known Dr. Dronne as our cherished friend during the months

154

we knew him. Friends are one of life's most precious treasures and the older we become, the more precious they become. Betty and I revere the gift of knowing Dr. Marc Dronne in life before he was called home. Losing a friend who was my colleague and often my companion is never easy, especially the way I found him sprawled on the road.

33

Worldwide Peace Corps Budget Cuts

During breakfast and dinner we always listened to worldwide news on Voice of America. In early 1972, we were certainly not pleased when it was being reported that President Richard M. Nixon, back in Washington, D.C. was having difficulty getting congressional support to pass his FY1973 budget. One of the ways he wanted to balance his proposed financial plan was to greatly reduce the Peace Corps budget. When this news reached Peace Corps/Chad, the Director informed the volunteers that if President Nixon cut the Peace Corps budget, there was no doubt that Peace Corps would be pulled out of Chad, meaning we would have to stop our work and go home or be transferred to another country if there were any vacancies. This created much dejection among Peace Corps Volunteers throughout Chad. There were about thirty volunteers in Chad who were well-drillers, health workers, an irrigation specialist, social workers, forestry specialists, an agricultural development officer, a home economist, and English teachers.

Betty and I were on a roll with our Peace Corps projects in 1972. We were beginning to feel that we were now well-received by the people as a part of the village and that our projects were beginning to contribute toward improving the quality of life of people living in Bessada and surrounding villages. Then came the gloomy news that President Nixon was setting the stage for cutting the national budget that would lead to major Peace Corps program budget cuts worldwide.

While the pit silo project was winning much attention and recognition throughout all of Chad and other sub-Saharan countries, one of the senators supporting President Nixon's budget-cutting ideas was our own Senator Hugh Scott. Betty and I were constituents of the influential Senator Scott who was leaning toward supporting President Nixon's maneuvers to sharply reduce Peace Corps budget. To show support for Peace Corps, Terence Todman, United States Ambassador to Chad, decided to travel to southern Chad to join the rhetoric of the popularity of the pit silo project, modern chicken house project, sewing project, seesaws and swings project, bread making project, horse drills, and other projects too numerous to mention. Ambassador Todman requested permission from the Peace Corps/Chad Director to visit the Diamonds in Bessada, the home of President François Tombalbaye. His timing was perfect to contribute toward portraying a positive image of Peace Corps efforts in President Tombalbaye's home village. The publicity that would result was his mode of assistance in urging the U.S. Congress to preserve the Peace Corps budget. The attention he received from visiting Bessada and the Diamonds certainly reached Washington, D.C. expeditiously and Senator Scott would surely become aware of Peace Corps efforts his constituents had achieved in Chad, especially when highlighted by Ambassador Todman's visit.

The arrival of the American Ambassador at Bessada was an exciting event, which required much preplanning and preparation. The first thing we had to do was inform the chief of the village, the *Sous-Préfret*, and the *Préfret* that the American Ambassador would be arriving in Bessada. We had to make sure there was transportation to take Ambassador Todman from the airport in

Fort Archambault to Bessada. We needed to plan a list of people in Bessada and surrounding communities, including the President's brothers and sister, who should meet the Ambassador with appropriate protocol. We had to determine the proper dress code. Ambassador Todman was scheduled to have a snack at our home in Bessada upon his arrival. For this event, Betty made a squash pie and hors d'oeuvres using her small gas stove and kerosene refrigerator, accompanied by beverages (water, tea and coffee) and other finger-food goodies. She spent two whole days preparing for the ambassador's arrival.

It was very exciting when the Ambassador arrived in a large black car accompanied by Chadian security officers. Betty and I greeted the Ambassador and welcomed him to Bessada, the home of President François Tombalbaye. The *Sous-Préfret* and chief of the village were each introduced and they too welcomed Ambassador Todman to Bessada. The Ambassador was escorted to our home and we all had homemade squash (pumpkin) pie and the other goodies Betty had made. As Betty served the coffee, she seemed to be nervous about serving the United States Ambassador to Chad. As she served the pie to Ambassador Todman and he took hold of the plate, the plate tilted and the pie slid off onto the floor. Ambassador Todman was dreadfully embarrassed but from that point on, Betty was no longer nervous. This incident proved that Ambassador Todman was human just like us.

After the brief rest with snack and beverage, we escorted Ambassador Todman to a pit silo nearby in the village where he could see for himself the farmer's success of making grass silage. When we arrived at the site, several farmers were waiting for us. We explained to Ambassador Todman how the farmers dug the pit, cut and transported the indigenous grass to the pit, how the farmers chopped the grass and covered it for storage and the concept of the ensilage (fermentation) process. Then the farmers began digging to open the silo. When they exposed the silage mass, it was beautiful. The silage was green and moist with a sweet-sour smell, just the way silage should look and smell. Ambassador Todman was very impressed with how we used indigenous skills, knowledge, equipment, and grass to introduce a modern concept. I filled and sealed a plastic bag full of silage for Ambassador Todman to take back to Fort-Lamy. He personally gave President Tombalbaye the silage sample while describing to him the success of the pit silo project in the President's home village.

We then escorted Ambassador Todman to Koumra to see a modern chicken house that was built using native skills, knowledge and resources. The chickens were totally confined on slats in a chicken house that was made from bamboo growing in the area. Because nails were not available the bamboo poles and slats were attached with bark from a native woody plant. This method had been used for hundreds of years. The nests were slanted down toward the backside of the nest causing the eggs to roll out into a homemade bamboo trough so that the farmer did not have to enter the chicken house each day to collect eggs. Ambassador Todman was so impressed with how this modern chicken house was made of indigenous materials and skills that he asked his photographer to take several pictures for a feature article in his monthly newsletter. Ambassador Todman departed Bessada after an informative three-hour visit. He was very gracious and seemed to be very pleased that he had an opportunity to visit two Peace Corps Volunteers in a rural Chadian village to see Peace Corps results supported by the American people.

Because Betty and I were constituents of Senator Hugh Scott, Peace Corps implemented several aggressive public relation blitzes to exploit the successes of Senator Scott's constituents. Peace Corps/Washington knew that Senator Scott was a rather influential person among his fellow contemporaries in the Senate and Betty and I were two constituents from his region; in fact he even belonged to our church. To counter President Nixon's strategy of cutting Peace Corps budget, a major Peace Corps/Chad public relations program unfolded to promote the strengths of Peace Corps

158

programs in Chad. Peace Corps/Washington hired *Los Angeles Times* Reporter Ron Harley to travel to Chad to develop a featured public relations blitz on the Peace Corps programs, which were implemented by Betty and Jim Diamond. It was hoped that Senator Scott's budget support could be swung away from cutting Peace Corps budget, and that he might have a major influence on President Nixon. Ron Harley traveled to Chad to visit and live with us for seven days to experience the gist of the uniqueness of our Peace Corps lifestyle, daily work routine, interactions with Chadian people and how our projects impacted the people in Bessada and surrounding villages.

Betty and I met Ron Harley at the airport in Fort Archambault and from the very moment of his arrival, he began the interview process and taking photographs. We took him to the Hotel de Chasse in Fort Archambault for a snack of fresh tropical fruit and a cold Gala beer before we began our journey part way across southern Chad into the bush to Bessada. While we refreshed ourselves, we became better acquainted and established his goals and how he planned to achieve them. This was important because his time was limited and we wanted him to hit the ground running.

For seven days Ron not only photographed our every move, he interviewed the local dignitaries and us. He also interviewed people in the village with whom we worked. He lived in our home for one week to experience the life of two Peace Corps Volunteers in a small rural village in southern Chad. Ron took several pictures of everything Betty and I did. He took pictures of Betty making breakfast, teaching women how to sew, village farmers opening their pit silos, boiling drinking water, demonstrating how to trim feet on a horse, the village marketplace, villagers making mud bricks using a Peace Corps Cinva Ram Press (see "Cinva Ram Press"), villagers using a brick oven made of mud brick and making bread using Betty's recipe. He photographed the chicken house that we built and the list goes on and on.

We sat outside of our house in our concession after dark un-

159

der clear starlit skies and talked about our lifestyle in Bessada, our feelings about the people, philosophical rationale of our approach to the people, how we identified the need for so many ongoing projects, whether we missed Bucks County, Pennsylvania, how Betty coped with household management without electricity or running water, and many, many other discussions. Often we stayed up until 11:00 even though we had to rise at 5:00 A.M.

When Ron departed Chad for the United States, he had a plethora of photographs, notes and ideas for stories. He wrote and published about our work in Chad in magazines such as *McCall's, The Farm, Successful Farmer*, and *Pennsylvania Farmer*. He produced a Peace Corps billboard for along highways featuring one of our pit silos and silage, wrote and published newspaper articles, all promoting Peace Corps and the work of Senator Hugh Scott's two constituents.

Betty and I were pleased that we were selected to play a role in promoting and supporting Peace Corps as an integral part of widespread efforts of many supporters who influenced President Nixon to decide that it was too much of a risk politically to cut the Peace Corps FY1973 budget. Supporters included Peace Corps lobbyists, Peace Corps Volunteers, returned Peace Corps Volunteers, Peace Corps Directors, ambassadors, international leaders who hosted Peace Corps in their respective countries, American citizens, U.S. senators and representatives, industry leaders, and many others who urged Senator Hugh Scott, along with his honorable colleagues in the U.S. Congress, and the President not to cut the Peace Corps budget. Ultimately the national budget passed and was signed by President Nixon. The Peace Corps budget was not cut but it remained flat. Thus Peace Corps/Chad remained in place and volunteers were able to move forward with their respective missions. Do not ever underestimate the power of an effective well-planned public relations program.

34

Fulani People and Zebu Cattle

The Fulani people of West Africa are reported to be the largest nomadic group in the world who are primarily herders and traders. Through their nomadic lifestyle, they established numerous trade routes in West Africa. The Fulani normally raise large herds of cattle and tend to be located in the large plains areas of Mali, Ivory Coast, Niger, Burkina Faso, Chad, and Guinea. Many times the Fulani go to local markets and interact with people to get news and share it with other Fulani. Recent readings seemed to indicate that there was a shift evolving from the traditional Fulani nomadic herder lifestyle to a more sedentary merchant, trader or farmer lifestyle.

The original Fulani people are of the North African or Middle Eastern origin and have light skin, thin lips and straight hair. Many Africans know them as "white people." They were the first group of people in West Africa to convert to Islam through jihads, or holy wars, and they were able to establish themselves not only as a religious force but also as a political and economical force. Historically the Fulani are a very proud people. They were the missionaries of Islam and ended up conquering much of West Africa. The Fulani hold to a strict societal caste system of four subdivisions. They are the nobility, merchants, blacksmiths, and descendents of slaves of wealthy Fulani.

Zebu cattle are an important component of the Fulani culture and there are many names, traditions, and taboos connected with their cattle. The number of cows a man owns is a sign of his wealth. Fulani men perceive a herd of Zebu cattle as their "walking bank account." Raising Zebu cattle is both their wealth and their livelihood. This form of wealth has caused significant conflict between the Fulani and other ethnic groups in African communities because their cows often destroy sustainable food crops grown by local sedentary farmers.

We were orally informed that the goal of a Fulani man is to raise a sufficient number of cattle to enable him to give each of his sons their initial herd. In the Fulani tradition an unmarried couple must first produce a son before they can marry. Following the birth of their first male child, the father gave his son cattle prior to the traditional wedding ceremony. The Fulani people were generally of the Muslim religion and according to the Koran, each man can marry up to four wives. However, the son gets a gift of cattle from his father only with the first wife.

Cattle are a medium of exchange for purchasing a wife in many African societies. The number of cattle is negotiable with the bride's father. The price of a wife can vary depending upon the girl's level of education, skill training, age, work experience, state of health and other ethnic variables.

In Chad and other countries in Central and West Africa, the nomadic Fulani people drive large numbers of Zebu cattle long distances following grass and water. This movement of cattle is known as a "transhumance." When nomadic Fulani people are on a transhumance it may take them thousands of kilometers over a three-to-four-year period to complete the cycle. They tend to follow the rains, which enable them to adequately feed and water their cattle.

A Fulani man may own several hundred head of cattle. For various reasons he will break the herd into smaller units and assign other members of his family to be the herders. Smaller herds may number up to one hundred to two hundred head of cattle. Each herd will be separated by several kilometers but all headed in the same general direction.

Fulani scouts walk several kilometers ahead of the cattle herds searching for grass and water. Scouts also search for signs of diseases, cultivated fields and villages so they can guide the herds away from such impediments. Scouts send messages back to the herders to inform them which direction to direct their herds. When crop damage does occur the owners of the offending cattle must pay sedentary farmers for any property or crop damages.

Fulani herdsmen prefer to keep a low profile and be inconspicuous as they move their cattle from region to region. They do not want government officials such as international border guards, military personnel, government veterinarians, civil service extension workers and others to know how many cattle they own. By dodging the attention of government officials, they often escape having their cattle counted and assessed a tax on each animal. The French veterinarian, Dr. Marc Dronne, and I, a Peace Corps Volunteer were trusted to work with their cattle because we were not affiliated with any government agency that required us to report their location or number of cattle. The late Dr. Dronne and I vaccinated hundreds upon hundreds of Zebu cattle in the bush because the herders were informed that we could be trusted.

Fulani men often take their wives and children on the transhumance. Their shelter in the bush consists of a small rounded igloo-type structure shaped by small saplings tied together with thin strips of peeled bark and covered with a thick blanket of dried grass. When it was time to move on, their meager structure was usually dismantled and packed onto donkeys to be used at the next campsite or it was burned. They left behind little or no physical evidence of their presence for fear that government or military officials would track and seek them out.

Their personal effects were certainly limited since living temporarily in the bush without running water or electricity is a challenging lifestyle. The Fulani men permitted their wives to milk a few cows. The wives poured the milk into large gourd containers and tied them to the side of a donkey or a Zebu ox. The donkey or ox was led to the local village market where raw milk was sold to sedentary village dwellers. Money the wives received for the milk was for their personal use. For example, it could be used to purchase needed commodities to survive in the bush or a beautiful piece of material for wrapping around herself.

I have seen hordes of Zebu cattle throughout Africa. This particular breed of cattle is tolerant of high temperatures, drought conditions and tick-borne diseases, and they can walk long distances. Zebu cattle do well on a grass-only diet and thrive on sparse grazing conditions. Because of their rather docile temperament, Zebu cattle are a multipurpose animal used for animal traction, milk production and meat. Zebu cattle calve easily and have a strong mothering instinct. A Zebu cow is expected to breed annually and rear calves for twelve or more years. It is normal for fifteen-year-old breeding cows to be sound and fertile. This breed has a strong herding instinct and can walk long distances.

Socrates once said, "He is richest who is content with the least, for content is the wealth of nature." The Fulani people are content with their lifestyle of raising cattle. Their large herds are perceived to be their "walking bank accounts" that go with them wherever they migrate just as we carry a wallet with cash or credit cards. As long as the Fulani have their cattle they are content.

35

Vaccinating Cattle

There were two types of cattle management in Chad. One type was that some fifteen to 20 percent of the sedentary farmers owned a team of oxen and sometimes a cow or two. The other type of management was a nomadic Fulani herdsman who owned hundreds of cattle. Regardless of the type of management, there was one common denominator: inoculation with vaccines to prevent them from being infested with local diseases, especially tick-borne diseases. The two diseases that were prevalent in Chad were stryptotricose and tyrpanosymiasis. These two diseases were deadly to many cattle.

Let's first talk about the cattle owned by the sedentary farmers. As a rule, a team of oxen was two bulls purchased from Fulani herdsmen for animal traction. Sometimes a farmer would have a cow or two. Normally a regional Chadian veterinarian was responsible for vaccinating them. However because he did not have funds to purchase vaccine, farmers lost their confidence in government veterinarian services because there was no money to support their efforts.

A French veterinarian named Dr. Marc Dronne worked for the ONDR (National Rural Development Office). He had a very good relationship with the Chadian farmers and Fulani herdsmen. He had access to vaccines subsidized by the French government. Because of my livestock background, the late Dr. Dronne invited me to assist in vaccinating oxen in rural villages on a regular basis and the Fulani herds found deep in bush country during the dry season. We normally did not take the regional veterinarian with us because farmers and the Fulani people did not trust government veterinarians. They were perceived as being representatives of the Chadian government and cattle owners were afraid of being reported as to how many cattle were vaccinated and they would be taxed accordingly. The Fulani trusted Dr. Dronne and myself because we did not represent the government.

To vaccinate oxen in rural villages, one had to have the means to restrain oxen because they were not easy to handle. They were especially dangerous with strangers. This was a risky task and we had to restrain those animals some way, some how. Remember, when working in bush villages, one has to improvise.

We asked each farmer to go into the bush and cut two wooden posts three meters long and twenty-six-plus centimeters in diameter. They were to bring their posts to the designated site in the

Homemade cattle chute made by Chadian farmers with local posts tightly tamped into the ground. Each post was directly adjacent to the other making a partial wooden wall. At each end of the chute, there are two short posts planted in the ground like the others, but they were forked. A post was horizontally placed into each fork forming a bar to keep the oxen from escaping the chute.

village on a certain day. All of the farmers worked together and planted each post into the ground one meter deep and tamped them tightly. Each post was directly adjacent to the other making a partial wooden wall. The bottom of the chute was one meter wide and the tops slanting outward were one-and-one-half meters wide. At each end of the chute, there were two short posts planted in the ground like the others, but they were forked. A post was horizontally placed into each fork forming a bar to keep the oxen from escaping the chute.

The chutes varied in length, but generally speaking and depending upon the length we could get six to ten head of oxen into a chute. We preferred to have the chute tightly filled with cattle because they could not move very easily. Each ox had a nose ring with a rope tied to it. The rope was tied to a post to hold the animal in place. We could easily examine them from the outside of the chute, give shots, spray for ticks, ear tag, take their temperature and other cattle raising tasks. That chute was not fancy to look at, but it worked and that is what counted.

Dr. Dronne and I would travel together to where the Fulani people had their cattle in a corral made of acacia branches and thorny bushes. They would drive thirty to forty cattle at a time into the corral for us to vaccinate. Cattle, under no circumstances, would go through an acacia barrier because of the long sharp thorns.

We entered the tightly filled corral among the cattle along with four or five Fulani men. After we filled our syringes, one of the men jumped onto a Zebu cow in front of the hump over the shoulders. He straddled the neck with his legs, slid forward and simultaneously grabbed the horns. Holding the horns, he twisted the head to one side while leaning sideways with his weight throwing it off balance, causing the cow to fall onto its side. After the animal was on its side, the others took hold of its legs and held the cow until either Dr. Dronne or I would vaccinate it on the rump. One of the men scooped up a handful of fresh cow manure and with his hand smeared it on the cows back to indicate that it was vaccinated. Remember we had to improvise because we did not have any other methods for marking cattle in the bush country. Those men could throw cattle as fast as we could fill our syringes. Once we vaccinated more than seven hundred head in one day.

At 10:00 everyone stopped for a morning break and we followed the men to a nearby grass igloo-type hut. We all sat on the ground in a circle and the women brought us a huge calabash full of raw milk. Drinking raw milk in Chad was a serious mistake. The Peace Corps nurse was adamant about not letting any volunteer drink raw milk. She told us it was undulant fever for sure if one drank raw milk because we were not immune to it like they were. Regardless of what the Peace Corps nurse said, I was in an awkward scenario and did not want to insult my Fulani friends by saying I did not want to drink their milk. Each person took a few swallows of milk and passed the halved gourd to the next person. When the milk finally came to me, I took the gourd and held it up to my mouth. I put my mouth on the rim, tilted the milk toward my mouth and then acted like I was swallowing gulps of milk. I even had a white milk mustache. I faked it and didn't swallow one drop of raw milk. I took out my handkerchief, wiped my milk mustache, and then went back to work.

At 2:30 everyone again stopped working for an afternoon break and we followed the men to the same nearby grass igloo-type hut. As we did in the morning, we all sat on the ground in a circle. This time the women brought to us metal teapots full of boiled milk. The milk was served in small glass cups and because it was very hot, it had to be sipped slowly. The milk had so much sugar added that it was almost too sweet for my taste. Since the milk was boiled, I drank it.

When one works in rural villages or the bush country, it is necessary to improvise. Teaching farmers how to make a cattle chute using available resources (wooden posts) and their skills (digging a hole to plant the posts) was a way to safely do a job without any cash outlay. These chutes could be used over and over. In the bush country using acacia branches to make a corral, throwing the cattle and marking them with cow dung was a way to safely do the same job without any cash outlay for the Fulani people. By using their own resources and skills, we were able to implement a modern technique of giving vaccinations to prevent cattle from acquiring diseases common to that region. Vaccinating cattle reduced losses from death and ultimately increased both the farmers' and the Fulanis' incomes.

36

Castrating Oxen

The definition of an ox is an adult male bovine, which has, preferably, been castrated. When French technicians introduced oxen into Southern Chad to be used as animal traction in 1960, they did not teach the farmers how to castrate their bulls. The ox teams that were used for animal traction were normally bulls and their temperament was feisty and they were difficult to handle. We had noticed at the Baptist Mid-Mission Hospital in Koumra that over a period of eight months, several people had been injured or gored by bulls. Betty had canceled her sewing class one day because she had to take a young boy to Baptist Mid-Missions Hospital. A bull had gored him that morning.

Oxen can be found as a source of animal traction throughout many parts of Africa. They are used for plowing cropland, pulling carts, and the nomads use them to transport their meager belongings. When choosing a bull to be an ox, it must be healthy and exhibit massive characteristics such as heavy muscling, well-developed shoulders, straight back, straight pasterns and robustness.

Castrating a bull is defined as the destruction or removal of the testicles so that male traits of a bull will diminish. The outcome of this process is that the ox will become more muscular, more docile and relatively easy to handle. In Africa, veterinarians normally wait until the animal is fifteen to eighteen months of age before it is castrated. By comparison, in United States and Europe, bulls are castrated at a much younger age. In most villages, bulls used for animal traction were four to six years of age and were still not yet castrated.

There was a reason the bulls were older and not yet castrated for domestic animal traction. Normally the bulls were purchased from nomadic Fulani herdsmen and they had no need or reason to castrate bull calves. Generally speaking, Fulanis owned large numbers of cattle and would sell an animal only when they needed money. That is when they would sell bulls to sedentary farmers for domestic animal traction.

Farmers had no means to castrate bulls nor did they know how. There are a number of ways to castrate bull calves (e.g. knife, elastrator bands, Burdizzo), but with older animals the methods become somewhat limited because of the risks and trauma to the bull. Because of full development of the testicles at maturity, the method was limited to using a Burdizzo. A Burdizzo is a heavy-duty clamp, which crushes the spermatic cord. This was the least invasive method to use on a mature animal. We didn't have anti-septics such as Jensen's violet to treat animal wounds and it was certain that a fly strike would result if there was bleeding. Crushing the spermatic cord using a Burdizzo was a bloodless and safest way to castrate mature bulls.

I was able to borrow a Burdizzo from a French veterinarian. We put word out in the village that on a certain day I would castrate bulls at no charge. The first day the farmers brought thirty-one bulls to be castrated.

First I explained to the farmers the advantages of castrating their bulls, how we were going to castrate them, why the testicles would atrophy, what atrophy meant and their personal risk. I made it clear (at least I think I did) that castrating the farmer's bulls was strictly a voluntary undertaking, it needed to be their decision to have their bulls castrated and they had to take responsibility for any risks that may have resulted in injury. I grouped the farmers around me to explain and demonstrate the principal of using a Burdizzo. I sandwiched a piece of narrow rope between two pieces of paper. Placed the opened Burdizzo jaws over the sandwiched rope and closed the Burdizzo. With a Burdizzo one can cut through the rope without tearing the paper. This showed that the spermatic cords were severed and no skin is broken. It is a bloodless castrating method.

After the ox is restrained, farmers learn how to grasp a testicle and pull it into the scrotum with the spermatic cord to the side and place the opened Burdizzo over the spermatic cord.

First the farmers had to restrain the bull. This was the most dangerous part of the whole process. I told them to throw the bull using their traditional method. One person placed a looped rope around the hind legs, another placed a looped rope around the front legs, another person grasped the horns and another grabbed the tail. Together they would begin the struggle of throwing the bull. Two people pulling the looped rope one direction on the hind legs, two people pulled the looped rope around the front legs the opposite direction and the person holding the horns twisted the head to throw the animal off balance. The bull would jump, kick and with everyone yelling and hollering the bull ultimately fell onto its side. Quickly they would wrap the rope around the hind and front legs then pull them together.

Once the bull was restrained, I taught the farmers how to grasp the testicles and pull them down into the scrotum, working one of two spermatic cords to the side. Then I showed them how to place the opened Burdizzo over one side of the scrotum, making sure the cord was in between the jaws of the Burdizzo then quickly closed the jaws. The farmers were taught how to use their thumb to push on the cord on the inside of the closed Burdizzo to make sure it was completely severed within the scrotum. Then the Burdizzo jaws were released. I did one testicle, and then I let a farmer repeat this process on the other testicle. When the farmer completed the castrating process, then the bull was released. No blood could now circulate through the severed cord into the testicles. Over a period of three to four weeks, the testicle will grow hard and begin to atrophy and be absorbed by the body.

After the farmers restrained three bulls using their method described above, I stopped the castration process and showed them a much easier way to restrain a bull. I took my seven-meter rope from the truck and explained to the farmers how two people could safely throw a bull. I asked a farmer to bring his bull to a spot close to a tree where a rope could be tied snugly around its horns using a square knot, and the other end tied to a tree.

172

The rope needed to be long enough to allow the bull to fall to the ground without injuring its neck or horns.

I tied one end loosely around the bull's neck using a square knot. I took the rope along the top of the neck to the top of the shoulders. There I held the rope with my left hand and let it drop to the ground and asked a person to reach from the other side and pull the rope under, up and around the bull's heart girth. I looped the rope under the hand held rope and pulled it snugly around the heart girth. Then trailing the bull's backbone, I placed the rope on top of the bull's loin and again grasped the rope with my left hand and dropped it to the ground. I instructed the same person to reach under and pull the rope upward around the hind flanks. I again looped the long end of the rope under what I was holding over the loin and pulled snugly around the hind flanks. Now I took hold of the long end of rope and stood directly in back of the bull and, standing aligned with the backbone, I gently pulled the rope until it was taut. The pressure of the rope over the shoulder and loin pressing down on the backbone caused the bull to sway and then lie over onto its side like a big baby. Quickly the farmers tied the legs together while one kept the rope taut. When the castration was completed, the bull was untied and released from the tree.

The first time farmers had seen me casting a bull using this method, they stood there and laughed almost uncontrollably. They had never seen this done before and thought it was very funny how easily that bull went down onto its side. This was a skill farmers learned very quickly, especially after first doing it their traditional way. Once I looked around and five bulls were lying on the ground and restrained, waiting to be castrated.

The farmers were very happy to have their bulls castrated and even happier that they had the opportunity to learn how to do this skill. Village farmers had perceived Chadian veterinarians as the only people who knew how to castrate bulls and only a veterinarian could do it. Veterinarians were scarce throughout Chad, another reason that there were so many bulls. One should never assume that African farmers could not learn how to become competent in performing animal husbandry skills. Farmers actually learned two new skills, how to castrate a bull using a Burdizzo and how to safely cast a bull.

37

Tick, Tick, Scratch, Scratch

Ticks were a problem on cattle and tick-borne diseases were prevalent, especially one known as *piroplasmosis*. This tick-borne disease caused cattle to have jaundiced mucus membranes, dark urine and a fever. This disease could be easily prevented if ticks could be kept off the cattle for extended periods of time. Generally the farmers were not aware of the fact that they had a practical means to eradicate ticks (*tiques*).

Most farmers had access to a backpack sprayer to spray their cotton or they could acquire one from ONDR for a short period of time to spray insecticides on their cotton fields. Their mindset was that spraying cotton was the only way this piece of equipment was to be used. Rotenone was available for farmers to purchase. It was an insecticide that was used on vegetables and it was also effective in killing ticks on cattle.

To get oxen sprayed to eradicate ticks I decided to teach farmers how they could do it without a government veterinarian. Even though government veterinarians were capable of performing this task, they were not readily available to farmers living in the hinterlands and did not always have the funds to purchase the insecticide. I decided to use the insecticide rotenone because it was safe to use according to its directions on the bag. The next time Betty and I went to Fort Archambault to purchase our monthly supplies, I purchased two bags of powdered rotenone. I needed a sprayer so I asked the chief of the village if he would lend me a backpack, which he did. The village chief made the announcement that on a certain day, if farmers would bring their oxen to the center of the village, we would spray them to kill the ticks.

I charged CFA 0.10 to spray each ox to cover the charge for the rotenone. This amounted to approximately one half of one U.S. cent and every farmer could afford this cost. It was not the amount of money that was important; it was the principle that farmers needed to pay something for the materials as opposed to giving it to them at no cost. Once farmers learned they could spray their oxen themselves they began to spray their oxen on a regular basis.

I simply explained to the farmers how much powdered rotenone, as stated on the package, was to be added to the water in a filled backpack sprayer and then mixed it with a stick until dissolved. The farmer restrained the oxen while I demonstrated how to spray an ox. It was very important to spray up under and between the hind legs around the testicles. In that particular area blood capillaries were normally close to the skin surface, making it easy for the ticks to suck blood. I personally had observed hundreds of ticks where the scrotum attaches to the body cavity. Around the neck, and especially the dewlap, was another spot where ticks congregated to suck blood.

Simply using a backpack sprayer as a means to spray rotenone on cattle to kill ticks was a very practical way to solve a tick borne disease problem. After the farmers observed how easy and practical it was to spray, I gave them the opportunity to get hands-on experience by spraying their own oxen. Most farmers had the mindset that only a government veterinarian could do this. No one had taught the farmers that they could easily perform this task. Drat, I had worked myself out of another job.

38

Zakouma National Park (a.k.a. Parc Zakouma)

Peace Corps Volunteers were given what amounted to a one-month vacation during a two-year assignment. For our vacation Betty and I planned an itinerary that evolved into a myriad of exciting, interesting, educational, thrilling, unusual and fascinating adventures. Our itinerary took us to Chad's Zakouma National Park (*Parc Zakouma*), Republic of Zaire, and Republic of Central Africa. Zakouma National Park was to be a highlight of the trip since it had been closed to tourists for more than a year. Frequent rebel skirmishes in parts of the park had made it unsafe for visitors. In March 1972, a portion of the park was reopened for tourists. In the Republic of Zaire, we planned to visit our dear Peace Corps Volunteer friends JoAnne and Paul (a.k.a. Sam) Samaduroff. We would experience being on the equator at Mbandaka, cross the Congo River in a hand carved pirogue, plus take a three-day trip on a riverboat down the Congo River to Kinshasa. In the Republic of Central Africa we wanted to visit the nomadic pygmies in the rain forest. The adventures that we planned to encounter are described herein and we hope you enjoy the experiences as you read about them.

In the first week of April, 1972 we drove to Fort Archambault where we met three Peace Corps Volunteers and a missionary who were good friends. We traveled by Air Chad Airlines to Zakouma National Park for an exciting three-day weekend. It was a short thirty-minute flight from Fort Archambault to *Parc Zakouma*. The plane had to first swoop over the landing strip to shoo away a couple of giraffes. After we landed and taxied to the end of the runway, we deplaned by climbing down a long ladder from the exit door to the ground. We deplaned and milled around getting organized. We did notice that there was a photographer taking pictures. We did not give it any thought then. At that time we had overlooked the photographer's activity because of our excitement of being at Zakouma National Park. But several months later we discovered that Betty and I among others were featured in a photo on the 1973 Air Chad Calendar.

There were four Land Rovers and drivers waiting for our arrival. After we were instructed to climb into an open Land Rover, everyone was informed that the luggage would be transported to the base camp. We immediately set off and began our first African wildlife safari.

Wow! What an experience it was sitting in an open Land Rover with Betty, our friends and a camera. The driver of the Land Rover was very friendly and described the fauna and flora as we drove. When we spotted an animal, he stopped and allowed us to get a good look at it, take pictures and ask questions. This was an out-of-the-ordinary experience such as we had only read about in *National Geographic Magazine*. We saw baboons, giraffes, lions, Cape buffalo, Kob (a.k.a. *Cobe de Buffon*) crocodiles and hippopotamuses. The bird life was phenomenal but unfortunately I did not have a good bird book to assist in identifying birds. At that time in our lives we were not as interested in birdwatching as we are now.

We were on safari until sunset when the driver began to drive us back to base camp. When we arrived at the base camp we were assigned to our surprisingly elegant "huts." They were absolutely wonderful. We each had a nice bed with clean sheets, shower with hot water, private bathroom and air conditioning. After a three-hour safari riding in an open-air Land Rover in Chad's dry season, we took a shower and then turned on the air conditioner. Wow! Was that an awesome treat! At 7:30 a scrumptious venison dinner was served outdoors on white tablecloths complemented by a red French wine. Chadian waiters and waitresses treated us like royalty. This was a radical lifestyle shift compared to Peace Corps Volunteer life in Bessada. After dinner we sat around in a nice lounge and talked until we went to our huts to bed down for the night. We had to rise and shine at 4:45 A.M. for our next scheduled safari.

At 5:00 there was a knock at the door from a waiter who had come to wake us in time for the early morning safari. He was holding a tray of hot water for tea or coffee. The Land Rovers were ready to depart by 5:45 for the morning adventures into the bush. The sun was peeping over the horizon in the east and the bush scenery across the lowlands and savannas were infinitely magnificent. As we began our safari, our first sighting was a Kob. As we ventured into the bush, we began to see more savanna fauna such as zebras, giraffes, elephants and baboons. We returned to the base camp at 9:15 where there was a hearty breakfast awaiting our arrival.

After breakfast we journeyed back into the bush for a couple hours before lunch. We were deep into the grassy savannas when suddenly our Land Rover had a flat tire. The driver was experienced and knew well how to change a tire. When he went to get the tire tool from under the wheel well in back of the Land Rover, he discovered that there was no lug wrench to loosen the lug bolts. Apparently the cook at the base camp that morning changed an empty gas tank in the kitchen and had borrowed the lug wrench to loosen the attachment on the empty gas tank. After he finished attaching the lines to a full tank of gas, the cook forgot to return the lug wrench to the Land Rover. So there we were in the middle of the bush with a flat tire, and no lug wrench or any means of contacting the base camp. (In those days there were no cell phones.) We were at least ten kilometers from the base camp. There was a degree of danger because there were many of wild animals among us, including lions.

It was decided that the women and Derek Brinkerhoff would stay on the Land Rover with the driver while Jean-Paul Marteau, an armed guard and I would walk to the base camp for help. We had some water but left it for the women. Jean-Paul, the armed guard and I began our long trek to search for help at the base camp. As we trekked, we heard animals in the distance. At one point a small herd of giraffes crossed the *piste* in front of us. What a gorgeous animal! They are so graceful and beautiful. As we continued on we heard elephants trumpeting not too far away but we did not see them. The birds were gorgeous. At that time of the year the flora was blooming everywhere and some of the wild flowers were certainly eye-catching. We walked and walked and the sun rose higher and hotter. After nearly two hours we spotted the base camp in the distance.

We arrived at the base camp where we learned that help was already on the way. Since our vehicle had not returned on time the game officers in charge knew there might be a problem. They had sent another Land Rover out to search for our group. Since Jean-Paul and I could do nothing else we went to our huts, turned on the air conditioner, took a shower and lay down on the bed. I thought I had died and gone to heaven. Half an hour later Betty arrived at our hut and told me that help had arrived and the tire was fixed. We rested awhile before going to lunch. I was pretty well tuckered out. One of the French visitors had heard that we walked all that distance and said, "Only a crazy American would do such a thing."

At 3:00 we all boarded the Land Rovers to begin our late afternoon safari. This is prime time to see wildlife. As we again drove deep into the savanna lands, the sweltering sun began to settle into the cloudless western skies. African sunsets are stunning and spectacular. We stopped at a spot where we could look far across the colossal vastness of savanna lands that hooked onto the horizon. After we sat quietly in our Land Rover for some thirty minutes, we noticed a herd of Cape buffalo meandering slowly in a southerly direction across the savanna, with the glowing sun setting in the west, followed by a small cloud of dust. There were at least three hundred of them. Suddenly out of nowhere came an immense herd of elephants, slowly trudging along behind the Cape buffalo. There were about two hundred elephants in that herd of colossal beasts. My camera could not capture the essence of such a phenomenal African spectacle. So many enormous animals in front of that dazzling sunset gave the impression that they were so secure and so much at peace. It made one think about how African fauna can be so serene yet at other times violent. What a capstone for the day! It has been thirty-seven years since we experienced such a panorama and I can still clearly envision that view in my mind's eye and sense the feeling of astonishment we experienced that memorable day.

Again we arrived at the base camp where we went to our rooms, showered, changed clothes, and had a delightful African shish-ka-bob dinner in the dining area. After dinner we all gathered in the lounge area sipping Gala beers and expressing to each other the excitement of that day. We finally all decided it was time to go to bed since we still had one more morning safari to experience.

At 5:45 A.M. we boarded the Land Rovers for our final safari into the savanna bush country. We had not yet seen any lions. The drivers were determined we would see one. We drove for two hours and finally we spotted three lions lying under an acacia tree. They had just made a kill that morning and we saw a gory sight. A small pride of lions had eaten a downed Kob and it was time for them to rest. That was the first time Betty and I had ever seen a lion in the wild. Whew! What excitement! Other than an armed guard, we had little protection if one or more of those lions had attacked us. Even though the guard had a rifle, we were not sure he had any shells. Nevertheless we safely got to see lions in the wild for the first time.

Our missionary friend Sandy was riding with us in our Land Rover taking pictures. We came upon a troop of baboons and some were mating. Sandy was standing next to the Land Rover cab taking pictures as quickly as she could snap the camera. Suddenly I said, "Sandy! I am so shocked by you!" She looked at me in amazement, puzzled with a quizzical look on her face. I said to her, with tongue in cheek, "You of all people, a missionary and a fine Christian, taking pornographic photos." Well, Sandy was slightly embarrassed, but she was a good sport and all of us, including Sandy, had a goodhearted laugh.

At 9:00 we returned to base camp to have breakfast and pack our suitcases. The excitement at *Parc Zakouma* had come to an end. We loaded our suitcases into the four Land Rovers and departed base camp for the landing strip where an Air Chad Plane was awaiting our arrival. We boarded the plane by climbing up the long ladder and we went to our seats. My last view of *Parc Zakouma* was the base camp as we soared off into the wild blue yonder for a short flight back to Fort Archambault. What a remarkable experience!

39

Mbandaka, Zaire

Betty and I flew from Fort-Lamy to Mbandaka, Zaire on 14 April 1972, to visit our friends Sam and JoAnne Samaduroff, Peace Corps Volunteers from the state of Washington. We met Sam and JoAnne at St. Thomas, Virgin Islands where we learned to speak French. Sam and JoAnne had been cattle farmers until a grass fire destroyed their ranch. Betty and I were sheep farmers and we too had experience raising beef cattle. We had much in common except that they had five children and Betty and I had none.

Because Peace Corps was having difficulties recruiting volunteers with an agricultural education and farming experiences, more mature and experienced agricultural volunteers were being summoned. Peace Corps opted to try recruiting older volunteers with more occupational and life experiences. To attract this type of volunteer, Peace Corps allowed spouses and families to travel with the volunteer to their assigned post. It was more desirable if both the husband and wife could both serve as volunteers. Officials were carefully monitoring the outcomes of this type of recruiting. It was a new approach to recruiting experienced volunteers and Peace Corps had to determine if it were feasible, practical and cost effective to recruit volunteers with families, especially volunteers having specific skills and experience.

Betty and I were assigned to work in Bessada, the home village of François Tombalbaye, President of Chad. Sam and JoAnne were assigned to work in the town of Mbandaka, Zaire, a three-day ride on a boat up the Congo River. Mbandaka is located precisely on the equator. While Mbandaka was under Belgian occupation, a monument with a bronze plaque was built on the equator. During the throes of the Belgian downfall in 1964, the bronze plaque was destroyed. We have a picture of Betty and me standing at that monument, with Betty standing in the northern hemisphere and me standing in the southern hemisphere.

In Mbandaka if you fill a sink with water, pull the plug, the draining water will spin counter-clockwise. If you put your hand over the drain hole to stop the flow, let it loose, sometimes it will spin clockwise. South of the equator water spins counter-clockwise and north of the equator water spins clockwise. Scientists claim this motion is caused by the earth's rotation and is called the "coriolis effect."

40

Rubber Trees

Shortly after we arrived in Mbandaka, we traveled into the bush about sixty kilometers to observe a rubber tree plantation. I had never seen a rubber tree or a rubber tree plantation other than those that we had observed at Longwood Gardens in Chester County, Pennsylvania. I could not pass up this extraordinary opportunity to study a rubber tree plantation near the equator in Zaire, Africa. As we approached the rubber tree plantation, we could easily identify the rubber trees (*Hevea brasilliensis*) of the spurge family. They are normally cultivated trees planted in plantations in hot, humid regions of the world. This particular plantation was established in 1957. There were thousands of trees planted in long rows. The trees were very tall, somewhat slender, having no lower branches, and it seemed as if the crown of the tree was reaching for the sky through the plantation's canopy to get light. The tree bark was light grayish tan and smooth. The trees had long dark green succulent leaves. Light at ground level was subdued because the canopy was tight and sunlight could not get through.

Collecting latex was a very interesting process. A man climbed each tree to its top and with a knife he cut a small groove that spiraled down and around the tree to about one meter from ground level. At that point a small aluminum spout was tapped with a wooden mallet into the tree's bark. Beneath the spout a wire holder was pushed into the soft bark and a round aluminum cup was placed into the holder. The latex would slowly flow down the spiral and drip into the cup. Once a day the viscous latex was collected from the cups by pouring it into a large can that resembled an old-fashioned milk can.

The cans of latex were taken to a dumping station near the edge of the plantation, where there was a large rectangular metal vat one meter wide, one meter high and two meters long. It was filled with water and sat on a rack over a blazing fire. The latex was poured into water and boiled until it formed a coagulated rubbery mass.

The rubbery mass was taken from the boiling water and while it was still hot, it was squeezed through two metal rollers which resembled a ringer on an old washing machine. The metal rollers pressed the gob of raw rubber into a long oblong form about two centimeters thick. It was hung on a metal bar to cool. When the bars were full, the lengths of latex were smoked. The smoking turned the latex to dark brown, oblong pieces of raw latex that varied somewhat in size but averaged one meter long and one-half meter wide. In this form the smoked raw latex was exported to rubber companies in Europe, Asia, Middle East and North America. The smoked latex was further processed and made into rubber products (e.g., tires, inner tubes, livestock mats, balls) and sold to wholesale and retail markets around the world

41

Why Did Two Peace Corps Volunteers Cross the Congo River?

Why did two Peace Corps Volunteers cross the Congo River? You will have to read on for the answers. I borrowed Sam's bicycle and rode it down the road in front of their house toward the Congo River. The river mesmerized my thinking, imagination and fantasies. Earlier, JoAnne had said she would just love to take a boat ride across the Congo River to see what was on the other side. Sam said that no way was he going to cross that river. I said to JoAnne, "I too would like to cross the river just for the hell of it."

As I rode the bicycle along the river's edge, I saw three men pulling their pirogue onto the river's bank. I stopped to see what they had in their pirogue and chatted with them a bit. I asked, "What would you charge to take two people across the river and back again?" He said six Zaires each (US $12.00). That was a reasonable price and I said, "Okay, you wait right here until I fetch my friend." I jumped onto Sam's bicycle and peddled hard to get back to JoAnne and Sam's house. I excitedly entered the house and said, "JoAnne, I have two people waiting to take you and me across the Congo River; do you still want to go?" JoAnne, now excited said, "You bet I want to go!" She stopped what she was doing and prepared to go. Sam and Betty had absolutely no interest in seeing what was on the other side of that river but they were good sports and accompanied JoAnne and me to the river's edge.

When we arrived at the river's edge, the two fishermen were waiting for us. We could not believe what we saw but there were two dark blue deck chairs in the pirogue, one for JoAnne and one for me. We did not have a clue as to where they found those two chairs so quickly. Betty and Sam snapped several pictures of JoAnne and me sitting on deck chairs in a hand-made dugout canoe. At the very back of the pirogue's bottom there was a hole the size of a home plate on a baseball field. We had to sit toward the front of the pirogue so our weight would keep the front end down and back end up. Keeping the back end high prevented the pirogue from taking on water and sinking into crocodile-infested waters. There were four people in that pirogue, JoAnne, two fishermen and myself.

We pushed off and began the adventure of crossing the exotic and intriguing Congo River with Betty and Sam watching from the riverbank. From where we pushed off, the Congo River was more than a kilometer wide. There were places farther south where one cannot see land from one bank of the Congo River to the other. The river is very deep, heavily infested with crocodiles and hippopotamuses and full of catfish that weigh up to sixty-five kilograms.

Because of the swiftly moving water, one cannot row directly across the river without being pulled down river by the current. The water flowed rapidly and caused a forceful eddy on each side of the river. To get to the other side, the two fishermen paddled their pirogue with its rather conspicuous passengers into the eddy near the river's edge. They rowed the eddy upstream about five kilometers. Then we reversed our direction. We started to go down river guiding the pirogue out of the eddy into the swiftly flowing Congo River toward a point diagonally across the river. As we were crossing the river, we saw huge islands of water hyacinths, which broke away from tributaries upriver, floating lickety-split down stream. During our adventurous ride across the Congo River, I kept my eye on the open hole on the bottom of the pirogues far-end making sure we were not taking on water. When we at last got to the other side, we were directly across the river from where we started.

On the other side we saw small fishing villages set back from the riverbank. Fishermen provided fresh, dried and smoked fish daily for the food market in Mbandaka. Yet Mbandaka seemed so far away on the other side of the river. The huts were made of traditional mud brick, each one with a grass-thatched roof with swirling streams of smoke meandering upward. Not far from each hut was a structure of bamboo poles to hang fish for drying and beehive shaped mud brick structures for smoking fish. There were no signs, advertisements, or flashing neon lights. We waved to the people as we passed by and they joyfully waved back to us. This was Africa! This was an exciting experience!

After our curiosity for seeing the other side of the river was satisfied, we decided to return to where we had set off on this adventure. Again the two fishermen paddled their pirogue into the eddy near the river's edge. They paddled up stream about three kilometers then again reversed our direction. We started down stream guiding the pirogue out of the eddy into the swiftly flowing Congo River diagonally toward our starting point. As we were crossing, there were still huge islands of water hyacinths continually floating down stream. During our adventurous ride back across the Congo River, I still kept my eye on that open hole in the bottom of the pirogue's far end. When we finally landed, yep, you guessed it; Betty and Sam were patiently and anxiously awaiting our return.

Wow! Crossing the crocodile-infested Congo River in a handmade dugout canoe with a huge open hole in the rear of the floor, sitting in a deck chair, two fishermen using the power of an eddy to get us upstream so we could diagonally cross the river was a sensational and awesome adventure. Being close to islands of water hyacinths rapidly floating down the Congo River, sensing the power of rapidly flowing water that bulged with huge catfish, seeing people on the other side eking out a living by smoking fish and seeing them joyfully waving back to us was a mesmerizing episode. All of this and more just to see the other side.

Now how many answers can you give for the opening question of this story; "Why did two Peace Corps Volunteers cross the Congo River?" If you can name four reasons or more, you are a very perceptive reader. If you can name two to three reasons, you're a good reader. If you can give only one reason, you are a so-so reader. If you cannot give any answers, you will have to reread this story, because answers can be found throughout.

Let me close this chapter with one more question. It is a given that Betty and Sam thought that we were off-center for wanting to cross the Congo River in a wooden pirogue with a large hole on one end. Do you think Betty and Sam enjoyed standing on the river bank watching JoAnne and me being paddled across the Congo River in a hand dugout wooden pirogue as much as we enjoyed being in that pirogue?

42

"Just Cruising Along"

After nearly a month visiting our dear friends the Samaduroffs it was time for Betty and me to say goodbye. We were to leave Mbandaka for Kinshasha, where we were scheduled to catch an Air Zaire flight back to Chad. Instead of flying, we opted to take a boat 1000 kilometers down the Congo River to Kinshasha.

When we arrived at the dock to board the boat on Saturday, 6 May 1972, we were told to purchase our ticket from the captain of the boat after we boarded. JoAnne and Sam advised us to spend the extra money and buy a first-class ticket because it was much nicer. We purchased two first-class tickets and were promptly escorted to the second deck and to a small first-class room. It was rather nice for a boat on the Equator in the hinterlands of Zaire. We put our luggage on a shelf and began to settle in for a long three-day boat ride.

An hour after Betty and I boarded, the boat was launched and we slowly began our voyage down the Congo River. We waved goodbye to the Samaduroffs from outside our room on the second deck. Shortly after we launched, a robust Zairian lady came to our room with her baggage and said this was her room. We said to her in French, "We're sorry but there must be some error. This is our stateroom." She departed in a huff and about an hour later she came with the captain of the boat and he informed us that this was her room, not ours. The captain and I exchanged the following words:

> *Jim Diamond* "There must be an error, because we paid for a
>   first-class room and were escorted to this room."
> *Boat Captain* "This lady paid for a first-class room and you
>   must get your belongings and go elsewhere."

Jim Diamond "Where are we to go?"

Boat Captain "In the dining room where you can sleep on the floor."

Jim Diamond "If that's where we have to go, I want a refund on my first-class ticket because sleeping on the floor in the dining room is not first-class."

Boat Captain "I will give you a refund later."

Betty and I had no choice, we had to go to the dining room and sleep on the floor and that is where we slept for two nights. Betty used her purse and I used my briefcase for pillows.

I climbed to the captain's cabin on the third deck three different times on that first day of cruising on the Congo River to receive my refund. Each time he said he would give it to me later. After two more requests on the second day, I was finally resigned to the fact that I was not going to receive a refund. On the third day he was nowhere to be found and I never did get my refund.

About an hour from Mbandaka, the boat began to cruise along at a faster speed. At this point it was pushing two barges packed full of people, bags of grain, dead monkeys, pigs, dogs, sheep, goats, fish, handcrafted items, cabbage, bananas, plantain, and other types of cargo. At the rear of the barges people dropped buckets tied to ropes for lifting water from the river to drink, wash clothes, bathe, cook and for whatever else water was used. At the front of the barge a person could be seen standing on the edge peeing into the river. I went downstairs a couple times to experience the ambiance of those compacted barges. The stench was awful; one could not walk on the barge without climbing over someone or something. People were cooking their meals and selling cooked food and other commodities to each other on the barge. All the while these activities and dealings were going on, the boat was "just cruising along," the captain paying no attention to what was going on within the two barges.

The Congo River is the drainage of the Congo basin and it is an intriguing body of water. This river made it almost impossible to believe it was the real thing. There were places one could not see land on either side of the river. The width at some places was fifteen to twenty kilometers wide. It is the second-longest river in Africa after the Nile and the fifth longest in the world. There were places where it narrowed and the water was deep, with tall jungle trees on each side. It flows through the second-largest rainforest in the world. The islands of water hyacinths were considered a serious river pest because they could create blockages at tributary outlets which caused flooding. They also became tangled in the rudders of boats, causing breakage and boat delays.

The river was deep and the volume of water flowing was mind-boggling. It is the second largest river in the world in terms of volume of flowing water. Its flow rate was calculated and reported to have over forty thousand liters (three thousand gallons) of water per second. It was heavily infested with crocodiles and hippopotamuses, two very dangerous animals. One does not normally think of a hippopotamus being dangerous. Hippos kill many people in Africa, especially if one gets too close to a young hippo or if one stands in the path that a hippo uses to walk to and from the grass.

Along the river in the jungle were small villages where people eked out a living from nature's bounties on the land, in the jungle or the river. Some were hunters, some were fishermen and some were farmers. Collectively they provided sufficient food for the people to survive in such remoteness.

Included in our "first-class ticket" were meals in the dining room. The dining room consisted of plain bare wooden tables for six people with salt and peppershakers in the middle of the table (no table cloth). The chairs were also wooden and both the tables and chairs were ripened with age. The meals were bland, cooked too long and were the same each day. Breakfast was usually served at 7:00 A.M. so Betty and I had to make sure we were up before the people started coming in for breakfast. We usually had bug-infested cereal and boiled eggs with bread and coffee. For lunch there was bread, soup, peanut butter, jelly, tropical fruits (bananas, mangoes, oranges, guavas) and hot tea. For dinner we usually had rice or beans with a sauce (gravy), and for variety we had rice and beans. A pot was plopped in the middle of the table and we helped ourselves as it was passed around. There were plenty of flies to go around during lunch and dinner but there were not too many during breakfast. By stretching the truth, I would be doing that dining room a real favor by calling it a "one-star" restaurant.

Yes, the floor was hard but looking back on this scenario in a positive frame of mind, it was good for the back. The pillow was my briefcase. It was hard, immovable, too high and very uncomfortable. Using my briefcase as a pillow gave me a secure feeling for its safety and its contents. Knowing that I had hold of it while sleeping made it difficult for a thief to steal it. I carried all my important documents and money in that briefcase and I simply could not afford to take any chances of having someone steal it or we would have been in a terrible quandary, especially in Zaire. The boat's mate gave us each a light blanket and a sheet to sleep on and to cover ourselves. It was not exactly like an American inn, but we managed. Because there was "no room at the inn," we were joined by a couple from Canada. Together the four of us slept on the restaurant floor.

As we lay on the floor, one could hear the drone of the boat's engines and the pounding of cylinders turning the propellers. There was a dim light left on all night in the dining room. After things quieted down, if we opened our eyes and looked around on the floor, there were hundreds of cockroaches scurrying around everywhere eating morsels of food. When they came close I flicked them away. If a person made a disturbance like someone waking, moving or swatting a cockroach, those rascals would almost immediately disappear and there was not a cockroach to be seen anywhere!

While we were cruising along on the Congo River after dark,

Betty and I, with our friends from Canada, stood on the deck looking into the night skies. What an incomprehensible experience! The boat had a very strong light beam coming from in front of the captain's cabin shining downstream over the top of its barge. This light beam enabled the captain to keep the boat and barges on course and enabled him to look for sand bars. There were times when we looked into the light's beam and saw what must have been millions of insects. There were so many insects that it looked like we were driving a car at night in a Pennsylvania snowstorm with insects looking like snow bouncing off car lights. At a couple points the river appeared to be in a white out because there were so many insects.

There were times when burning fires in either the village or the bush painted the sky reddish orange. Villagers built fires within the village at night to ward off wild animals. Bush fires are common in many African countries. Sometimes fire is used to drive animals to hunters. Other times it is used to clear land for farming or to generate green sprouts for livestock to browse. At still other times fires are a natural phenomena caused by lightning. Nearly all fires are uncontrolled and burn for many days.

In the middle of the first night, the boat stopped at a small town and docked for a couple of hours. The dockworkers attached two additional barges in front of the two already connected to the boat. Scores of additional passengers boarded the two new barges. As the boat continued its journey down the Congo River with tons of cargo, it pushed four barges packed full of people and multitudes of assorted cargo. There always seemed to be room for more cargo and people.

It was pushing four barges, fully loaded with tons of cargo and an estimated 1,000 passengers toward Kinshasa. Among all those people were six Caucasians, two from the United States (us) two from Canada and two nuns from Italy. The two nuns did not go all the way to Kinshasa; they disembarked late Sunday afternoon at a jungle village somewhere in the bowels of Zaire. That left the four of us as the minority on the boat. Generally speaking we never felt any animosity, threats or insecurity when we were among the passengers.

As the boat was cruising along pushing its four barges, with thick jungle on both sides of the river, I was overwhelmed by the remoteness and density of the jungle. I looked up ahead and suddenly there came scores of pirogues, each with several people standing up paddling the canoes toward us. They resembled warriors attacking the boat. Instead of bearing arms for an attack, the canoes were laden with all kinds of commercial commodities grown in, harvested from, or made in the jungle to be sold to passengers on the boat and barges. As the canoes rowed to the boat and barges, they tied up to its side. There was a boisterous flurry of activity and commotion from the passengers on the boat and barges and the people in the canoes.

After the canoes were attached to the side of the boat, they were bombarded by passengers throwing a handkerchief or rag or towel wrapped around a small stone or something heavy into a canoe containing, for example, a stalk of plantain or a dead monkey or a bag of millet. This meant that that particular stalk of plantain or a dead monkey or a bag of millet was to be sold to the person who threw the handkerchief. Passengers actually got into fights over who claimed or owned whatever it was they were trying to buy. Some even tried to steal items. The goal of the people in the canoes from the jungle villages was to sell their commodities to passengers on the boat. Some boarded the boat or barges and themselves purchased commodities from the passengers to take back to their jungle villages. All the while this flurry of bartering and haggling over price was taking place, the boat kept cruising along. When the boat approached the village where the people came from, they climbed back into their canoes, detached from the barge and paddled to shore with their newly purchased wares or commodities or money they earned.

As the boat progressed down the river, more and more people

from jungle villages paddled upstream several kilometers to meet the boat and barges to do an encore of the marketing. Each village had its specialty. One of the villagers approached me with an ivory smoking pipe (In those days I smoked a pipe). After some traditional bartering, I purchased a carved ivory pipe with a cow horn stem. It was rather attractive and different. However I smoked it only two times, the first and last time. What a horrible tasting pipe! When the tobacco was lit it tasted and smelled like burnt horn. I still have that pipe, but I never again smoked it.

Watching this entire flurry from the second deck of the boat was an experience that was interesting, entertaining, intriguing, colorful, cultural, spectacular, educational, comical and exciting. But above all this experience gave us a greater appreciation and a different perspective of people's lifestyles in another society that was different from mine. As citizens of the world we must learn to understand, respect and appreciate the culture, traditions, foods, religions and lifestyles of people in societies that are drastically different from those in Europe or North America or Asia.

Swimming in the Congo River are tons of what I call catfish, a favorite food for crocodiles and an untapped food source for people. Passengers were fishing off the barges as the boat cruised along. Sometimes the people from the jungle villages who paddled their canoes to the "floating shopping center" had huge catfish for sale. I ventured down to one of the barges in the afternoon of the second day where I saw stacked like firewood a pile of the largest catfish I have ever seen. Some of those fish weighed at least forty-five to sixty kilograms. They had huge heads, mouths that were thirty centimeters or more wide and long thick whiskers. These fish were enormous! Then there were live fish kept in huge basins covered with woven-vine lids and were stacked seven and eight basins high. They kept some of the fish alive until the boat arrived in Kinshasha and were sold as fresh fish. People bartered fish for other commodities or sold them outright. Most of the fish were sold upon the boat's arrival in Kinshasha.

During the middle of the second night, the boat again stopped to attach two more barges. Again they were loaded with similar cargo and scores of people climbed on board. Near daybreak three hours later, the boat started its engines and began to push six heavily laden barges on its journey down the Congo. By now we were seeing more open land where agriculture had encroached into what was once a jungle. We saw small villages with people standing on the riverbank waving at the passengers as the boat and barges passed.

Various species of monkeys were usually found in the jungle. Young men in the villages hunted monkeys and killed them for food for their families. Sometimes they would sell harvested monkeys to make money. As the jungle people boarded our "floating shopping center," many had dead monkeys for sale. The monkeys had been gutted and the body cavity washed out before they were brought on board. Passengers haggled over the price before buying one or more monkeys for their meals on the barge. Many of the monkeys were sold upon arrival in Kinshasha.

To prepare the monkey for roasting the hair had to be singed off before it could be placed on a rack over a small barrel containing hot charcoal on the barge deck. An energetic middle-aged chap would climb up onto the roof of the captain's cabin to where the exhaust pipe came through. The diesel exhaust had an occasional flame and was hot enough to singe off the monkey's hair. He tied the monkey's tail around its neck, grasped it like a handle and held it over the hot exhaust pipe. When the monkey was completely singed, this chap climbed back down onto the barge and placed the singed monkey over the charcoal fire to be roasted.

As the boat chugged behind six fully loaded barges and headed downstream toward Kinshasha, every once in a while one would feel the barges or the boat hit a bump. Once I heard the captain say, "Oops." The bump was an "oops" caused by sand bars. Sand bars shift when the water is high. Turbulent currents stir the sand and silt causing it to become dispersed within the moving water. The sand and silt is dropped when the current slows or the water level recedes. Where the water drops sand and silt it builds up to form what are called sand bars. Sand bars are unpredictable and they can appear almost anywhere, especially where there is a bend in the riverbed. Sometimes boats can slide over low sand bars. Passengers hear a sliding, grinding sound as the momentum of the boat pushes itself over the sandbar. Boat captains try to avoid hitting them. The captain can see most but others are under water and cannot be easily seen from the captain's cabin. Boats can go aground when they hit a sand bar. A forward-moving boat can easily ride up onto a sand bar and the boat will sit there for several days until it can be pulled off by another boat or wait for rising water level. Even though the Congo River is an important waterway for Zaire, its government has never budgeted funds to purchase a river dredge to keep boat channels open. Traveling by boat on the Congo River and arriving at your destination depends on the time of the year and the luck of the draw.

Late morning, Monday, 8 May 1972, we arrived in Kinshasha. There was bedlam on the barges and dock as the people started to disembark with their cargo. A boat mate came up to Betty and asked her for our passports. After Betty gave them to him he turned and briskly walked away. I was very concerned that a stranger had our passports and I didn't have a clue who he was, where he was or why he had them. Carrying our luggage and briefcase, we jogged after him down a long corridor until we came to a room that said "*Douane*" (Customs). There he stood at a desk with two gentlemen sitting behind it. They began to interrogate Betty and me by asking questions such as:

- "Why were we at Mbandaka?"
- "How long were we at Mbandaka?"
- "How long were we in Zaire?"
- "Where did we travel while in Mbandaka?"
- "What were the names of the people you visited?"

- "What did we purchase in Mbandaka?"
- "What did we purchase on the boat?"
- "When were we departing Zaire?"
- "Where were we going after departing Zaire?"
- "Why we traveled by boat and not Air Zaire?"
- "Who did we travel with on the boat?"

And the questioning went on for nearly an hour. All the time the person doing the questioning had our passports. Finally he said, "Wait here until I return." Betty and I had no choice but to wait. The other two gentlemen stayed in the room with us. About fifteen minutes later he returned with our passports, stamped them and handed them to me. Then he simply said, "*Merci beacoup*." All in all, this three-day trip was one of the most unbelievable events one could ever have in a lifetime.

We worked our way through the mayhem on the docks and found a taxi to take us to United Missions Hostel where we stayed until Friday, 12 May 1972. The United Missions Hostel was like an American motel sponsored by nine different Protestant churches. We had our room and three meals a day for US$10.00 per person. This hostel was certainly reasonably priced and a very nice place to stay in Kinshasha. It was wonderful to hear Americans speak English at the hostel.

I was particularly interested in seeing the market where people daily sold and purchased their vegetables, fruits, meats, flour, baked goods, fish and other food items. The town market tells me a lot about the culture of a particular society. It shows what they eat, how they purchase their food and the kinds of crops grown and sold in an area or region. The affluence of people is measured by the price they can afford to pay for food.

This market impressed me because it was well-organized and paved. The concrete stalls were under a tin roof which provided shade where people set up to sell fruits, vegetables and other food items. There were several water taps which enabled the merchants to hose down their stalls at the end of each day, making this facility easy to keep clean. There was no dust, very few flies and the appearance of the market was rather attractive. This market could have been used as a model for towns and villages in other countries, especially in Chad.

We did a great deal of sight seeing by walking here and there in Kinshasha. We visited the ivory market, the copper market and just looked at several other places which sold trinkets and "stuff." There was always someone trying to sell something. One gentleman approached us and wanted me to buy from him a set of copper plaques to hang on a wall. I had absolutely no intention of purchasing those plaques simply because I did not want them. I very stupidly asked, "*Combien?*" (How much?). He said ten Zaires (US$20.00) each. I said, "No, that's too much money." He said, "Then make me an offer." Hoping he would go away, I said, "I'll give you two Zaires for both of them." He said, "*Donne-moi l'argent*" (give me the money)." I knew then and there I was duped. We were Peace Corps Volunteers and did not have much extra money to spend. However US$2.00 for two copper plaques was not a bad price. We have them hanging in our home as a reminder of that market.

On a street near the market, a man approached me with a black and white oil painting. It was a fishing village scene along the Congo River painted on a flour sack. The artist of that particular piece captured the ambiance of an unnamed fishing village along the Congo River either at dawn or dusk in a more uninhibited way than a complex camera could. It was gorgeous! The artist had to use a flour sack because he had no easel or canvas. I paid him his asking price of US$20.00 because it was so well done. I was almost ashamed to give him only $20.00 for that fine piece of work but to him it was a large amount of money. I also knew he would exchange those American dollars on the black market and would get a bonus. That is the reason I paid him in American dollars.

When Betty and I returned to our farm in Bucks County, Pennsylvania in June 1973, I asked the carpentry teacher at Upper Bucks County Area Vocational-Technical School if his students could make a frame for that painting using weathered rough-cut eastern red cedar boards from an old pigpen at our farm. They agreed to do it for the experience at no charge. They did a wonderful job framing that unique oil painting. We gave the carpentry club at the school a donation as a token of our appreciation for a job well done. We have had that framed oil painting hanging in our home since 1974.

We were scheduled to fly out of Kinshasha on Air Zaire on Friday, 12 May 1972 for Bangui, the capitol of the Central Africa Republic. We waited and waited in the lobby of the airport and there was no one at the counter. Finally a lady came to the counter to take our ticket and issue us a boarding pass. We asked, "What time is the flight scheduled to take off?" She said that it would be announced. We went through customs and got our passport stamped that we were leaving Zaire. Again we waited and waited for the announcement of the flight departure time and flight number. Still there was not anyone in the area where Betty and I were directed to wait. I spotted an Air Zaire plane at the far end of the tarmac and some people walking toward it. I said to Betty, "That has to be our airplane." So we walked through a turnstile and the lady standing at a table stamped our passports again saying we entered Zaire. When we saw people boarding that airplane, I said to Betty, "Come on, we're getting on that plane." To get to the tarmac, Betty and I had to walk through a door with a sign posted above it saying, "Do not enter." We walked through it and across the tarmac to the airplane. Sure enough, it was our flight and we boarded. We departed Zaire with our passports stamped that we entered Zaire and yet today they are still stamped that we're there. So ended our extraordinary expedition to the Republic of Zaire which is profoundly etched into our minds.

43

The Only Time Betty Ever Felt Big and Tall

Whew! What an experience! We landed in Bangui, the capitol of Central African Republic, on 12 May 1972. Inside the airport were travel posters advertising tours to the Ituri rain forest to visit nomadic Efe pygmies. Since this was our first time to visit this remote country and possibly the only time, Betty and I thought this would be an interesting educational voyage. The Efe pygmies lived approximately two hundred kilometers south of Bangui in the Ituri rain forest which borders the Democratic Republic of the Congo (Zaire). Unfortunately the travel agents informed us that they were closed for the season and trips were no longer available.

At our hotel we met an embassy official from Austria who indicated that he also wanted to visit the pygmies in the rain forest. In our discussion we agreed to hire a taxi and split the costs and travel together to the rain forest. That afternoon we hired a driver and planned to leave the hotel at 6:00 A.M. on 14 May 1972.

The three of us anxiously waited until the next morning for a fascinating encounter that we will remember forever. As planned, we left the hotel with the driver and car we hired. We headed south on a gravel road toward the Ituri rain forest for a total of 162 kilometers. It was raining and the road became narrower and narrower. As the road passed through poorly drained areas, it was completely flooded. It was an awesome journey! There was jungle on both sides of the narrow gravel road and a torrential rain pounding the roof of the car. We arrived at a river where we had to board a ferry with our car to cross over to the other side. After crossing the narrow river, we disembarked the ferry and drove a short distance to a small river village called Loko.

The rain forests of northern Democratic Republic of the

200

Congo and southern Central African Republic are where the larger concentrations of nomadic Efe pygmies can be found. It had been reported to us that the pygmies historically were the original inhabitants of Africa. As the Negroes from the coastal areas of Africa escaped the slave traders, they migrated deeper into the mainland. This migration drove the pygmies deeper into the rain forest where they still lived in 1972. In some areas according to our guide, particularly villages, the Negroid people consider pygmies not to be true human beings and they look upon them condescendingly.

Some of the pygmies had left their traditional nomadic lifestyle, built mud brick huts and became sedentary in villages of northern Congo and southern Central African Republic. They can always be identified by their huts because they are lower in height, especially the doors, and are always located on the peripheral edges of the village. Sedentary pygmies can never get a fair paying job, public or private. They can only get menial, low paying jobs that no one else wants.

At Loko we used proper protocol by first going to the village chief, introducing ourselves and describing to him why we were in his village. We asked him if we could visit the pygmies who lived in the rain forest nearby and that we would need a guide who could also be our interpreter. The pygmy chief by coincidence was nearby and the Loko village chief sent for him. We waited nearly an hour for the pygmy chief to arrive. Our driver could speak the language of pygmies and they began to talk. We assumed he was obtaining permission for us to visit his people in the rain forest. Before we arrived in Loko, the driver informed us that we should take gifts to leave behind. We were advised to take salt, sugar and cigarettes. We finally got the nod to move ahead and began our trek on a narrow slushy footpath in the rain into the forest.

As we trekked into the rain forest on the narrow footpath in single file, Betty and I became very soaked from the rain. This hike was so exciting and interesting that we did not mind getting wet. The density of the undergrowth and the height of the trees were extraordinary. I only wished I had been more educated in horticulture to be able to identify the many exotic wild flowers, shrubs, vines and trees we observed. We had to rely on our guide to know where we were going and how to return. If anything happened to us in that rain forest, nobody would ever have found us. It was so easy to become disoriented because one could not see the sky. We had walked approximately two kilometers into the forest when it started pouring rain again. Still it did not matter.

At long last we reached a small settlement of nomadic pygmies deep in the rain forest where they were living at the moment. Whoa! What an encounter! This was the first time Betty ever felt big and tall. The pygmies were no taller than 136 centimeters and Betty was 146 centimeters tall. Betty said that it felt good to be among adults smaller in stature than she was. Their settlement in the forest was about the way I had envisioned, from what I had read.

The people lived in small igloo-type huts made of grass thatch or large overlapping leaves. They were easily disassembled and transported or were discarded when they departed from the settlement site to seek out a new food supply.

Nearly all of the people were naked except two men who wore groin straps and the chief, who wore a ragged pair of tan trousers. One lady, possibly a wife of the chief wore a skirt. One man had on a red football jersey with the number 21 on it. Nakedness was an accepted way of life and no lewd behavior or pretenses were observed among the people.

Being there in the rain forest with a society that exhibited no signs of twentieth century influences was a humbling experience for us. There were no transistor radios, wristwatches, pots, pans, clothes, jewelry, telephones, water wells, tin roofs, automobiles or tools. Their baskets were woven with vines, utensils were fired clay pots or halved gourds and rope was woven using bark from small woody vines.

202

This was the first and only society I had ever visited which had no agriculture. These people were hunters and gatherers. For a period of time they would temporarily settle where sufficient food was available. Being nomadic in nature, when the food became scarce, they would simply gather up their meager belongings and move on to where they found food in another section of the rain forest. There were dangers in the rain forest but they learned from childhood how to cope with wild animals, poisonous snakes and swift-flowing water.

A couple of men showed me how they hunt with their cross-bows. The crossbows and small arrows were handmade from indigenous materials. The hunters hunted for animals by setting a crossbow so the animal would trip it. The arrows were short, thin and razor-sharp on one end. The arrows usually did not kill the animal. Their function was to pierce the animal's skin to inject a lethal dose of poison smeared on the end of the arrow. The poison was made before the hunt began. They told us the hunters went into the rain forest looking for certain white grubs which were found in rotted logs on the ground. They would put the grubs into a container until it was nearly half-filled. The grubs were dumped into a container of boiling water on a small fire, killing them. They instinctively excreted a substance, which was deadly poisonous, before the boiling water killed them. As much of the water was boiled off, the poison became concentrated. Then the grubs were mashed into a paste. The hunters would dip their arrow tips into the lethal poison before mounting them onto the crossbows. The question I have always posed was, "How did these people learn to make and use such a deadly poison?" "How did these people discover crossbows?"

The people we observed seemed to be content, healthy and happy. They were very friendly and seemed to be pleased that we came to visit them. To express their delight at our visit to their settlement, all the women and some of the older children sang and danced for us.

When we were about to begin our trek through the rain forest back to Loko, we decided to give the people their gifts. They appreciated the gifts of the salt, sugar and tobacco but the chief wanted an additional 1,000 CFA (US$4.50). We wanted to get back to Loko safely and with a guide, so we gave him 1,000 CFA. Our gifts were the only thing in the settlement that truly represented western civilization.

We began our walk back to Loko with the guide. We walked at a pace that was comfortable for Betty. It began to rain again. This time it rained hard and we really were soaked but the temperature was warm and we didn't mind. By the time we arrived at Loko, we were all starting to become tired from walking and the excitement of the experience, plus we were hungry.

Upon our arrival at Loko, the chief invited us to his "*case de passage*" (guest house). Most villages have a guesthouse for people to rest in when passing through their village. We had taken our own food with us and we decided to eat there while it was raining. We were all very wet and hungry at that point. After we ate a late lunch, we rested until the rain stopped. Then the driver arrived with the car and we began our ride to the river, onto the ferry and on to the same gravel road back toward Bangui.

As we were riding on that gravel road, each time we passed an occasional oncoming car or truck, the driver would place his thumb onto the windshield. I watched him do this all the way to Loko from Bangui. The curiosity was getting the best of me so I asked the driver why he put his thumb onto the windshield when an oncoming vehicle passed us. The driver said to us, "I put my thumb there in case a piece of gravel flies up from the road after an oncoming vehicle passes us. If a piece of gravel hits the windshield, my thumb absorbs the shock and prevents the windshield from breaking." Well, I thought that was a pretty interesting theory until forty-five minutes later. That was when an oncoming car approached us. Yep, sure enough, an ordinary piece of gravel flew up hit the windshield and the windshield safety glass exploded into thousands of little pieces. After the aggravated driver stopped the car, he opened the door and began to clean glass off the front seat, floor, dashboard and his clothes. Betty, our Austrian friend and I sat in the back seat and we did not have any of the glass on us. I leaned over toward Betty and softly said to her, "Well, this shoots that theory all to hell!" With no glass in the windshield, we continued an uneventful journey back to Bangui to end a remarkable experience that we will forever cherish.

The time came when we needed to begin bringing a magnificent, enlightening, thrilling and fascinating expedition to its conclusion. When we left Bangui and headed northward towards Fort-Lamy, Chad, I looked out the window and in the far southerly distance I could see the beginning of the tropical rain forest, the home of the pygmies whom we had visited two days earlier.

After nearly two hours in flight we arrived in Fort-Lamy. There the Peace Corps staff driver met us and took us back to the Peace Corps/Chad Office. What a phenomenal, once-in-a-lifetime opportunity we had, and will forever remember! Now we had to get back to reality and finish our business in Fort-Lamy and drive back to Bessada to carry on with our Peace Corps duties and responsibilities.

44

"Cinva" Ram Press

For hundreds of years traditional round huts in Chad including Bessada were constructed of handmade mud bricks. Mahogany upright poles latched to the roof's bamboo pole frame supported the structure. The round roof was covered with a thick layer

These men are making traditional mud bricks by placing mud into a wooden frame using their hands to pack it firm. The wooden frame was gently lifted off to allow the brick to dry in the hot sun for two to three weeks.

of dried thatched grass. A decree was made sometime in the late 1960s by President Tombalbaye that all new huts were to be rectangular in shape, preferably with a tin roof as opposed to the traditional round hut with a grass thatched roof. The President's rationale for this decree was to portray western-shaped homes and the tin roofs gave the impression of affluence throughout the villages.

The traditional method of making mud brick during the annual dry season was done by digging soils with high clay content. Such soils made bricks that withstood weather elements longer. The loosened clay-type soil was piled in the middle of a rather large hole from where it was dug. A large depression was hollowed out on top of the pile where water was added. Water was poured into the depression on top of the piled soil and a hoe was used to mix the soil with water. Additional water was added until the soil became a semi-stiff slurry. With a spade the slurry was placed into a wooden frame until it was full. Using their hands, men packed the slurry firm. The wooden frame was gently lifted off to allow the brick to dry in the hot sun for about two to three weeks. Traditional mud bricks generally lasted three to four years before they began to disintegrate from climatic elements.

Peace Corps/Chad provided a Cinva Ram Press for us to use in the village. The press was a steel box with a steel lid and false bottom plate attached to a long pipe-like lever. After watching how traditional mud bricks were made, we decided to try making bricks using the Cinva Ram Press. First I attached the press with lag bolts to two rough-cut mahogany boards 8 cm. x 26 cm. x 185 cm in size. The boards provided the necessary stability and weight for the press. It could be moved, but not easily. At the southeastern edge of the village was a stratum of gray clay soil where everyone made mud bricks. If this Cinva Ram Press worked the way we envisioned, it would be permanently placed for all the villagers to use.

The box was filled with traditional semi-stiff mud slurry; the lid was closed and locked. The lever had its fulcrum point on top of the lid. As it was pulled down, the false bottom plate pushed upward, compacting the mud against the lid. Then the lever was pushed back releasing the pressure on the mud. The lid was opened and turned outward to completely open the box. The lever again was pulled to lift the false bottom plate, pushing the compressed brick out of the box. The brick was lifted from the steel box and laid on the ground to dry and harden in the sun. The sturdiness and strength of bricks made in the Cinva Ram Press were much greater than the traditional bricks. The number of people who visited the clay pit to look at and study the newly made brick was amazing. In a short time, these new bricks became very much preferred by the villagers. When all was said and done the Cinva Ram Press became a popular piece of equipment at the clay pit for all the people to use.

It has been said that, "Where we cannot invent, we may at least improve." The villagers were not able to invent a new brick-making machine, or a new material to make brick, but at least they were able to use their clay soil to improve their mud bricks by using a "Cinva" Ram Press. Thanks to Peace Corps/Chad for providing the people in Bessada with the press to make stronger mud.

45

Plow Rentals

One day between Christmas and New Year's, in December 1972, while I was in Fort-Lamy the manager of the United States Embassy warehouse told me there was a heavy wooden box in the warehouse that he was going to discard if no one wanted it. He apparently needed the space and was tired of moving that heavy crate. He invited me to the warehouse to take a look at "stuff" in that crate, which had never been opened, "stuff" that the Embassy had purchased at one time for a project but was never claimed.

It was very, very hot the day I went to the Embassy warehouse to look at whatever there was to find. Wow! Did I find a trove of goodies! In that unopened heavy crate were brand new unassembled green plow parts from France. They were the same kind of plows I had occasionally seen being pulled by oxen in southern Chad. The warehouse manager told me that I could have them if they were of any use to Bessada farmers or myself. Making the decision to take the plow parts was a no-brainer.

I went back to the Peace Corps Office to borrow the Peace Corps Land Rover and drove it to the warehouse. With the help of another Peace Corps Volunteer, we loaded the wooden crate onto the Land Rover. We hauled the plows back to the Peace Corps shop to assemble them. We opened the crate and took out enough parts to assemble one plow. There were enough parts in that crate for a total of seven plows. Since I had the proper tools in my toolbox to assemble the plow, we decided that I would finish that job after we returned to our village. Wow! What a find! The total cost to Peace Corps/Chad for seven plows was $0.00.

Peace Corps/Chad Director, John Riggan, allowed Betty and me to borrow the Peace Corps Land Rover to haul the plows back to Bessada. I was going to need a four-wheel drive vehicle anyway for driving on deep sandy roads to get to villages in the Canton of Bessada to open pit silos for farmers. Driving a Land Rover for eighteen hours from Fort-Lamy to Bessada on a rough dusty dirt road was very tiring. Betty and I arrived safely back in Bessada late at night after a long day. We went into our house and straight to bed.

The next morning I unloaded the parts for seven plows and stored them in the warehouse attached to our house. A few days later I found some time to begin assembling the plows. I was surprised at how quickly the parts went together. Only a couple of

Jim Diamond demonstrates to a farmer how to use an ox-drawn hand plow.

hours were needed to assemble the plows and make them ready for use. At that point we planned a new project for the plows.

The cost to a farmer to purchase a new plow at that time (1972) was CFA 5,000.00 or approximately US$166.00. This was a major investment for a farmer who would use it only once a year to plow three to five hectares (1 hectare = 2.47 acres). Many farmers had a team of oxen but could not afford to purchase a plow.

Our new village plow project was to rent all seven plows to farmers who lived in and around Bessada. We charged a very small affordable fee on a per day basis for each plow. The fee was CFA 0.50 or US$0.16 per day. At 5:30 each morning farmers would come to our house to rent their plow for the day. The plows were rented on a first-come, first-served basis. A farmer could plow in one day approximately one-half hectare (1.23 acres) with a team of oxen and a hand plow. It previously had taken a farmer nine to ten days to till the same area using the traditional small hand hoe. Those plows provided a real time saving service for the village farmers.

The rental fee collected from the farmers was kept in a separate "blue sugar box" as a cash reserve to purchase plow parts as they wore out or had become broken (e.g. worn plowshares, broken chains). Plow parts for that particular plow were available at the markets in the larger villages.

I knew the plow project would be very effective as long as we managed it from our home. To ensure project continuity of renting plows after we left Bessada, we solicited the village chief and farmers to form a committee to be responsible for managing the rental plow project. All the farmers and the committee knew the rules for renting the plows. They knew how much to charge, where the plows were stored and when they were to be returned. When we turned the plows and funds over to the committee, they were well-organized and well regarded by other farmers. I often wondered whatever happened to those plows and the plow rental project after we terminated our Peace Corps duties. When helping people help themselves, there comes a time when the helper has to get out of the way and let it happen. The people being helped must at some point take responsibility for their progress.

46

Demonstration Cotton Field

Southern Chad's environmental conditions were conducive to growing cotton and it was Chad's only exported commodity and the government of France subsidized it. Each farmer was required to grow one hectare (2.47 acres) of cotton and one cord (1.23 acres) for each wife. The National Organization for Rural Development (ONDR) officers was equivalent to County Cooperative Extension Educators in the United States. They were responsible for teaching farmers how to grow cotton by using approved agronomic practices established by Chad's Ministry of Agriculture. They were also the community overseers to document and report the amount of cotton that was being grown in their assigned zone and making sure that the farmers were growing their fair share of cotton according to the government mandate.

In Chad, farmers do not own titled land as in other countries. The village chief controlled agricultural fields. The land on both sides of a selected road leading out of the village was staked out into one-hectare blocks, each designated with a number. The village chief assigned numbered blocks of land to farmers in the village. Every farmer would receive at least one hectare for himself and one cord for each wife in the household. However, the total number of hectares that a farmer received depended upon how much land he requested above the minimum as mandated by the government. Every household was assured they would get a portion of land. Usually the older, more influential villagers were assigned land closest to the village; the younger farmers would have to walk two or three kilometers each day to their fields.

In a land where its society had not yet been exposed extensively to western agricultural practices, it was interesting to observe intuitive conservation practices, which prevented degradation of the soil's capability to grow crops. The practice of placing large tracts of land into a system of fallowing for four to six years came into being from within the Chadian society. Normally in most rural villages of Chad, there were dirt roads that went in a northerly, southerly, easterly or westerly directions from the village. For the sake of discussion, lets begin with large tracts of land on both sides of a road leading from the village in a westerly direction. Assuming that it had been cultivated to grow crops (cotton, sorghum) for the past four years, the following procedure would transpire:

1. The village chief would inform the villagers that he planned to take that land out of production after all the crops were harvested and will let it fallow for no less than four, preferably six years.
2. The following growing season, the village chief would select land on another road leading from the village where the land had been fallowing for four years.
3. The ONDR officer would measure and stake out fallowed land into one-hectare fields and assign each field a number.
4. The chief assigns the numbered fields to households within the village.

The fallowed land ultimately becomes overgrown with grasses, shrubs and trees. Over a period of years the nutrients in the soil are recharged from plant residues and legumes.

Usually two to three months prior to the beginning of the rainy season, farmers began clearing their new plots for tilling and planting. Usually the following would come to pass.

1. Beginning in early April, farmers would begin the slash and burn process of clearing their land. Slashing trees and shrubs was normally accomplished with a machete.

213

Dead trees were set afire and would smolder for several days until there were only traces of white ash. One needs to note that no heavy equipment was used to clear land; there was no compaction that formed impenetrable hard pans.

2. Burning the dried grass, dead trees and stacked brush cleared the land.

3. Westerners often frowned upon burning a field. They claimed that it affected the soil structure by destroying the organic matter in the soil. This may be true to some extent, but in reality, under the farmer's limitations of circumstances that existed in southern Chad, there were several valid advantages for farmers to burn herbage on their fields. Some of the advantages were as follows:

> Fire helped to control weeds by destroying indigenous weed seeds.
>
> Fire destroyed insects, their eggs and pupa.
>
> Residual ash provided fertilizer (potash) on the soil.
>
> Burned fields were much easier to till because the herbage was usually so thick that it was difficult to turn under with either an oxen-drawn plow or a hand hoe.
>
> Cleared land was safer for the people to work because they could see if a dangerous wild animal or serpent might be lurking in the distance.

In summary, these agronomic practices evolved through trial and error over many years and seemed to have suited farmers who were mandated to produce crops with very limited resources and technology. This is the reason it is important to study traditional practices before one introduces new methodologies. Whatever an outsider decides to introduce, it must fit into or add to traditional husbandry practices already in place. One must never perceive

Chadian farmer tills his land the traditional way by using a short-handled hoe. It took him and his wives nine-ten days to till one-half hectare (1.23 acres).

A Chadian farmer plows my field with a team of oxen using a rented moldboard plow. Farmers could till one-half hectare (1.23 acres) in one day with a team of oxen and a plow.

African farmers as being incompetent. They do what they can with what they have and get what they can from what they bring into being.

During the 1972 growing season, I was asked by President Tombalbaye to plant a demonstration cotton field using all of the approved practices so farmers in Bessada and surrounding villages could see how cotton should be grown. As fate would have it, I had never grown cotton, and as a matter of fact, had never seen cotton grown, especially in Pennsylvania. Nevertheless I was being perceived as the Chadian expert cotton grower. I had no choice but to learn pronto how to grow cotton and grow it properly because the village chief gave me six hectares (14.82 acres) of land on which to grow cotton.

The field was located along the road where everyone in the

village walked past it daily to reach their own fields. Everyday as farmers walked by my field they watched what I was doing. Everything we did in that field was apparent to the villagers and no matter what there was no margin for errors.

Under normal circumstances in Chad, tilling was done with a short-handled hoe. This was a very difficult, laborious and time-consuming task. It took both the husband and his wives nine to ten days to till one-half hectare. A team of oxen hitched to a plow could till that same amount of land in one day. A very limited number of farmers were beginning to use teams of oxen to pull hand plows. The farmers who used a team of oxen to till their land were affluent enough to purchase both a team of oxen and a plow. More often than not the amount of money needed to purchase a team of oxen and a plow was far beyond the financial capability of typical village farmers. We paid two farmers a fee for their labor and two teams of oxen to till six hectares of land with rented plows for the "President's Demonstration Cotton Field." It took seven days and two teams of oxen to till the demonstration cotton field. Our purpose was to illustrate to village farmers the efficiency of using a team of oxen and a plow. When the soil was tilled, we began to make plans to plant the cottonseed.

In Chad there was no mechanical seeder to plant cotton. Farmers would go across the field walking backwards with a long handled hoe making holes within the rows at various distances ranging from thirty to eighty centimeters apart. The rows were crooked and the distances between the rows varied greatly. Sometimes they even crossed over one another. These distances did not enable the farmer to get the proper plant population to achieve maximum production. The planting process started after they made the holes. A wife or two and older children holding a hand full of cotton seed against their belly buttons, placed four to six seeds in each hole with their free hand. They would use their bare feet to cover the seed with the loose laterite soil. This was a time-consuming task and inefficient. It was inefficient because the

A Chadian farmer prepares to plant cotton by digging holes with a hoe. The distance between the holes varies greatly and negatively impacts the number of plants per hectare.

A Chadian farmer pushes a small-cleated wheel with six cleats on it making holes exactly twenty-five centimeters apart. The purpose of the wheel was regulating the distance between the holes with each row.

government recommendation was that seeds be planted twenty to thirty centimeters apart within the row and sixty to eighty centimeters apart between the rows. Plant population did not seem to be a concern to those planting the cotton. Following are their methods with my suggestion for improvement.

Weeding cotton by pulling weeds by hand or by a short handled hoe, it made no difference whether the row was straight or crooked. If the rows were straight and the cotton planted the proper distance apart across the field, a cultivator could be used to weed the cotton.

When cotton was planted too far apart, it affected the plant population and had negative impact on the yields. The distance between rows of cotton should be sixty to eighty centimeters for maximum production. If the cotton were to be weeded by hand or with a hoe, then sixty-five centimeters would be acceptable. If the cotton were to be weeded with an animal drawn cultivator, then eighty centimeters was recommended.

When cotton was planted too close together within the row, it would not fully develop because of crowding. Proper spacing of cotton plants within the row should be twenty to thirty centimeters for maximum yields. Without a ruler, one could make use of an open hand and the distance from the end of the thumb to the end of the little finger would usually be close enough to plant cotton seeds in what they called "seed pockets within the row."

A volunteer from Switzerland had developed a small-cleated wheel with six cleats on it. As it was pushed it made holes in sandy soils exactly twenty-five centimeters apart. The purpose of the wheel was to get farmers to increase their plant population by planting cotton the proper distance within the row. So we asked him if we could borrow it. He went one step further and donated one to Bessada to be used for the demonstration cotton field and by anyone in the village who wanted to use it.

We went into the bush and cut a couple of hundred thin sticks for marking rows. At side A of the field along the road, we pushed the first stick into the sandy soil then measured eighty centimeters and pushed another stick into the soil. We continued this process until we reached the other end of side A. Then at side B, on the other side of the field, we repeated the same procedure. With a long rope, we stretched it across the field from the first stick on side A to the first stick on side B. We took the wheel with six cleats and pushed it along the taut rope making holes every twenty-five centimeters. It worked beautifully. When side B was reached the rope was moved to the next stick and this process was repeated until all the holes were made. After the holes were made in the first eight rows, eight of my workers each took a row and began planting cotton by dropping four to six seeds into each hole and covering them with soil using their foot. Once we started planting cotton, anyone who wanted to visit me, had to talk with me while we planted cotton, including my wife Betty.

Granted it took some effort to measure the distance between the rows and push the sticks into the ground, but this system certainly gave us straight rows so we could use a cultivator. Also by using the cleated wheel, we were able to obtain the proper plant population. There were several farmers who borrowed the cleated wheel to try it in their own fields. Many of them decided they did not care to use it because it made too many holes and it took longer to plant the cotton (at this point they simply did not understand the concept of proper plant population).

When the cotton seed germinated and grew about fifteen centimeters, those straight rows of cotton plants properly distanced from each other was an appropriate model for comparing neighboring fields planted the traditional way. Shortly after the cotton sprouted, my farmers went down each of the rows and inspected the plants. If all four or five or six seeds germinated, two of the healthiest plants having at least four leaves were selected and the others were pulled out and discarded, being careful not to harm the two desirable plants. This was called "thinning" the cotton. This task was usually done when the soil was wet because the

A Chadian farmer uses a trained horse to pull a cultivator as an efficient way for controlling weeds in our cotton field.

undesirable plants were much easier to remove without disturbing the two desired plants. The goal was to have two healthy plants per "pocket." Yields would be hampered if all of the seedlings grew because of crowding.

I was pleased with how our demonstration cotton field had evolved. The cotton looked lush and healthy but the weeds were out of control. I had eleven laborers working in the cotton field and the weeds were unmanageable. Hoeing nearly six hectares of cotton with a hoe or pulling weeds by hand were never-ending and time-consuming tasks. In Chad weeding cotton had been accomplished by pulling weeds by hand or using a short-handled hoe. Throughout the region including our village, there were many Arabian-type horses owned by villagers. These horses were used primarily for riding from village to village or for pleasure. Not once did I see a horse pulling a cart, wagon or any kind of farm implement. An idea came to mind. Why not use a horse to pull

222

a cultivator to weed the cotton? Animal traction was limited to using oxen. Horses were used only for riding. A horse-drawn cultivator would certainly be a much more efficient method of keeping weeds under control (See "Giddy-Up," "Whoa-Haw," "Gee," and "Whoa"). With the introduction of a horse-drawn cultivator, weeding was not as labor intensive. The horse performed beautifully! The cultivator tilled the soil and dug out the weeds between the rows and in less than ten minutes the horse was across the field and one row of cotton was weeded. After the weeds were cultivated with a horse drawn cultivator between the rows, all the workers had to do was hoe the weeds within the row.

To encourage farmers to apply expensive fertilizer to their cotton, the Ministry of Agriculture used this promotional scenario: "A man who eats good will be strong and work good. A cotton plant who eats good will be strong and grow good." The government lent money to the farmers for purchasing fertilizer, cottonseed, and insecticide. After the cotton was weeded and thinned the first time, the ONDR officer recommended that cotton be side-dressed with fertilizer. It was best to place fertilizer about ten centimeters from the base of the plant stems to obtain optimum benefit. Fertilizer was very expensive and great care was taken not to waste it. Chadian farmers usually carried a halved calabash (gourd) or a small box filled with fertilizer and applied it by hand to the base of the cotton plant.

Farmers relied on recommendations from ONDR officers for controlling cotton insect infestations. As a rule southern Chad had many different species of insects which attacked cotton. In most cotton-growing areas in our region farmers had access to an insecticide that was recommended by the government for controlling most of the common cotton insects. Often three to five applications were necessary. This particular insecticide was not only expensive but very dangerous to people if not properly handled. The farmer mixed it with water and filled a knapsack sprayer with the solution. The sprayer was mounted on the worker's back and they walked along each row spraying cotton. The workers had no facemask, body protection (e.g. long-sleeved shirts, long pants) or gloves to protect themselves. In addition there was no way to properly measure the amount of chemical being mixed in water nor properly calculated rates of chemical being sprayed onto the cotton plants. Yes, there were instructions on the container; however most of the farmers could not read. This is an example of how agricultural pesticides are often used in developing countries when there are no controls or regulations on agricultural chemical usage. Yet farmers are mandated to use them!

In early October we began to notice that some of the cotton capsules were beginning to open. The last week of October we began harvesting the cotton. Whew! What a job this was. Each morning after the dew dried, each picker (including Betty and myself) had a sack, which was attached to our side. We picked cotton and placed it into the sack. When the sack was filled, it was carried to the end of the field and dumped into an oxcart. When the oxcart was filled we filled our sacks one more time and placed them on top of the cart. At the end of the day we transported the cotton to the large warehouse attached to the end of our house. At this time the farmers saw how much cotton we were harvesting from our demonstration field. They began to understand the importance of proper plant population and weed control. We picked cotton again in November and again in January. The brightest and largest bolls of cotton were harvested during the first two pickings. The pickers were careful not to mix leaves, hulls or other organic material in the higher quality cotton because a higher price was paid for large bolls of bright, clean white cotton. Each time we picked the cotton, its quality diminished.

All harvested cotton was transported to one of several gins strategically located throughout southern Chad. In Koumra was *Coton Chad*, a cotton gin which was owned by a French company that purchased the harvested cotton from local farmers, usually in January or February. *Coton Chad* scheduled one or two days each year for farmers to bring their harvested cotton crop to a collection site in the village. Farmers brought their cotton to the collection site in ox-drawn carts or in large baskets carried on their heads or in filled bags transported in a wheelbarrow or in pickup trucks. They dumped their cotton into piles and there it stayed until their names were called to bring their cotton to the scales. Cotton was sold by the kilogram (2.20 pounds). The farmer brought his cotton up a ramp and had it weighed. Then it was dumped into a huge trailer truck. The farmer was given a receipt and a sum of cash money for his product. The farmer then walked to the next table and there he paid the government loan for the fertilizer, seed and insecticide. At the next table he paid a tax. When the farmer departed, there was very little money left, if any, for his toil, trials and tribulations of growing cotton.

When we hauled our cotton to the collection site, there was no question that we had the largest pile of cotton (six hectares of cotton is a lot of cotton compared to their standards). When we weighed the cotton and loaded it onto the truck, cash was paid for it. Then like everyone else, we went to the next table to pay for our seed, fertilizer and insecticide. Because it was the presidential demonstration cotton field, we didn't have to pay any tax. The president was pleased with both the cotton yields and the amount of money (net profit) received for cotton produced in his Demonstration Cotton Field managed by an "authoritative" American cotton greenhorn. Life is certainly full of lessons, including how to grow cotton.

47

Why Don't You Use a Long-Handled Hoe?

Whew! What a back breaking job. Weeding cotton was a dreaded, time-consuming task that involved all members of the household. Men and women would be bent over with a short-handled hoe weeding cotton beginning in early morning while it was cool. Because women were responsible for taking care of infants, it was common to see them weeding cotton with babies tied to their backs. Children old enough to do the task would also be weeding cotton. This was a never-ending job because weeds were virtually unmanageable. It didn't take long for weeds in a cotton field to get out of control. I had eleven laborers and a horse-drawn cultivator working in the cotton field and it was all they could do to keep weeds under control on six hectares of cotton. One day I asked my laborers why they did not use a long-handled hoe. They told me that a short-handled hoe was easier to use. I did not buy that response and decided to do something about it.

One day while my laborers were working in the field I went back to the village and purchased eleven new hoes from the village blacksmith. I asked him to bend the hoes just above the top and below where it is attached to the handle. You might have thought I had asked him to do something really horrible. I said to him, "Look, these are my hoes and I would like them bent as I described." He looked at me as if I were out of my mind as he began heating the metal to bend the first hoe. I stood there to make sure he bent the hoe enough the way I wanted. He did a very good job and I said to him, "*Madjingaye* (great) this is the way I want the other ten hoes bent." By the expression on his face, he really thought this American was lacking good judgment and was quite inexperienced in using hoes.

While the village blacksmith was bending my hoes, against his better judgment, I went into the bush and cut eleven poles 154 centimeters long. When I returned to the village all eleven of the hoes were bent and after I paid the blacksmith, I commended him for doing a good job. I took the hoes and poles back to our house and fitted them together, making long-handled hoes. I had to do a little trimming on the poles but all eleven were comfortable to hold. I put the eleven long-handled hoes into the storage room for distribution the next morning when the laborers reported for work.

The next morning at 5:45 when the laborers arrived at our house, I greeted them with my usual hearty *bon jour* (good morning) and handshake, then gave them their instructions for the day. We started to bring out the long-handled hoes to be used for the day. When I brought out the first three long-handled hoes, those fellows were really surprised and did not know what to think. They thought that the handle had not yet been shortened on those new hoes. While I was inside getting more long-handled hoes, one of the men got a machete and began chopping off the long handle. When I came outside I saw what was happening and I yelled, "*Arrêt, arrêt!*" (stop, stop). I then explained to the men that today I was going to teach them how to use a long-handled hoe. The look on their faces indicated that their minds thought this American must be some kind of idiot!

When we all arrived at the demonstration cotton field, I got the hoes out of the car and gave each laborer a long-handled hoe. I explained again how I was going to teach them how to use it. Those fellows were not too excited about using those hoes because this was a major change in their traditional way of weeding cotton.

I took a hoe and explained how much easier it was to hoe cotton without having to bend all day using a short-handled hoe, and how to hold the hoe. I demonstrated how to use the new hoe. I said to the men, "I want you to try this long-handled hoe until noontime today. If you like it, you can continue using it. If you

A Chadian farmer learns how to use a long-handled hoe to control weeds.

do not like it, you can shorten it to your liking." They seemed to agree reluctantly with this proposal so I lined them up at the side of the field and got each of them started hoeing one row of cotton with a long-handled hoe. After they began to get used to the hoes, I left so I would not make them nervous.

At noontime when I returned to the cotton field, they were all waiting for me. I asked them, "Well, how did you like the long-handled hoe?" One said, "I liked it." Another said, "My back is not as tired." Still another said, "I never thought of using a longer handle on a hoe, this worked well with me." Not one of the workers cut off the handle of their hoe. During the remainder of the weeding season, they used long-handled hoes. Amazing!

A couple days later, after they became competent in hoeing one row at a time, I demonstrated to them how they could hoe two rows at a time. Following the demonstration they were each assigned to hoe two rows at a time. When I arrived at noon, I asked "Well, how did you do hoeing two rows at a time?" Their response was, "It took too long to go across the field." I said, "Yes, that's probably true, but you did two rows and only had to walk across the field one time." Their response was, "Oh." Each day thereafter they hoed two rows at a time.

A week later I demonstrated how to hoe three rows at a time. You straddle one row with your legs and hoe it, then hoe the row to the left, then the row to the right. This was too much for them to fathom, so I agreed to let them hoe only two rows at a time. Between the laborers and the horse-drawn cultivator, we were able to keep the weeds under control.

Each day people would see the laborers using long-handled hoes as they walked by our cotton field. Some even stopped and tried using them. Three weeks later, I was walking on the road looking at other cotton fields and to my surprise, I observed— yep, it is true—I saw a lady using a long-handled hoe with a baby tied to her back. By the end of the weeding season, there were several people using long handled hoes. I have always wondered what that village blacksmith must have thought when other people in the village wanted their hoes bent? A change process is never easy.

48

"Giddy-Up," "Whoa-Haw," "Gee," and "Whoa."

"Giddy-up, Whoa-haw, Gee and Whoa" were commands for a team of horses my father taught me as a young lad on the home farm back in Woodside, Pennsylvania. Most draft horses were taught these commands when driven as a team or a single horse pulling an implement, a buggy, a wagon or a sleigh. The horse responds to "Giddy-Up" by starting to pull forward. "Whoa-Haw" means go to the left, "Gee" means go to the right and "Whoa" means stop. These were common commands used by farmers who used draft horses.

Each Chadian farmer was mandated by the Chadian government to grow two cords of cotton and one cord for each wife because France subsidized it. In review, I had been asked by President Tombalbaye to plant a demonstration cotton field using all of the practices recommended by the Ministry of Agriculture (See "Demonstration Cotton Field"). The weeds were especially difficult to control. It was a never-ending, time-consuming task. My idea of using horse-drawn cultivators would certainly be a more efficient method of weed control.

I asked a farmer why he did not use his horse to pull a cultivator in his cotton field instead of weeding by hand. He told me that horses are not used for animal traction. I told him that early

America was built with draft horses. After obtaining similar responses from other horse owners, I wondered how many people would like the idea of using a horse for light work. It was time to find out. It seemed that a practical approach would be to teach farmers how to use a horse as a means to reduce their manual labor and mine. Although these horses were small in stature, they could do light work without jeopardizing their well-being. These Arabian-type horses were certainly capable of doing light work such as pulling a cultivator or pulling a small lightly loaded cart.

The first task was to meet with the village chief to explain the proposed idea of demonstrating to the people how to train a horse to pull a cultivator. Even though the chief was a bit skeptical, I explained to him that early America was built by using draft horses. He gave me his blessing. This cleared the way to begin the horse-training project. I needed a horse, a harness, a singletree, a cultivator and a field of cotton.

I knew the *Sous-Préfet* owned several horses in Bessada. I explained to him the idea of training a horse to pull a cultivator. I asked him if I could borrow one of his horses for about three months. He was a progressive person and agreed to lend me a horse. Now that I had a horse what was needed next was a harness. Where was I going to get a harness? There was not a harness available anywhere in Chad, let alone Bessada. I was walking through the village one afternoon wondering how I was going to hitch this horse to a cultivator. At that moment, I walked right by a dried cowhide hanging on a *secca* fence. That's it! I'll make my own harness, I thought to myself.

I asked Pierre if he would ask the owner of the hide if he would sell it to me. Also I wanted to know how much he would charge. Pierre returned from the hut and told me he would sell it and it would cost 300 CFA (US$30.00). I am sure I could have bought it more cheaply, but the asking amount was reasonable and I agreed to purchase the dried cowhide. We carried the cowhide back to our house for safekeeping. The hide was stiff and needed to be softened before we could work with it. I placed the hide into a large puddle of rainwater outside our house and soaked it for four days, turning it over once a day. Finally the hide softened enough so that I was able to cut it with my pocketknife.

I laid the hide flat on the ground with the hair side down and measured it so I could make four side-straps, each one 154 centimeters long, one end ten centimeters wide and the other end twenty centimeters wide. In addition, two smaller straps, five centimeters wide, were cut from the hide. Whew! What a job! Four hours of cutting (sawing) a thick stiff cowhide with that pocketknife was a very difficult job. Finally all four side-straps were cut and paired. I cut thin slivers from the rest of the hide for sewing.

Using a small leather punch on the pocketknife, I punched small holes every three centimeters around the outside edge of each side-strap. With the slivers of rawhide threaded through the holes, I sewed the paired side-straps together as one. The side-straps needed to be strong, since all the draft stress would be on the double-sewn straps.

The wide ends of the two double side-straps were sewed together end to end with the hair side facing out. This formed what is known as a breast-band harness. On the narrow ends of the two side-straps, metal rings were sewn onto each strap. The five-centimeter-wide straps were sewn onto each of the long side-straps so that one would straddle over the horse's withers and the other over the croup. Now we had a completed breast band harness.

We needed a singletree so the cultivator could be properly pulled. We went into the bush and cut a one-meter-long branch from a fallen tree which was ten centimeters in diameter. In the exact center we drilled a hole and inserted an eyebolt where the cultivator would be attached. On each end of the singletree we attached a hook where a short chain would be attached to the rings on the ends of the breast band harness. A singletree is used to distribute the draft equally to each side of the horse.

When a horse pulls a cultivator or other like implement for-

232

ward, all the draft pressure would begin at the cultivator hoes, equally transferred to the ends of a singletree, to a short chain attached to the ring on the side-straps to the side-straps. From there the draft is transferred on each side of the horse and ultimately to the breast.

Medar (who worked for me) was the keeper of the horse. We began training the horse by first leading it with a rope halter. After a few days the horse was used to walking and being led with a rope halter. Then we put the breast band harness on the horse so it could get the feel of the harness. Every day for three weeks, Medar placed the breast-band harness on the horse and then took it for its daily walk. At the end of three weeks the horse was used to the rope halter and walking with a breast band harness attached to its back. The next step was to put some pressure onto the breast band harness. At first we attached the singletree and had a person walk behind the horse holding the single tree pulling gently on it to give the horse the sensation that it was pulling something.

Simultaneously we searched for a horse-drawn cultivator. They were few and far between in southern Chad. I found a cultivator at the French ONDR headquarters warehouse in Koumra. I asked the Director, M. DePeux if I could borrow one for a few months. M. DePeux was very cooperative and lent me a cultivator and said I could keep it as long as I needed it.

We attached the cultivator to the singletree on the breast-band harness and let the horse pull it a short distance. The first few times the horse pulled the cultivator, someone lifted it so that only the guide wheel rolled on the ground. Its shovels were lifted, limiting the amount of draft on the harness. We gradually let the shovels drag on the ground to put more pressure onto the harness. Finally, after another week of training, we were ready to take the horse and cultivator to the cotton field for its first official day on the job.

Everyone in the village knew we were going to take the horse and cultivator to the field early the next morning. They wanted to see this horse perform. Normally it took twenty minutes to walk to the cotton field. But this particular morning it took nearly an hour. People were everywhere looking at that harness and watching the horse drag the cultivator to the field.

When we finally arrived at the cotton field, the people stood along the road to watch this unnamed horse pull the cultivator while wondering all the while if that American knew what he was doing. I said to myself, "Horse, if you do not pull that cultivator like you were trained, I'm going to have all kinds of names for you." Medar took hold of the lead rope on the halter, Nestor took hold of the handles on the cultivator and together with the horse they went across the field. The horse performed perfectly, the cultivator tilled the soil and dug out the weeds and in just ten minutes the horse was across the field and one row of cotton was cultivated. Normally it would take a farmer with a hoe an hour or more to work his way across the field once. With that horse and cultivator plus the men hoeing weeds, within four days the entire six-hectare cotton field was completely weeded. Then we started over to keep fast growing weeds from competing for natural and applied soil nutrients that were so vital for proper growth of cotton. What a success! That horse worked for five months pulling that cultivator, three to four days a week, with Medar leading it.

Need is the mother of invention. Do not ever say, "I can't," because "can't" never did anything. Acquiring a horse, cultivator and a field of cotton in a village where resources were scarce at best was both a challenge and an opportunity. Making a harness and singletree would have never happened if I had said, "I can't."

49

"Madame. Stop!"

When we arrived in Chad, the President's office provided us a new car to use in Bessada. This was a special privilege because Peace Corps Volunteers normally are not assigned motorized vehicles unless they were needed for their work. As part of our basic training, we were informed that if we ever hit a person with our vehicle, we were not to stop but to drive quickly to the nearest police station and immediately report what had happened. The rationale for this rule evolved from earlier times before there were established governments and courts of law. When tragedies, attacks on people or acts of revenge happened, often the perpetrator(s) went unpunished, especially those who lived within remote hinterlands of Chad. Since many Chadian tribes lived by the philosophy of, "An eye for an eye and a tooth for a tooth," they often took the law into their own hands.

If a driver of a motorized vehicle hits and injures or kills a person, there are many documented cases in Chad where the local people killed the driver on the spot. It mattered not the language spoken, religion or skin color. It is a way of life in Chad.

Seeing a car being driven through the village was a rare sight for children. Often when they heard a vehicle approaching their village, they gathered at the edge of the village and chased it or tried to outrun it. Although this was a dangerous activity, the children were just having fun.

While returning from teaching her sewing class in Sebe, Betty along with her interpreter, was driving our car through a tiny village outside Bessada near the south side of my demonstration cotton field. As Betty was passing through, she noticed the village chief was sitting under a shade tree and she waved and with his usual smile, he returned the wave. A couple young boys dashed across the road in front of the moving car. Suddenly, Nestor hit Betty's arm and shouted, "Madame, Stop!" Just as Betty looked forward, she saw the child go down and he appeared to be under the front left wheel of the car. She instinctively hit the brakes and immediately stopped the car, stalling it.

A young boy had darted in front of the car and the bumper knocked him off balance and he fell down but the wheel did not go over him. It caught the end of his shirt. The frightened boy stood up, cried loudly and ran away toward his hut. The chief saw this incident happen. Betty was petrified! The chief told her, "It is okay, it is okay, the boy is okay." Betty offered to take the boy to the hospital if he were injured. The chief assured her the boy was not injured. Relieved, but still fearing revenge from the boy's family, Betty and Nestor returned to Bessada.

When Betty came into our house, she was white with fright and still concerned. When she and Nestor told me what happened, I said, "Okay, let's settle down and decide what to do next." I asked Nestor if he would, on my behalf, report this incident to the chief of Bessada and ask what we should do. Nestor immediately went to the chief and informed him of the incident. The chief's instructions to Nestor were, "Tell the Diamonds everything will be okay. The boy was not injured, he was not supposed to run in front of the car, the chief witnessed the incident and Betty stopped." I told Nestor, "That was very kind of the chief." I would have felt better if I could go to the tiny village where the incident occurred because I wanted to see the boy with my own eyes to make sure he was not injured in any way. If he had had any injuries, I would take him to the hospital in Koumra. Nestor said, "That would be good." We got into the car and drove a short distance to the village where I met with my friend the chief of the village. He appreciated my returning to inquire about the boy; he sent for the boy and his mother. He was about 10 years of age and appeared to be just fine. I said to the mother that if her son became ill tomorrow to please send for me and I will take him to the hospital. Everyone was happy and appreciative and Betty settled down after having the experience of her lifetime.

50

"Jim, How Do You Stand with the Lord?"

Generally speaking I have found missionaries of various faiths to be very dedicated, loving, caring, thoughtful and unselfish international human resources. They were to be commended and held in high esteem for the excellent work they do in addition to bringing their versions of God's word to local people. Modern day missionary practices now bring to the mission field a set of practical life skills as an integral component of religious teachings to convert people who have animistic or other beliefs. They teach people to be automobile and truck mechanics, carpenters, farmers, medical practitioners, livestock managers, nurses and homemakers. Religion was an important, integral part of their teaching programs. In my opinion this was a more holistic approach and a more practical means of contributing to the economic development of people within a society.

This being said, missionaries are human beings and they too unknowingly and sometimes knowingly make blunders. There was one missionary who did not understand the mores of the Chadian society where she lived and worked. For example there were many large mango trees on the property owned by Baptist Mid-Missions. Owning deeded land in Chad was unheard of by the Chadian people. Their method of distributing land was different from that of America or other countries. According to Dr. Dave Seymour the mission station actually had a deed for a piece of land outside Koumra. Obtaining title for the land was a condition which the original missionaries insisted upon before they would invest money in buildings for developing a mission station and hospital on the premises.

The Chadian people had an ancient tradition whereby if a person planted a fruit tree, that tree belonged to the person who planted it. They normally would protect the tree from being damaged by animals, people and pests. It was clearly understood by the locals that any fruit produced on the tree(s) belonged to the person who planted it. Furthermore it is against the law in Chad to cut down any kind of fruit tree because they are a source of food for people. When the land was originally deeded to Baptist Mid-Missions, there were several mango trees growing there. According to Chadian tradition they belonged to those who planted them, deed or no deed. A few missionaries were under the impression that the mango trees belonged to the mission station. This is how and why the issue I'm about to explain unfolded.

Customarily, each afternoon between 1:00 and 3:00, most everyone took a siesta during the heat of the day. During the dry season when mangos were ripe, children would sneak onto the station grounds and pick mangos during siesta time. The missionaries were irritated that children were not only disturbing their siestas, but were "stealing 'their' mangos." The missionaries were constantly chasing the children from the property during that time of the year. One missionary was so furious regarding those kids stealing the mangos that she bitterly complained to the director of the Mission Station. Regardless of her many complaints, the children continued to pick ("steal") mangos.

Knowing full well that it was illegal to cut down a fruit tree, this one missionary hired a Chadian worker and instructed him to cut off all the branches from each mango tree surrounding her house. In her mind she did not cut down the trees, but for all practical purposes, destroyed their capability of producing fruit. What she did caused quite a stir among the locals and upset the director of the Mission Station. I also frowned upon what she did with those once-beautiful mango trees but said nothing because it was none of my business. I was not a missionary; Betty and I were Peace Corps Volunteers stationed in another village. Each time I passed by the stems of those once magnificent mango trees I cringed. I understood the Chadian tradition; I sincerely believe she understood the tradition but apparently did not respect it.

After two weeks a new husband and wife missionary candidate team arrived in Koumra to observe the station and see what life was like in Chad, especially the Koumra area. They were from the state of Georgia and were giving very serious thought to becoming a missionary team somewhere in southern Chad. Every Wednesday evening Betty and I traveled to Koumra to the mission station to pick up our weekly mail and attend the weekly prayer meeting with the American missionaries at the home of Dr. Dave and Ruth Seymour. On one occasion, Betty and I were invited to have dinner with one of the missionaries before prayer meeting. The other guests were the new missionary candidates. What a delightful dining experience we had! There was laughter, thought-provoking discussion and good food. After dinner the houseboy began cleaning and washing dishes with most of the guests trying to help. There seemed to be plenty of help in the small kitchen so I went outside and sat on the veranda to get out of the way. The wife of the new missionary couple joined me on the veranda and we began to continue our conversation as it took place at the dining table. Suddenly, out of the blue, she changed the topic and said to me, "Jim, I was wondering, how do you stand with the Lord?" Here was a lady I had known for only two hours and she was asking me this kind of question. Quite frankly, I was mystified by her inquiry and asked myself, "Why is she asking me this question? Did I say something wrong?" Simultaneously as I looked across the grounds to the next house where the stems of those magnificent mango trees stood, I thought about her question. Without thinking, I blurted out, "You know, sometimes the actions of you missionaries speak so loudly that I cannot always hear what you are saying." Well! That was obviously the end of that conversation! She knew very well what I was referring to because she had previously learned from another missionary what had happened to the mango trees and she saw me looking intently at their barren stems.

51

M. Le Président...

Betty and I had arrived in Fort-Lamy from Bessada in December 1972, for a meeting with the Peace Corps Director John Riggan. We were invited to use the guest room in his home during our stay. The first thing we did was take a most welcome shower after our long arduous seventeen-hour drive over 660 kilometers of rough dusty dirt roads. The telephone rang and it was M. Ouagadjuo, *Counseilleur Diplomatique* (Diplomatic Counselor) who wanted to speak to John. M. Ouagadjuo said to John that he had heard the Diamonds were in town. John said, "Yes, they just arrived and are getting showered." He informed John that the President would like the Diamonds to visit him at the Presidence at 6:00 P.M. John responded, "...only the Diamonds?" M. Ouagadjuo said, "Yes, only the Diamonds." John said, "I'll inform them and they will be there."

M. Ouagadjuo was our direct link to the President. All our communications to the President went first to the *Counseilleur Diplomatic*. We had previously described to him the projects which were in progress at the time. They were: silage making, the cotton-growing demonstration, the vaccination program for oxen, sewing classes for village women, an individualized homemaker training program, making a mud brick oven for the villagers, a bread-making project, the modern poultry house project, see-saws and swings for elementary schools, horse hoof trimming, castrating oxen, spraying oxen for external parasites and the plow rental program. The purpose of the meeting was to describe to the President the progress we had made in Bessada, his home village. This visit evolved after the *Counseilleur Diplomatic* had reported our projects to the President. This was considered an official visit to the *Présidence* (equivalent to the White House in Washington, D.C.) to meet with President François Tombalbaye.

Betty and I arrived at the front gate of the *Présidence* at 5:35 in the Renault that President Tombalbaye provided for us. Several guards were dressed in fire-engine red coats, black trousers and plumed hats with solid black hat bills. Each guard had a ceremonial rifle but we did not know for sure if they were loaded. However, behind them was a chain-link fence where several battlefield-dressed soldiers holding loaded machine guns stood at attention.

We were cordially greeted by one of the smartly dressed guards who asked our names and why we were there. I said, "I'm Jim Diamond and this is my wife Elizabeth Diamond, we are Peace Corps Volunteers from United States of America and we're here to see the President." The guard replied, "What embassy are you from?" I said, "We're not representing an embassy, we are Peace Corps Volunteers." He replied once again, "But what embassy do you represent?" At about that time Mr. Ouagadjuo spotted us and came out from the *Présidence* and told the guard who we were and that we had an appointment with the president. We were motioned to drive our car through the gate and entered the grounds through a well-locked and guarded chain-link fence. We parked our car inside the compound.

After we left the car, we were directed to walk to an outdoor veranda where there were several chairs. We were seated there to wait for the President. We had assumed that because of the number of chairs, we would be only two of several people to whom the President would speak. After we waited twenty minutes, Mr. Ouagadjuo came out and said to Betty and me, "The president will see you now."

Betty and I entered the *Présidence* and there we met President Tombalbaye. The president greeted us very warmly in a beautiful reception room. The chairs and sofa were white, the floors were highly polished and the furnishings and decor were well-coordinated. The president sat in a chair with his back to a window-less wall, Mr. Ouagadjuo sat on the opposite side of the room and Betty and I sat in the middle on a sofa. Mr. Ouagadjuo served each

241

of us a glass of champagne. The four of us discussed the progress of our Peace Corps projects and discussed agricultural issues of Chad as they related to the well-being of Chadian people.

During our conversation, we talked about how important agriculture was to the economic development of Chad and the welfare of Chadian citizens. I said to the President,

> M. le Président, before any nation can become economically strong, it must first develop its agriculture. When your people are hungry, you will always have unrest. America's real economic strength is not its huge corporations. It evolves from the vast agricultural production capabilities of the American farmer.

This statement is as true today as it was in January 1973. He was very much concerned about the issue of desertification. We talked about how the government of Chad could stop desertification in a practical manner. This brought up the topic of the Israeli nursery where Israeli horticulturists did a magnificent job raising tens of thousands of eucalyptus (Eucalyptus) tree seedlings. I went on to say to the President,

> M. le President, your people have a wonderful tradition where if they plant a fruit tree, it is their tree for life and it is passed on to their family when they die. They supervise the management of their trees and protect them. M. le President, would you consider declaring a 'National Arbor Day?' At the middle of the annual dry season attempts to plant seedling trees from the Israeli nursery is a noble effort. However the efforts are futile because for various reasons, there is a ninety percent mortality rate. Before a scheduled National Arbor Day, at the end of the dry season, load military trucks with eucalyptus seedlings at the Israeli nursery and send them on roads north, east and south. When they arrive at a village, the driver will ask the village chief, 'How many people do you have living in this village?' The driver will give the chief one tree per person living in the village with instructions on how, where and when to plant the trees. The driver then moves on to the next

242

village and repeats this process until all the trees are distributed. On National Arbor Day, you make an inspiring speech on Radio Chad in front of an audience, sponsor a parade in Fort-Lamy with your military carrying seedling trees supported by employees of the *Ministère des Forêts* (Ministry of Forests). You plant the first tree, followed by the audience, employees and military each planting one tree. Then each person in all the villages will have planted one tree. *M. le Président*, in one day you can have three million trees planted at a time of the year when the survival rate can be ninety-five percent. It makes no difference if those trees are planted in straight rows. The fact is they get planted and have an excellent chance to survive because of the forthcoming rainy season and the people will take care of them.

During this conversation, the President continually made a clicking sound with his mouth. At the time Betty and I did not know the significance of those clicks, since it was the first time we had heard them. We later learned from Dr. Seymour, who was President Tombalbaye's personal medical doctor, those clicks meant he was agreeing with what was being said.

After a half-hour, Mr. Ouagadjuo politely informed us that our time had expired and the President had other appointments. Overall the President seemed to be pleased with our report. Betty and I were impressed with his politeness and mannerisms. We felt at ease with him while we talked. We politely bid President François Tombalbaye farewell and invited him to our home the next time he traveled to Bessada. The President said, "The next time I come to Bessada, I will stay with you."

After we left the *Présidence*, we returned to the home of John Riggan. John was excited about the fact that the President wanted to meet with Betty and me and particularly what we reported to the President. John was so pleased with how our amiable relationship unfolded with the President that he called the American Ambassador to inform him of what took place.

The American Ambassador immediately invited us to his residence, and there we reported to him our successful visit with the President. The Ambassador seemed to be pleased about our visit but I could sense an undertone feeling that he was a bit miffed since he had not been informed that we were to visit the President at the *Présidence*. It was not the fault of John Riggan or Betty and I that the Ambassador was unaware of our visit with the President. The appointment had come into being so quickly. The Ambassador had reason to be a bit miffed because according to international diplomatic protocol, President Tombalbaye's Office should have notified the American Embassy that Betty and I were scheduled to meet with the President. It didn't happen. *C'est l'Afrique* (That's Africa). Nevertheless Ambassador Terence Todman was not offended. Our visit with him was very friendly and constructive.

52

Arbor Day In Chad

The term "desertification" is a word not normally used in the United States. However, in Central and West African countries south of the Sahara Desert, it is a commonly used term. It means that the harmattan winds blow from a northerly direction across the Sahara Desert to the Atlantic Ocean repositioning sand in a southerly direction toward where people live and grow their meager food crops. The Sahara Desert in some places moves south at an incredible rate of about eight kilometers annually. There are pictures of houses half buried in sand, and crops completely lost under the sand. The scarcity of natural forages and trees fail to hold the sand in place. Agricultural practices that contribute to desertification include over-grazing sparse grasses, cutting down trees to make charcoal, a lack of trees to hold the sand in place, lack of crop rotation and improper soil management.

To combat the movement of the Sahara Desert from moving south, the Government of Chad made a decree that a Green Belt of eucalyptus and other tree species indigenous to the region would be established across Chad north and east of Fort-Lamy. Eucalyptus trees are native to Australia. This species of tree was selected to be the preferred tree because they were tolerant to an arid environment, had deep root systems, were tolerant to some insect infestations and grow rapidly.

A short distance south of Fort-Lamy was a nursery sponsored by the Israeli Embassy. The horticulturalists there grew outstanding eucalyptus tree seedlings by the hundreds of thousands. It was well-managed and the trees were healthy when they left the nursery. At the Chadian government's request, the Israeli Ambassador agreed to produce eucalyptus seedlings at their nursery for the Green Belt.

The eight-month annual dry season in Chad normally begins at the end of September. There will not be one drop of rain until the beginning of the following June. The environmental landscape becomes parched and herbage is desolate during the last three months of a normal dry season. Water wells go dry, river flow diminishes or slows to a trickle and the bush is completely burned. The temperature soars into the nineties. during the afternoons and dry winds carry much dust that transmits disease such as spinal meningitis. Life in general becomes sluggish.

Cadres of people were recruited to plant the eucalyptus seedlings across northern Chad in January 1972. Those who planted the seedlings came from *Bureau de Eau et Forêts* (Department of Waters and Forests), Peace Corps Volunteers, Swiss volunteers, French volunteers, missionaries and many others. Thousands upon thousands of seedlings were planted daily from January to the end of May.

To facilitate the survival rate of the seedlings, the employees of *Bureau de Transport* (Department of Transportation) filled tanker trucks with water from an already low-flowing Chari River and hauled it to the areas where the seedlings were planted. The men used a long hose from the tanker to water the seedlings with the anticipation that the seedlings would survive until the rains arrived in early June. The watering was a futile effort. The soil and air were so dry that the water from the tankers rapidly evaporated with little or no benefit to the seedlings.

The mortality rate of the eucalyptus seedlings that were planted was about 90%. So many variables destroyed the seedlings that it was a wonder anything survived! The seedlings that did survive were planted near the end of May just before the rains arrived. When the rains did arrive, there was enough water for the root system to be established. Now the seedlings began to grow. If eucalyptus seedlings survive one rainy season, their chances of growing were good because of their deep root system and tolerance to arid conditions.

The nomadic Fulani herdsmen commonly pass through northern Chad with their cattle. They move their livestock thousands of kilometers following the rains, available herbage and water for their cattle. A watershed containing a river is one of their favorite passageways for keeping their cattle alive. Fulani herdsmen passed through the parched landscape north of Fort-Lamy near the Chari River with their huge herds of cattle, flocks of sheep and goats. Their livestock eats almost anything that is palpable, moist or has a green leaf. The hungry livestock destroyed entire areas planted with eucalyptus seedlings.

The annual dry season placed much stress on wild animals as well as people. Rodents were a serious problem. They had a negative impact on the survival rate of the eucalyptus seedlings. The bark was moist, small rodents such as mice and sugar cane rats, as well as rabbits, girdled the seedlings. Girdling destroys the cambium layer, killing the seedling.

Termites are very common in the semi-arid and savanna areas of Central and West African countries. They eat dried woody material with gusto. The eucalyptus seedlings were so dry during the dry season that termites killed them by feasting on the roots, especially those that had been planted in February, March, and April.

Normally during the dry season, the people set fire to the dry grass and it burned for days. Hunters used fire to drive animals from the bush into their well-placed nets for the kill. After the hunt was completed, the fire was left to burn sometimes for days until it burned itself out. Herdsmen set fire to the bush and burned the dried grass. About ten days later, green sprouts would emerge from the blackened landscape. Nature has a way of storing enough moisture in the root system to cause sprouts of grass to grow about seven centimeters high. This practice generates browse so hungry livestock can graze. Farmers set fire to their fields to destroy the tall grass and crop residue. This controls insects and diseases, improves the pH of the soil with burned ash and increases the ease of tilling the land. Whatever the reason for burning the bush, fire killed newly planted eucalyptus seedlings.

Villagers, to make charcoal, cut down five- or six-year-old trees which survived the above variables. Charcoal in large burlap bags was sold along the road to people who drove by the village in pickup trucks, ox-drawn carts or large trucks. Villagers carried charcoal-filled bags on their heads to their mud brick huts. Charcoal was the only fuel used by the Chadian people for cooking, boiling water and keeping warm during the cooler nights. The vast number of trees cut for making charcoal caused the landscape in some areas to be devoid of trees to hold back the desert sands.

President Tombalbaye apparently took my suggestion for sponsoring a National Arbor Day seriously ("M. Le President...") and went to his ministers to discuss its ramifications. Betty and I terminated our wonderful Peace Corps experience in Chad on 2 May 1973 and returned to the United States. The Arbor Day idea we left behind with the President became their idea and was perceived to be an economic, practical and efficient method to quickly establish a Green Belt. Later, we learned from missionaries that in June 1973, President Tombalbaye had an "Arbor Week" approved to establish the Green Belt across Chad. We hope and pray that the Green Belt was established and that the Arbor Week has continued after their horrendous civil war in the late 1970s.

53

"Mmmmm Good!"

Bessada was not always the easiest place to exist. We had no electricity or running water. At night we used a Petromax lamp for light in our house. Each day our two employees, Nestor and Pierre, drew our water from an open well in the center of the village. Each morning our routine included building a fire outside at the crack of dawn and bringing a container of water to a rolling boil for twenty minutes. Then it had to be filtered before it was fit to drink. Betty had a small kerosene refrigerator to keep her food cool and she used bottled gas to cook her meals. Every week Nestor and Pierre helped Betty do the laundry by hand and hang it out to dry on a clothesline.

There was a small market in Bessada. It featured local women selling food products grown or made in or near Bessada. At Koumra there was a larger food market where one could purchase meat one day a week. In Fort Archambault there was an even larger market. Once a month we traveled east 136 kilometers to Fort Archambault to fill a 55-gallon barrel with gasoline for our car. Betty stocked up on our supplies so we could survive for the next four weeks before we could return. In Fort Archambault we pur-

Medar plasters the domed mud-brick oven with stiff mud.

chased freshly made loaves of French bread. Fresh out of its beehive mud brick oven and still warm, it smelled and tasted so good.

The only time we got bread in Bessada was when someone brought dry, hard two-day-old bread to the Bessada market. It tasted better if it was first dunked in coffee or tea. The people of Bessada rarely had fresh bread at their local market.

A villager named Medar had expressed an interest in learning how to bake bread after he tasted Betty's homemade bread. He also was interested in learning how to build an oven in the village to bake bread so he could sell it in the village market. When I sensed he was serious about learning how to bake bread, Betty and I agreed that we would conduct a joint project. I would teach Medar how to make the oven and Betty would teach him how to bake the bread.

Peace Corps had given me a VITA (Volunteers for International Technical Assistance) handbook written by professional engineers at major universities. They had a sense of how to make practical items using indigenous materials in remote villages around the world. The VITA handbook was full of ideas and plans and one plan in particular showed how to build a mud brick beehive oven. After studying the plans and directions, I concluded that the compressed mud brick would be the perfect size for building a beehive oven.

With Medar we decided to build the new oven near his hut where his family lived. Using the plan in the VITA Handbook, we calculated how many bricks would be needed to build the new oven. Medar went to where the villagers made mud brick and began to make brick using the Cinva Ram Press (see "Cinva Ram Press"). It took Medar, Nestor and Pierre one week to make the required number of mud bricks. They waited about three weeks for the bricks to dry in the sun. I used my car to haul the baked mud bricks to the construction site near his hut. Medar, Nestor, Pierre and I studied the plan and discussed how we would begin.

We used a ruler to determine where the exact spot for the oven would be located. Then we cleared the site and laid a solid square of brick on the ground. We filled and sealed the joints with stiff mud slurry. The second layer of mud bricks was laid the opposite direction to make the structure more solid. Stiff mud slurry was placed under each brick and in the joints. The third layer of brick was laid in the same direction as the first layer. The platform for the oven was now a solid, three-mud brick high base. Then we calculated the center of the square. We took a piece of cord three-fourths of a meter in length, placed one end in the exact center of the mud brick square and stretched the cord with a piece of chalk tied to its end. We made a circle one-and-one-half meters in diameter. The chalked circle was the inside brick line for the beehive oven.

The first circular layer of brick was laid on the platform. The second layer was about three centimeters over the inside edge of the first layer leaving an overhang. Each layer was pulled inward

Betty Diamond teaches Medar how to make bread using locally made flour.

Medar proudly exhibits his first loaves of fresh French bread made in his new beehive oven.

the same distance, forming a beehive-shaped structure. The twenty-five-centimeter hole at the top remained open to allow a draft for making the fire burn hotter.

After all the circular layers of brick were laid to form the domed-shaped structure, the entire outside wall of the oven was plastered smooth with a stiff mud. As the oven was being built, an opening for a triangular door forty-six-centimeters wide at the base and seventy-seven centimeters in height was built into the bricks. After a few days, the mud-brick oven dried and was ready to use.

Meanwhile I was able to find a piece of thin plywood that was used to make a triangular door. This triangular wooden door was used to seal in the mud brick oven's heat. A wood fire was made inside the oven and it burned until there was a five-centimeter layer of hot coals on the platform. The oven was sealed with the wooden door and a metal cover on the top hole to allow the oven walls to absorb the heat. When the oven's wall was hot it was time to bake bread. We used a hoe to pull out the hot coals from the oven.

Betty taught Medar how to make bread using a mixture of wheat flour purchased at the market in Fort Archambault and millet flour made locally. This was a whole new experience for Medar, so Betty slowly walked him through the process, explaining every term in the recipe. She taught him how to measure the flour, mix in water, add a little salt, add the yeast, how to let the bread rise and how to knead bread dough. Betty had no bread pans for baking the bread so we had to improvise. I found a piece of aluminum roofing and was able to cut it into pieces large enough to hold up to six long loaves of bread dough which would bake into six loaves of French bread.

Medar and Betty very proudly took their first homemade bread tray of six loaves of French bread dough and placed it into the hot oven. After less than ten minutes, they took the bread out of the oven because it was plenty hot. As he proudly held his first tray of six French bread loaves, we all circled around Medar and gawked at him with a cheeky predatory look on our faces. It was absolutely beautiful and tasted "Mmmm" Good!

Because of the taste-bud-titillating aroma, word spread very quickly throughout the village that Medar and Betty were successful at making the long awaited bread. The first six loaves were quickly gobbled down by Medar's family, friends and us. The next batch of bread yielded twelve loaves of bread. He took them to the village market, placed them on a small table and sold freshly made French bread for the first time. Betty assisted Medar for two weeks, then she backed away and let him make bread himself. Medar's bread sales soared, making his business endeavor very successful. To help him out a bit, Betty and I fetched his flour and yeast from Fort Archambault when we traveled there to get our personal supplies.

Medar sells fresh homemade French bread at the market in Bessada.

Medar established a routine of baking bread every other day with his new beehive oven. His new enterprise was a hit with local villagers. This is another example where local people became capable of addressing a need by using domestic knowledge, materials and skills.

54

Corny Story

Sorghum is the major food in Chadian daily diets. Women prepare *boule* by mixing flour from pounded sorghum grain mixed with water and boiled for an hour. Then it is poured into a calabash to set. *Boule* is eaten by dipping chunks into a gravy-like sauce. My workers once told me, "If we have not yet eaten *boule*, we have not eaten." During the growing season, maize (corn) is grown on a small scale and is eaten to supplement the sorghum diet. The maize is normally roasted over hot coals with the husks on. Then the husks are peeled back, the ear is held by its husk and the roasted maize is eaten directly from the cob. I have tasted it and after acquiring a taste for it, I found it to be tasty, even though it was what we considered to be field corn in Pennsylvania.

Back in Ottsville a very dear friend and neighbor near our farm named Matt Schaeffer sold seed corn to farmers in the local townships. I once sent him a letter that described how corn was grown and eaten in Chad. He decided to sponsor a sweet corn trial in Chad and sent me a two-pound bag of sweet corn seed. There were three purposes for the trial. One was to determine if American varieties of sweet corn would grow effectively in Chadian soils, the second was to identify pest problems and the third was to determine if the Chadian people liked American varieties of sweet corn.

After consultation with the village chief, I gave the sweet corn seed to the Chinese to plant at their research farm near Bessada. They were very pleased to receive it and agreed to plant it, manage the trial plot, harvest the ears and share it with Chadian people as a taste test. Periodically I visited the Chinese Research Station to check on the progress of the sweet corn. Each time the Chinese told me the maize was not doing well. At about the time

I thought the maize should be ready to harvest, I visited the Chinese researchers and again they informed me that the sweet corn did not grow well. I looked at the stalks and they seemed normal to me but suddenly I realized that they had never seen American varieties of sweet corn grow and did not know that our sweet corn stalks do not grow very high. In their minds maize stalks should be no less than two meters high. I looked at the cobs and they were at their peak for harvesting and eating. We picked a couple dozen ears and put them into boiling water with the husks on. When the corn was ready to eat, we pealed back the husks and ate the steaming corn the usual Chadian way. According to my taste buds, the sweet corn was delicious. The Chinese agreed that the sweet corn tasted like the sweet corn grown in Taiwan. However the Chadian participants in the taste test were not as impressed. They told me the sweet corn was *trop sucré* (too sweet). The American sweet corn was much sweeter and was a major flavor change to their learned tastes. The farmers and their wives showed no interest in the need to grow American sweet corn in Chad. It was concluded that the sweet corn grew very well, there were no major pests and the people did not cherish the sweet corn taste. Based upon the findings, Matt's idea of introducing American variety of sweet corn to Chadian people fizzled.

55

October 20th Bulldozer

One evening Betty and I heard an unusual noise and commotion in the village not too far from our house. We went to investigate to find out what was happening. We quickly found out. A large tractor-trailer truck with a flatbed trailer had backed up to a small embankment along the dirt road in front of our house. On the trailer were a large bulldozer-type tractor, a four-bottom moldboard plow, a disk harrow and a huge wooden box of spare parts.

One of the men said to me, "Here is your tractor and equipment." I exclaimed, "My tractor? I'm not expecting any tractor!" He responded, "It is a tractor from the president for you to use." I said, "There must be some mistake, but I will find out in the morning."

Meanwhile it was getting dark and these men had one end of a cable tied around a tree and the other end attached to the heavy steel frame on the four-bottom plow. The truck driver was going to pull forward and drag it off. Obviously they did not have any experience unloading heavy equipment. I said, "Whoa! We need to stop to study this situation because you are going to bend the frame on that plow if you drag it off." Equipment on the trailer was in this order from the rear: first the plow, then the wooden box of spare parts, the disk harrow and next to the truck's cab was the tractor. I said, "Gentlemen, it is now dark and I'm going to ask that you wait until morning when we can work in the daylight to properly unload this equipment." The driver was not too keen on this idea, but the village chief and the president's brother agreed with me, so he agreed to stay over until morning.

Early the next morning I went out to examine what was on that truck. Wow! This equipment was brand-new and was manufactured by a company in Yugoslavia known as "October 20th." When the men arrived we properly off-loaded the plow by lifting the tongue and pushing it off on its wheels. Then we put two pieces of pipe as rollers under the heavy wooden box and pushed it off the truck onto the ground. We lifted the tongue of the disk harrow and steered it while three men pushed it off the truck. We started the tractor and drove it off the trailer. This was a more sensible method of unloading farm equipment than hitching it to a cable tied around a tree.

Now I began the task of trying to find out who was supposed to receive this equipment. I drove into Koumra to ONDR and spoke with the director, M. DePeux and described to him what had taken place in Bessada within the past eighteen hours. I asked him if he were expecting this equipment. He replied, "*Non.*" He knew nothing about new equipment arriving in Bessada. Then I drove to the Baptist Mid-Missions and asked Dr. Seymour if he knew anything about this equipment. He had the same response, "No." Then I drove to the Chinese farm and asked them if they were expecting the arrival of this equipment. Their response was the same "*Non.*" Then I drove to Bedaya and stopped at the Catholic Mission Station and asked *Père* Corti (Father Corti) if he was expecting new equipment from Yugoslavia? His response sounded like a recording, "*Non!*" By early afternoon I still did not know who was to receive this equipment because I had not received any word from Fort-Lamy that it was to be assigned to me.

Finally late that afternoon I learned from the *Sous-Préfret* that this equipment was manufactured in Yugoslavia and it was a gift to President Tombalbaye from President Tito of Yugoslavia. President Tombalbaye sent the equipment to Bessada for me to use in our Peace Corps agricultural development program. On another truck, eleven fifty-five-gallon drums of diesel fuel for the tractor arrived at the President's personal residence, a short distance from Bessada. Also I was informed that in two weeks, the October 20th Company was sending a Yugoslavian specialist to Bessada to teach us how to operate and maintain this tractor and equipment. This gift was certainly a noble gesture on behalf of both President Tito and President Tombalbaye. This equipment was also the last thing I needed in Bessada. Nevertheless, it was there and we had to make our best attempt to use it.

To prevent any theft, two days later we started the tractor and pulled the four-bottom plow and disk harrow from the center of Bessada to the President's residence to await the arrival of the Yugoslavian specialist. No one dared to enter the grounds surrounding the President's residence, plus it was guarded. I was one of the few foreigners who was permitted access to the grounds.

Three weeks after the arrival of the tractor and equipment, a company specialist arrived to teach six men who worked for me plus myself how to service, drive and maintain the new Yugoslavian equipment. We had a very difficult time understanding his heavy Yugoslavian-accented French. Nevertheless he was a very talented, patient, and competent mechanic. He taught us how to service the tractor and equipment, change filters and oil, clean fuel lines, minor repairs, adjustments and other maintenance tasks listed in the operator's manual.

While they learned how to drive the tractor, the men cleared forty hectares of trees, brush and termite hills. After the land was cleared, the men were taught to use the four-bottom plow. Due to lack of experience, one of the men accidentally hooked plow number four onto a root. Instead of stopping to put the tractor in reverse, he kept the tractor moving forward and sprung the beam on the fourth plow. That was the end of the four-bottom plow because there was no spare beam in the wooden box or in all of Chad, for that matter. There was no money budgeted to purchase one from the October 20th Company in Yugoslavia. With the plow out of commission, the trainees used the disk harrow to till the remainder of the land. When the training program was finished, the field was ready to plant.

Chad's President Tombalbaye and President Mubutu Sese Seko of what was then known as Zaire were good political and personal friends. President Mubutu Sese Seko had been sponsoring a horticulturist from Zaire to develop a palm tree nursery in Bessada. He was propagating and growing thousands of oil palm seedlings. The forty-hectare field which was cleared during the tractor-training program was to be an oil palm plantation. In essence, we were killing two birds with one stone. "Learning to do and doing to learn" was an effective method for teaching six men to operate the tractor while they cleared and tilled for the new plantation.

The wooden box containing all the spare parts such as belts, transmission oil, hydraulic oil, oil filters, air filters, hydraulic hoses, water hoses, cotter pins, bolts, wrenches, pliers, and the like was stored in a small building near where the horticulturist was growing oil palm seedlings for the plantation. One morning the horticulturist discovered a swarm of wild African bees under the building and he decided to try harvesting some honey. Generally African bees can be kept calm in the evening or early mornings by using a smoker. He obviously was not an apiculturist because instead of using a smoker, he built a fire next to the building where the bees entered. The building caught fire and burned to the ground, including the wooden box from Yugoslavia with all the spare parts. After all the commotion ended and I assessed the damage, the horticulturalist did not get any honey.

So now we had a problem. We had that wonderful new tractor, disk harrow and plow, but now we had no spare parts. There was no budget to purchase parts from October 20th company in Yugoslavia and there was no October 20th dealership in Chad. All parts had to be ordered from the October 20th Company in Yugoslavia and shipped to Chad. It took at least three to five months for them to arrive in Bessada. Furthermore, only three of the original eleven barrels of diesel fuel remained. There was no budget to purchase diesel fuel.

After the land for the oil palm trees plantation was prepared for planting, the men assisted farmers. They used the tractor and disk harrow to till their fields for planting crops, especially cotton. One day a fan belt broke and that was the end of using the tractor. There were no available fan belts because they were lost in the fire. The local officials used the remaining diesel fuel in their Land Rovers and trucks. So ended the Yugoslavian equipment experience. That tractor and disk harrow sat there in the field where the fan belt broke for the last seven months of our stay in Chad and it was still there when we departed. The following lessons were learned:

1. The people were not ready for that kind of technology. The French had introduced the use of oxen a mere ten years earlier and only ten percent of the farmers were using animal traction.
2. There was no money for purchasing diesel fuel.
3. There was no October 20th dealership in Chad for acquiring spare parts or supplies for the tractor or equipment.
4. Only six men learned how to operate the tractor.
5. The only real task accomplished with that equipment was preparing the site for an oil palm tree plantation.
6. All that investment ended up sitting in a field of no use to anyone.
7. The villagers were disappointed. They had great expectations for how that tractor was going to assist them in preparing their fields for planting crops.

It has been said that the old ways are the safest and surest ways. There is nothing wrong with a change process that would assist a society to move forward, but the change process needs to be a gradual process and the people must have ownership of the process. Imposing a large tractor, four-bottom plow and a large disk harrow upon a society that still has no electricity, running water, medical facilities, schools, proper housing, roads or transportation seemed to me to be an attempt to appease the people. Instead it was a superficial fix for a short period of time. The people were simply not ready for this type of equipment and there was no economic infrastructure to support the introduction of tractors and farm equipment. One can say that this was "putting the cart ahead of the oxen."

56

"Was Silage Feasible in Mali?"

Dr. Dialre, Director of Livestock Services (*Directeur du Service de l'Élevage*) for the Republic of Mali was in Washington, D.C. on government business in July 1972. He heard about a Peace Corps Volunteer in Chad who had a successful silage and pit silo project in the southern part of the country. He became very interested in this project and when he returned to Bamako, he scheduled a meeting with Mr. Jack Burch, Director, Peace Corps/Mali to discuss what he knew about this project. He also asked Jack Burch to bring me to the Republic of Mali to meet with Malian government officials. We were to discuss my silage and pit silo project and determine if such a program would be feasible in Mali.

During our tenure in the Peace Corps/Chad, there were no fax machines, e-mail, cell phones or, for that matter, telephones. Beginning in October 1972, I began receiving a flurry of telegrams from Jack Burch requesting information about my silage and pit silo project. He also asked if I would be interested in traveling to the Republic of Mali to do a feasibility study. In addition, I began receiving telegrams and letters from Baudouin de Marcken, Director, Peace Corps/Chad wanting to know if I would be interested in traveling to Mali at Peace Corps expense to do a feasibility study. I said to Betty, "Why not. As long as we have the approval of our Peace Corps/Chad Director and the President of Chad."

I was very pleased that there was such a strong interest in expanding Chad's Peace Corps Silage and Pit Silo Project internationally to Mali. During our Peace Corps Volunteer meeting at Christmas time in Fort-Lamy we were able to discuss doing a feasibility study in Mali. Once agreement was reached, it was decided that Betty and I would travel to Mali on 2 January 1973.

It was now necessary to get the required approvals, visas, travel documents and airline tickets.

We departed Fort-Lamy on 2 January 1973 by Air Cameroon Airlines to a small town called Garoua, Cameroon for a forty-five-minute layover. We left Garoua and flew to Cameroon's capitol, Yaounde for another forty-five-minute layover. We flew out of Yaounde for Douala where we had a one-day layover. That afternoon Betty and I walked all over Douala. We found the Cascade Restaurant, noted for its seafood, so we decided to have dinner there. When we walked in, strictly by coincidence, we met up with our Chinese friend Tzou Ming-Jhie, of Taipei, Taiwan and his five colleagues, all of whom had worked near our home in Bessada, Chad. They too had a layover in Douala and were destined for Taiwan. Our Chinese friends were so excited to see us that they asked Betty and me to join them for dinner. After a lovely seafood dinner, fairly good wine, good friends and good discussions, we went our separate ways and that was the last time we ever saw or heard from our Chinese colleagues.

That evening Betty and I stayed at the Cocotier Hotel in Douala. That was a special treat for us because we had electricity, electric lights, running water, a shower, a bathtub, a clean bed with sheets and no termites or cockroaches. These are small amenities according to our western standards but they are missed when one has to do without them for a long period of time.

Douala is an important seaport located on Cameroon's Atlantic Ocean coast. Goods for landlocked countries pass through there, bound for Chad, Republic of Central Africa, Burkina Faso and Niger. In addition, commodities produced or manufactured in Cameroon for export are loaded onto ships which sail from Douala for ports around the world.

We saw much of Douala but we were not really that impressed with the city as a whole. It was dirty, the buildings were in need of repair and maintenance, people were always pestering for handouts or money, the streets were full of holes due to heavy truck traffic and garbage was everywhere. The ambiance of the city was not pleasant.

In the afternoon at 4:00 on 3 January 1973, we left Douala by Air Afrique and landed at Cotonou, Dahomey for a one-hour layover. Our next stop was Abidjan, Ivory Coast. After arriving at the airport late that evening, getting through customs, and settled in the Grand Hotel, we were ready for a quiet meal and then bed.

The next morning we walked around Abidjan until noon. During that time we visited the Peace Corps/Ivory Coast Office and there we talked with the Peace Corps Director and some volunteers. Abidjan is the capitol of Ivory Coast and is on the coast of the Gulf of Guinea. We really liked Abidjan! It was a city which was well-developed by most western standards. It certainly did not look or feel like Africa. I purchased a wristwatch in Abidjan because my old one wore out from the African elements (e.g. dust and moisture) and abuse.

After lunch we departed Abidjan, Ivory Coast at 1:00 on 4 January and flew directly to Bamako, Mali. There by chance we met the Peace Corps nurse at the airport. Our flight plan was changed to have us arriving in Bamako at 3:30 P.M. instead of the originally scheduled 5:30 flight. The Peace Corps Director was not there to meet us as he had planned. Mali's Director of Livestock Services in Bamako had made arrangements for us to obtain "airport visas" upon arrival. When we showed our passports to the police without visas, things became a little sticky. The Peace Corps Director had all of the necessary papers but he was not there to meet us. Fortunately I had in my briefcase a telegram indicating my daily itinerary from Mali's Director of Livestock Services. I showed this itinerary to the customs police, he gave me a paper to let us in but kept our passports. Otherwise Betty and I would have had a real problem at the airport. The next day the Peace Corps Director submitted the necessary documents and our passports were returned.

We arrived at the Peace Corps/Mali Center where we would

264

be housed while we were in Bamako. We were welcomed to the Republic of Mali by Jack Burch, Peace Corps/Mali Director. At the same time Leslie Temanson, Peace Corps/Mali volunteer, welcomed us. Leslie, Betty and I had studied French together at St. Thomas, Virgin Islands. It was wonderful to rekindle our friendship with Leslie. He was very much interested in my silage and pit silo project in Chad and wanted to learn more about the technique.

Because of Leslie's strong interests in making silage, Jack Burch instructed him to accompany Betty and me at all times during our stay in Mali and to learn as much as possible about making silage and pit silos. Beginning the next day, Leslie accompanied me to all meetings and travel within Mali. During this time Leslie was taught how to make silage from local plants, the biological principles of how silage evolves, what kinds of plants could be used and how to store them in pit silos. He learned how to make a pit silo, when to open a pit silo, how to open a silo, how to remove the silage from the pit silo and how to feed it to cattle. We discussed in detail the complications he could encounter and how to solve them. Because of his interests in making silage, Leslie was the perfect Peace Corps Volunteer for implementing this proposed project.

Dr. Dialre, Director of Livestock Services, was responsible for making our travel itinerary. Wow! What an itinerary! He wired each regional veterinarian, government officials and all the other people we were to meet. He informed them when we would be arriving and at the same time made lodging reservations. He also gave us our travel orders, which gave us authorization to travel within the Republic of Mali. Travel restrictions in Mali required people, especially foreigners, to show their travel orders to the road barrier police, confirming that they had authorization from a government official to travel within Mali. We had to stop at many road barriers during our travels but we had no problem. The itinerary that Dr. Dialre gave to us follows:

REPUBLIC OF MALI

Ministry of Agriculture

Bamako, Mali

Travel Itinerary

for

James E. Diamond

Peace Corps/Mali Consultant

5 Jan 1973	Meet with Director of Livestock Services, Bamako
	Meet with Dr. Anglo Traore, Director of Sotuba Farm, Bamako
	Meet with Mme. Beye, Director of Mali Lait, Bamako
6 Jan1973	Meet with Mr. Albert Traore, Coordinator of Agricultural Workers, Samanko State Farm
7 Jan 1973	Rest and make preparations for six-day trip
8 Jan 1973	Travel to Segou.
	Meet with Dr. Kouma, Livestock Services
9 Jan 1973	Meet with retired veterinarian at Segou
	Travel to Mopti
10 Jan 1973	Meet Dr. Issa Amagjuire Ongoiba, Veterinary Director, Mopti Region and Dr. Diam Oumar, Mayor of Mopti
	Meet with Governor of Mopti Region.
11 Jan 1973	Visit Dogon Country and Bandiagara Fault
12 Jan 1973	Depart Mopti
	Visit mosque at Djenné
	Travel to Sikasso
13 Jan 1973	Visit Dr. Kansaye, Director of Livestock Services.
	Visit a remote village in southern Mali.
	Return to Bamako

We met with Dr. Dialre, *Directeur du Service de l'Élevage* on 5 January 1973. During this meeting I presented him with a detailed overview of our silage and pit silo project in Chad. After answering a plethora of questions about making silage and pit silos, I presented a description of a proposal we put together for a "pilot pit silo and silage project" which could be sponsored by Peace Corps/Mali. Dr. Dialre expressed a great deal of interest and enthusiasm toward developing a pilot program in Mali. He was particularly interested in developing a practical and economical means of preserving native grasses. My proposal obviously met Dr. Dialre's needs and he was aware that such a program could be very important in developing the economic potential of Mali's livestock industry. He indicated that he would give Peace Corps/Mali his full cooperation in implementing a pilot silage and pit silo program in Mali provided the concept was feasible. First he asked that I travel throughout the Republic of Mali to do a "feasibility study" and, based upon my findings, make recommendations as to the practicality of such a program in Mali.

We met with Dr. Anglo Traore, *Directeur du Ferme Sotuba* (Director of Sotuba Farm) on 5 January 1973. Sotuba Farm is somewhat similar to the United States Department of Agriculture Research Station at Beltsville, Maryland. All agricultural research for the Republic of Mali takes place at Sotuba Farm. Dr. Traore expressed his support for our proposed pilot project and he said it would be good for the country. However he did not seem to me to be sincere with his comments. I sensed that his hospitality and stance on the pilot project was artificial and not trustworthy.

On the same day we met with Mme. Beye, *Directrice de Mali Lait* (Director of Mali Milk). She was extremely receptive to our proposed pilot project because grass silage would be an important feedstuff for dairy cattle in Mali, especially during the dry season. Milk production in Mali drops drastically at the onset of the dry season and milk collection by Mali Lait is halted by the end of January of each year. According to Mme. Beye, farmers plan for their cows to stop lactation at this time of year (end of January). Then they hire nomadic Peul herdsmen to take their cows on transhumance in search of grass and water. At the onset of the rainy season, the Peul herdsmen return the dairy cows to the farmers when the local grass was again growing and milk production once again commenced.

To meet the consumer demands for milk during the dry season while the cattle are on transhumance, Mali Lait must process imported powdered milk. The Mali Lait staff was enthusiastic about the prospect of producing fresh milk year round and gave our proposed pilot silage and pit silo project its full support.

Our next scheduled visit was *Ferme de l'etat Samanko* (Samanko State Farm) where we met Mr. Albert Traore, *Ingénieur des Travaux Agricoles, Institute Economique Rurale* (Engineer of Agricultural Projects, Rural Economics Institute). Our visit at the Rural Economics Institute was interesting because, to our surprise, we found two trench silos fourteen meters by four meters x two meters already filled with an estimated four hundred tons of silage. Mr. Traore was very knowledgeable of silage and trench silos. He informed me that he had filled those two trench silos since 1968 for the dairy herd there on the institute's state farm. He was very interested in our proposed pilot silage and pit silo project.

I asked Mr. Traore if farmers in the immediate area around the institute farm used silage as well. His response was, "No." I asked him if they were aware of his silage-feeding program. His response was, "No." I asked why farmers did not know of his silage program and why they did not make trench silos. His response was, "Because it is not my job to teach farmers." He further told us that the lack of agricultural extension officers was the main reason farmers were not aware of silage and pit silos. This was the understatement of the day. With his attitude toward teaching peasant farmers, it is no wonder educating rural farmers was a major issue. I had a difficult time grasping the rationale of why this technology was so close to surrounding sustainable farmers and they were not aware that Mr. Trarore fed his dairy cattle grass silage stored in two trench silos. Mr. Traore did favor our proposal and encouraged us to go ahead with it.

We were off Sunday morning so we used that time to prepare for our six-day trip by Land Rover into the hinterlands of the Republic of Mali. In the afternoon we visited some other Peace Corps Volunteers and learned more about their respective projects. We walked to Bamako's *Grand Marché* (Great Market). Seldom does one leave the market without buying something. The salesmanship tactics of the Malian merchants were persistent, unique and effective. When they spot a westerner, believe it or not, the westerner is hooked. Their salesmanship skills are to be admired.

The next morning we left Bamako and drove north to a town called Segou. Outside of Segou, we were stopped at a road barrier and had to show our travel documents to the police. All our documents were in order and we were waved on.

At Segou we met with a Dr. Kouma, *Directeur du Service de l'Élevage*. Dr. Kouma expressed a great deal of interest toward our proposed pilot project for the Segou Region. He explained to us the availability of various feedstuffs in the region. They included dried grass, peanut vines, bean vines, rice straw and *san du riz* (by-product of cleaning process of rice). Except for the peanut and bean vines, nutritionally speaking, *san du riz*, rice straw and dried grass were very low in nutrients and very high in cellulose. They had practically no digestible protein and other digestible nutrients. Dr. Kouma was particularly interested in dovetailing our proposed pilot silage project with a cattle-feeding experiment. He mentioned that he budgeted 10 million Malian Francs (US$10,000.00) to instigate a cattle-fattening experiment in the Segou Region. He planned to purchase rice by-products from the Mopti areas and mix local grains as a fattening ration. But due to a shortage in the total rice production of 1972 in the flood plains of the Mopti Region, rice by-products were not available, thus stalling his proposed experiment. He was enthused about incorpo-

269

rating my proposed pilot silage and pit silo project into this same experiment the next year (1974).

While at Segou, we met with a retired veterinarian who was very knowledgeable about trench silos and silage. He was encouraged that Peace Corps/Mali had shown interest for instigating a pilot pit silo project. He had made pit silos before but a little differently. His pits were "V" shaped and he did not cover the grass with anything after the hole was filled. I doubted the success of his "V" shaped pits because the silage mass must be covered with soil to form a seal to allow the fermentation process to take place. In the western world this can also be accomplished with a heavy plastic cover but it was not available in Mali.

During the afternoon, we continued to drive north to the flood plains of Niger River that surrounded Mopti. Mopti is located just south of the Sahara desert along the Niger River. We stayed in a very nice motel just south of Mopti.

We met with Dr. Issa Amaguire Ongoiba, *Directeur de la Region, Veterinaire de Mopti* (Veterinarian Director for Mopti Region) and Dr. Diam Oumar, *Chef de Secteur de Mopti* (Mayor of Mopti) on 10 January. After two hours of discussions they were very enthusiastic and receptive of our proposed pilot pit silo and silage project. Dr. Ongoiba was very knowledgeable about silage and pit silos and had much experience with feeding silage to livestock. He studied and got his degrees in Egypt and United States (Texas A&M).

During our conversations with Dr. Ongoiba, it was obvious that he was very knowledgeable about livestock issues in his region, cultural characteristics of his people and the implications of a pilot project if instigated in his region. I asked Dr. Ongoiba if nomadic Peul herdsmen had feed and water available for their animals during the dry season, would the Peuls discontinue their annual transhumance. Since Dr. Ongoiba was a Peul himself, I couldn't think of a better person to whom I could pose such a question. His response was, "Absolutely!" The only reason Peuls go on transhumance during the dry season is to search for feed and water for their livestock.

At this point of our discussion, Dr. Ongoiba brought forth the need for dovetailing a water project with the silage and pit silo project. He pointed out that without water sources, silage alone would not benefit the farmer. He suggested that constructing windmills be included in our pilot project as a means of pumping water for livestock. Although his suggestion was well taken and in my opinion, was valid, I felt that what he was actually implying that more US dollars be added to the Peace Corps silage project. He later showed us how the regional government (equivalent to a state government in the U.S.) had already begun providing water supplies by constructing a series of small dams to conserve water from the rainy season for dry season use. These dams were sixty kilometers east of Mopti at Bandiagara, and they were effective. Having this water available had already somewhat stabilized the movement of cattle on transhumance.

After a lengthy and involved meeting with Dr. Ongoiba and Dr. Oumar, we met with the *Gouverneur de Mopti Region 5* (Governor of Mopti Region 5—equivalent to a state governor) and explained to him the purpose of our visit and our meeting with Drs. Ongoiba and Oumar. We were quite impressed with the Governor's interest in our proposed pilot project. The Governor stated that in 1972, Federal Economic Development did a study of Region 5 for the possibility of developing a controlled pasture-grazing program. If the results of this study were to be accepted by the Mali Minister of Production in Bamako, the International Bank for Development would finance this program. At that time the Minister had not yet received the results from the Paris meeting. The controlled pasture-grazing program was stalled until the Minister of Production received those results and approved them. If the results of the Paris meeting were approved and adopted by the Government of Mali, the Governor stated that he would like to dovetail our pilot pit silo project with the controlled grazing pro-

271

gram. The Governor even offered to assign an area in the Mopti Region to activate our pilot project. The Governor received our proposal with open arms.

The only day we had free was 11 January. Since we were not too far away from the Dogon Country, we all agreed that by virtue of our location, we should see the Dogon people and the Bandiagara Fault. After breakfast we drove 110 kilometers on a dirt road north-northeast of Mopti to the Bandiagara Fault. Near the base of the fault is where the Dogon people lived. They are known as cliff dwellers. As we got nearer and nearer to the fault, all we could see was rock. The rocks were large barren slabs having absolutely no vegetation. As we wound around a narrow rocky road we finally arrived at the fault. What an awesome experience! The escarpment (fault) was no less than five hundred meters high. After we parked we walked to the edge of the fault. Being afraid of heights, I was not about to walk to the very edge like the others did. But I could look still off into the horizon. Halfway to the horizon, there was a meandering river, which made its way across the arid plains to within walking distance of the village. People literally lived on the cliffs near the bottom. Dogon people migrated to the top of the 150-kilometer long fault several hundred years ago to hide from the Arabs. The Dogon people refused to convert to Islam and they were fair game for the slave trade by organized merchants. This was a place where they could hide among the rocks and easily defend themselves with their crude weapons.

We walked a long way on top of the rocky fault. Suddenly we noticed agriculture being practiced on those barren rock slabs. A large number of small *barrages* (barricades) and many manmade dams had been built. This enabled the Dogon people to do onion farming on a solid rock environment that previously could not support food production. To protect their food supply, the Dogon people grew their food crops on top of the escarpment plateau where they could be safeguarded. They carried soil on their heads from the river bottom up a narrow crevice on natural crude steps to the top of the fault. There they placed about twenty centimeters of soil on rock slabs forming ninety by ninety centimeter plots. To keep the soil in place around each plot, a small stone *barrage* surrounded each plot where the crops were planted. There were several hectares of the rocky plateau covered with precious soil in small plots. During the rainy season, they would again carry soil back up to replace what was lost to erosion. Soil on top of that rocky fault was a very treasured commodity. None was wasted.

Onions seemed to be the dominant crop with tobacco growing around the edges of the plots. The onions looked lush because they were irrigated with water that was carried from manmade dams on the plateau or up that crevice from the river. After the onions were harvested, the women pounded them into a mash and with their hands formed onion balls about the size of a softball. The onion balls were placed on a rock slab to dry. The Dogon women sold the dried onion balls at their local market.

After walking an additional kilometer from where we parked the Land Rover, we arrived at the infamous crevice where we unsteadily began our decent to the bottom of the fault. In this crevice were crude steps, some of which were sixty to seventy centimeters high. We hired a Dogon villager to assist in guiding us as we descended to the village to be among the villagers. While we went down those steps several children pestered us by saying, "*Donnez-moi une cadeau* (give me a gift)." Betty was about to whack a couple of those youngsters because she was concentrating on every step, since she was so afraid of falling. They distracted her and made her nervous. I was very proud of Betty for accompanying us down through that crevice to the bottom.

When we were nearly to the bottom, we arrived at a small village nestled in the side of the cliff. We visited the Dogon people in their tall, square, narrow, side-by-side homes made of mud brick. The women were spinning wool by using a small, round fired-clay ball with a long wand-like piece of wood through its middle. They spun the wooden wand with their thumb and forefinger while the ball provided a gyroscopic force. As the women simultaneously twisted strands of wool into yarn, the spun yarn wound itself onto the wooden wand.

Traditionally the ladies did not want their pictures taken. We were told that Muslims do not like to have their pictures taken because photos capture their soul. When Betty asked them to show her how to spin wool, they were thrilled to teach her. Because the women were elated that a white lady would want to learn how to spin wool, they allowed me to photograph Betty spinning wool. Soon they wanted their pictures taken of them teaching Betty how to spin wool.

Looking toward the face of the cliff, one could see caves that pocked the cliff's side. It was in these caves where the dead were buried. Traditionally washing and wrapping it in a white shroud prepared a corpse. Then it was hoisted up to a cave where a Muslim cleric presided over the burial ceremony.

What an interesting experience! Visiting the Dogon people was a special adventure that we will forever cherish. Getting to know and appreciate a different culture with rich traditions and intriguing customs broadens one's views of people's lifestyles in that part of the world.

We left Mopti the next morning and traveled south all day toward Sikasso. As a side trip, we drove forty kilometers to D'jenné on a rough dirt road across a dike above the flooded rice fields. There we visited the largest mud brick mosque in the world. This mosque was built in 1907, but the first mosque was built in the thirteenth century and more recently (1988) has been designated a World Heritage Site by UNESCO. Apparently in the twelfth and thirteenth centuries at D'jenné there was a highly developed civilization. The people of D'jenné had one of the few universities of that period in history. There remained only remnants of the university but the mosque was still a functional place of worship and prayer. We had a rare opportunity to go through the mosque. Normally only Muslims are permitted to enter this mosque. I was given rare authorization to photograph not only the outside of the mosque but the inside as well. I gave the guardian five hundred Malian francs as his fee to authorize me to take pictures. We were required to remove our shoes prior to entering for a walk through tour. All I could think of as we walked in our bare feet was getting hookworms (walking in bare feet is how one acquires hookworm). Visiting this mosque was a very important and special stopover. We learned much about the Muslim religion and were able to better understand it and show more respect to the Muslim people.

After our long day of traveling we arrived at Sikasso from Mopti via D'jenne. Sikasso is only seventy kilometers from the Ivory Coast border. There we met Dr. Kansaye, *Directeur du Service de l'Élevage*. He lacked experience in both silage and pit silos and was the most uncooperative Malian official we met on the entire trip. He told us he was not interested in farmers who had only a few head of cattle. Dr. Kansaye said his priorities focused only on large herds owned by the Peuls of which he was one. He told me "…if you Americans were really interested in developing a silage program in my region, you would bring in tractors and machinery." He said he had already talked to the Chinese and French about bringing in machinery. I was sure that Dr. Kansaye was trying to use international politics to pressure me into recommending to both Peace Corps/Mali and USAID to send silage machinery such as tractors, wagons, choppers and blowers to his region. In his next statement, Dr. Kansaye said that he would be the first to try out this new machinery. He said we should send this machinery into his region on a trial basis and "if" this machinery were to work well, they would buy it on a cooperative basis. Just for fun, I asked him, "How much do you think your people would be willing to pay for such machinery?" He replied by saying they would be willing to pay between 45–50,000 Malian francs (US$1,000.00). What this Director of Livestock Services was trying to do was explore ways to get the USA to hand out gifts without first making an attempt to urge people to help themselves. Dr. Kansaye did give us an interesting bit of information that was significant. During the annual dry season, many cattle were stolen while they were browsing in the bush. The cattle were then driven across the nearby Ivory Coast border where they were sold.

After our meeting with Dr. Kansaye, we had lunch and prepared our gear for moving on. We had planned to visit one more area but we were not sure if anyone was expecting us. It was a bad road all the way, this town was small, we were not sure about available lodging or meals and we were all rather tired of traveling at this point so we canceled this part of our trip. I said to Leslie Temanson that I had enough data and had seen enough to write my report and that we should begin heading north towards Bamako. Everyone agreed so we headed north and arrived in Bamako by 7:30 that evening. After everyone had a welcome shower, we went to a restaurant and enjoyed a Malian gourmet dish of hotly spiced goat meat and rice.

At the Peace Corps/Mali guesthouse, we slept in a little the next morning. We were all exhausted after six long days of traveling a total of 2,160 kilometers. After breakfast I immediately began compiling all of my field notes and from them I began analyzing the data before writing my report for Peace Corps/Mali and Mali's Director of Livestock Services.

Mid-afternoon that day, I took a break from my work and we traveled fifty kilometers north to a state vegetable farm to visit several Peace Corps Volunteers who were assigned to work there. We had a very delicious cookout and a wonderful visit. There I met Bill Schweighofer of Honesdale, Pennsylvania.

Early that evening we returned to Bamako and I continued my work on my report. At 8:00 Betty, Leslie and I went to an evening church service at a Protestant mission in Bamako where we met several American missionaries.

By 6:00 the next morning, I was working again and spent all day developing and writing my report for Peace Corps/Mali. At 8:00 A.M., on 16 January 1973, Leslie Temanson, Jack Burch and I once again met with Dr. Dialre, Director of Livestock Services at Mali Ministry of Agriculture. We gave him a synopsis of our six-day trip through north central, eastern and southeastern Mali. I presented him with an executive summary of my Peace Corps/Mali report, including recommendations. I informed him that a complete report was forthcoming and that any decisions for implementing the proposal in the report would be dependent upon his office and the Director of Peace Corps/Mali. Dr. Dialre was very pleased with our findings and recommendations.

Following our meeting with Dr. Dialre, we returned to the Peace Corps/Mali office where I used the remainder of the day and a portion of the evening to finalize my report. Betty and I had been invited to a 7:30 dinner at the home of Mr. and Mrs. Chedder, who were American missionaries. We enjoyed a lovely evening of fellowship.

It was now time for Betty to contribute an important role to this whole effort. She devoted the entire next day at the Peace Corps/Mali Office to typing my report, that included all recorded observations, conclusions and recommendations.

While Betty typed my report, the Peace Corps Director, a representative of United Nations Education, Science and Communications Organization (UNESCO) from Holland, *Sous-directeur de Mali Lait* (Assistant Director of Mali Milk) and I traveled sixty-five kilometers south of Bamako to visit one of their milk collection points. Mali Lait is Mali's nationalized milk industry. In addition we visited two dairy farmers, and a state-operated agriculture school. During this trip, we discussed the implications of my proposal toward the dairy industry in the Republic of Mali. These people were so enthused that they were proceeding on their own to make a few pit silos on a trial basis. We returned, had lunch and rested a while. Meanwhile Betty finished typing my report and we went into Bamako and did some shopping until evening.

Jack Burch had planned a reception at 7:00 that evening to honor Betty and me at the Peace Corps/Mali Center in Bamako.

He invited Malian Government Officials, veterinarians, the Minister of Production, United Nations officials, USAID Officials and U.S. Embassy officials. It was truly an honor for Betty and me to have had this *soirée* dedicated to us. There were some fifty people attending and we had a wonderful experience with these people during our last evening in Bamako, Mali.

The next day Betty and I boarded an Air Mali plane and we flew to Abidjan, Ivory Coast and had a one-hour layover there. We then took off and landed at Accra, Ghana for one hour. We flew on to Douala, Cameroon where we had a one-day layover. At the hotel we discovered that Betty's jewelry had been stolen from her suitcase. We suspected that it was the houseboy at the Peace Corps/Hostel in Mali who stole it, but at that point there was nothing we could do about it. So we did some shopping in Douala and later went to a hotel restaurant for a drink. There we bumped into four Peace Corps Volunteers. When we all heard each other speaking English, we introduced ourselves and had an enjoyable evening with them.

We departed Douala at 10:00 in the morning on a Cameroon Airlines for Fort-Lamy. First we landed at Younde, where we de-planed to have lunch at the airport. We went on to Ngaoundere, and Marona, all in Cameroon. It was an all-day flight and very tiring. We finally landed at Fort-Lamy at 5:00 P.M.

Our trip to the Republic of Mali was a wonderful experience and very educational. We were pleased and happy that the Malian people were becoming interested in the idea of using pit silos. I had hoped that interest would continue to generate momentum in other African Savanna Nations.

Now is the time to answer the question, "Is silage feasible in Mali?" Looking back over the whole experience of doing a feasibility study in the Republic of Mali, I honestly could say with confidence that we made some progress in convincing appropriate Malian government officials, dairy farmers, Mali Milk officials and Peace Corps/Mali that the digging and filling of pit silos with chopped grasses to ferment into silage in southeastern Mali, were both possible and needed. My official recommendation was simply, "Go for it."

In February 1973 Peace Corps/Mali and Mali's Ministry of Agriculture gave their approval to implement the proposed Silage and Pit Silo Project for one year. Leslie Temanson was asked and he agreed to extend his time for one year to implement the silage project. He became very interested in the project and was chomping at the bit to start it in Mali. He had just completed his two years in the Peace Corps and by law, he had to go home for one month before extending for an additional year. When Leslie returned to Mali, he officially began to implement the Silage and Pit-Silo Project on 1 June 1973. The project was very successful and after Leslie left the project, Peace Corps Volunteers who followed him continued it for the next seven years.

This project was documented in the 1975 August issue of *National Geographic Magazine*. The Republic of Mali was featured on the cover and it was the main article for that issue. The article mentioned that Peace Corps Volunteers taught Malian farmers how to make silage and store it in pit silos to feed their oxen.

57
A "Hare" Raising Story

A lady who lived in Lewistown, Pennsylvania read about our Peace Corps projects in an article written by Ron Harley, a reporter for the *Los Angeles Times* and published in the *Pennsylvania Farmer Magazine* (see "Worldwide Peace Corps Budget Cuts"). She was moved by what she read and out of the kindness of her heart, she sent us a check for $50.00. There was a note with the check saying that she had read about us in the *Pennsylvania Farmer Magazine* and that the money was to be used for a project which we felt was appropriate for helping the Chadian people. Betty and I were pleasantly surprised that someone totally unknown to us would send a check to support a project in Chad. We immediately sent her a letter and thanked her profusely and assured her that the money would be used appropriately for a project in Bessada.

We sent the check to Betty's parents in Doylestown, Pennsylvania to be deposited into our checking account at Doylestown Federal Savings. It would have been nearly impossible to have the check cashed at our bank in Chad. We used the equivalent of $50.00 in Chadian money from our checking account at the bank in Fort Archambault.

The big question on our minds was, "What kind of project could we do with $50.00 that would be appropriate for the people of Bessada?" The $50.00 donation translated into 600 CFAs (US$1.00 = 12 CFAs). This was not a large amount of money but it was enough to do something. What that something was needed to be identified. We decided to hold the money until we found an appropriate use for it.

Two months later, Betty and I made our monthly trip to Fort Archambault to purchase supplies and visit friends. We stayed overnight with a Peace Corps Volunteer whose husband had three horses. At the crack of dawn Jean-Paul and I took an early morning horseback ride several kilometers to the edge of the Chari River to observe wildlife and birds. We had been riding about two hours when we returned for breakfast. On the way back to Fort Archambault, we rode past a house that had what looked like rabbit cages on its side. I said to Jean-Paul, "I wonder who those people are who live there that raise rabbits?" Jean-Paul said, "Oh, those are my friends from France and they raise rabbits for themselves." I responded, "Really!"

In my mind I said, "That's it!" We could purchase rabbits

with that $50.00 and start a rabbit project in Bessada. I did not say anything to Jean-Paul about my idea until I first talked it over with Betty. Betty thought it was a great idea but we decided it would be best if we first went back to Bessada and talked with some of the people to determine if there was any interest among the villagers for raising domestic rabbits.

A few days after we returned to Bessada I asked some of the people I knew if they had a good understanding about domestic rabbits. Much to my surprise they were well acquainted with domestic *lapins* (rabbits). I asked, "Would you like to raise domestic rabbits here in the village?" The response was always a resounding, "Yes." When we determined the interest level was high, it was time to determine a practical way to build an economical hutch for the people to raise domestic rabbits. Also we had to determine a fair and equitable method of distributing the rabbits.

After identifying an enthusiastic volunteer farmer, I assisted him in building his hutch. My goal was to make sure he followed the plan. We placed it under the east side of a mango tree so that during the heat of the day it would be in the shade. We used traditional mud bricks to build the structure with inside dimensions of 180 centimeters by 95 centimeters. On the fourth tier of mud bricks, we laid halved bamboo slats across the entire tier with one-and-one-half centimeter spacing between the slats. The rabbits would live on the bamboo slats and their droppings would fall through the spacing. We laid mud brick another four layers high so there would be enough height to keep the rabbits from jumping over the top. The top was covered with a woven grass mat to keep out predators (e.g. snakes and raptors). There was no cash outlay for this hutch because we used indigenous resources (mud brick, bamboo and woven grass) and skills (making and laying mud bricks).

Management of domestic rabbits is rather easy. Commercial rabbit feed was certainly not available anywhere in Chad. Rabbits could easily survive on a diet of fresh, palatable, green grass or

281

legumes supplemented with an occasional vegetable such as carrots, celery, or radishes. One of the most important factors in raising rabbits successfully is having a constant supply of clean fresh water available at all times. Domestic rabbits are easy prey for predators such as dogs, large snakes, leopards and raptors. They must be protected within a well-built structure.

After we built the hutch, Betty and I traveled to Fort Archambault to purchase domestic rabbits from the French family with whom we became acquainted through our friend Jean-Paul. We were able to purchase four New Zealand White does (females) and one buck (male) with the $50.00 which was donated to us for an appropriate project. New Zealand White rabbits are a hardy breed and could withstand the warmer climate of Chad, especially the dry season months. The total cost was a bit more than what was donated but we added the difference. The rabbits were healthy and in good condition. I was very pleased with our purchase. We put them into a box and off to Bessada we drove.

Next came the question, "Who gets the rabbits?" Since we had only one hutch built, we put all the does into the hutch and we cordoned off one side to keep the buck separated from the does. The question lingered in my mind as to how these rabbits would be distributed in an equitable and fair manner. I was very familiar with the "Heifer Project International" based in Perryville, Arkansas, USA. We decided to adopt their model of distributing animals in villages and established the following rules:

1. Family A needed to have a sincere interest in raising domestic rabbits.
2. A suitable hutch would first be built.
3. Family A would agree to learn the approved management practices of raising rabbits.
4. Betty and I, on behalf of the donor, would give two female rabbits to family A.
5. Family A would raise the rabbits and have them bred.

6. After the does kindled and the litter was weaned, family A would give two does to family B within the village. Family B must agree to rules 1–6.
7. Family A had satisfied the terms of the agreement when Family B received two female rabbits. The remainder of the litter and does would then become the personal property of the family A.

The gestation period (period of time from breeding to kindling) for a rabbit is thirty to thirty-two days. Litter sizes could range from one to fifteen and they could be weaned at eight weeks of age. A doe can be rebred thirty-five days after kindling. This all means that from this meager beginning, hordes of rabbits could have been available to people within one or two years if they took this project seriously by sticking to the rules.

Six weeks later, I stopped by Family A to see how the rabbits were doing. I looked into the hutch and noticed that one of the does was missing. I inquired as to where the doe was. The head of the family told me the following story:

Head of Family A: You know, *patron* (everyone called me patron, it means boss), "One day we had a very, very bad wind storm here in the village. You know, *patron*, that wind came by this tree, reached down into that hutch and picked a doe up and carried it all the way to the other side of the village before dropping it into the bush.

Jim Diamond: Vraiment (really)! Then what happened to the rabbit?

Head of Family A: Well, one day *mon frère* (my brother) was walking on a path in the bush and he spotted a white rabbit and he thought it was a wild rabbit. He killed it and took it to his hut for his wife to cook and it was fed to his family.

283

Thus ended the saga of one New Zealand White doe that had been donated to Family A. One doe and the buck still remained in the hutch. The Head of Family A was able to satisfy the terms of the agreement described above. Domestic rabbits could be a valuable food source for villagers at a low maintenance cost. The mission for the donor of $50.00 from Lewistown, Pennsylvania was accomplished. We thanked her profusely for her benevolent concerns of people less fortunate. Sadly, we learned the donor had passed away before we returned to Pennsylvania and had a chance to meet her. We were able to speak with her daughter on the telephone and reported how the money was spent.

Betty and I departed Chad three months after we initiated the domestic rabbit project. This project had much potential to unfold into a widespread source of protein for villagers in the region. There seemed to be a lot of interest among the villagers in obtaining a domestic rabbit. Whether that interest contributed to the success of the project still needs to be explored. How long that project continued after our departure from Chad will be forever unknown. Patience and honesty are virtues.

58

Took the Ginger Out Of My Snap

During our stay in Chad, each afternoon from 1:00 to 3:00, everyone took a siesta. Working in the mid-day heat was a *faux pas*. People needed their rest to maintain good health and well-being in the tropical climate. Even when visiting friends, they were always provided a place for taking a nap. Sometimes one would sleep on a mattress or a mat on the floor.

Malaria during the rainy season is very prevalent in parts of Chad, especially near rivers, swamps and bodies of stagnant water. Some Chadians tended to build a mild tolerance to this horrid disease. Thousands of people, especially children and elderly people, died each year from malaria. Those people who lived in Chad's hinterlands do not have access to malaria prophylactics or can they afford to purchase them. Betty and I were very fortunate that Peace Corps provided us with a sufficient supply of Aralen to take weekly. Aralen was a prophylactic that helped to prevent us from getting malaria. As directed by the Peace Corps nurse, every Sunday morning Betty and I very religiously swallowed our two malaria pills.

Because I was so determined to complete all our projects before leaving Chad, I was skipping my daily siesta. One day in March 1973, I was very tired so I decided to take my siesta. While lying on our bed, I ached everywhere. Then I began to perspire and shiver at the same time. I pulled a sheet over me and that didn't seem to help. I said to Betty, "I think you should take my temperature." She found that I had a slight fever. Betty said, "I think you should go to Baptist Mid-Missions in Koumra and have Dr. Seymour examine you for malaria." I agreed and got dressed and ready to go. I asked Betty if she would mind driving the Land Rover because I was not feeling too well. As she was driving it felt like she purposely hit every bump and hole in the road between Bessada and Koumra. I complained to Betty, "Do you have to hit every hole?"

At the Seymours' home, I was wiped out. Ruth was a nurse who had lived in Chad most of her life and had much experience treating people with malaria. She immediately recognized my symptoms and put me to bed. She gave me two Kenomax pills and I went to sleep almost immediately. I was so tired, achy and cold, yet I was perspiring. I lost my appetite and developed diarrhea. I never had an illness that "took the ginger out of my snap" like malaria. I drank many glasses of water because I did not want to become dehydrated. Fortunately, I had been taking my prophylactic and recovered in about ten days.

While I was recovering from malaria, the President's brother came to Dr. Seymour's home where I was bedridden. He informed Betty that the President's wife was coming to Bessada and she wanted to use our house during her stay. Betty said that would be okay (because it was the President's house) but we would have to move our personal belongings before she could give him the keys. When Betty told me she was going out to the village to move our personal belongings into our kitchen, I said to her, "I will go with you and help." Ruth Seymour said to me, "Jim Diamond, you are not going anywhere!" As I stood up, I became dizzy and said, "Ruth, you're absolutely right." I laid down on the bed and stayed put. Betty said, "Ruth, I have never seen Jim obey anyone so easily." One of the other missionaries, Sandy Banasyk, went with Betty to help her move our belongings out of the rooms the President's wife would be using during her stay in Bessada. It took all of ten days to recover from my malaria attack.

When we departed Chad, the Peace Corps nurse gave both Betty and me a pill to take after we returned to the temperate climate of Pennsylvania. That pill cleansed our blood of any malaria organisms. To this day, I have never had a reoccurrence of malaria, even though I have traveled and lived in the tropics for extended periods. The World Health Organization recommends that those who live or visit the tropics where mosquitoes are prevalent, must have plenty of rest and take malaria prophylactics regularly without fail. The rule of thumb for expatriates in malaria-prone countries is everyone takes their malaria prophylactic on Sunday mornings. Most people are home at that time and they tend to remind each other to take their pills. Had I not been taking my malaria pills on a regular basis, I would have been ill for much longer. Do not mess with your health! Remember, do what the doctor or nurse tells you. Without your health, you are not able to help others or yourself.

59

Impoverished! Yet a Proud People

After Betty and I got to know the Chadian people, experienced living with them for two years in their village, attended their celebrations, acknowledged their holidays, attended their weddings, watched the girls dance during their baya ritual, shared their joys and sorrows, ate meals with them, worked side by side with them and attended their funerals, we began to appreciate and better understand their customs, traditions and the difficulties in their way of living. One cannot get a true sense of such an impoverished lifestyle in a small rural Chadian village by hearing a guest speaker talk about it at a banquet, reading about it in a book, or news magazine, or newspaper, or seeing it on television or a web site. Unless one is there to see it, smell it, feel it, hear it and taste it first hand, everything else is abstract.

These people had dreadfully little to survive on and worked unbelievably hard to provide enough to sustain their wife or wives, children and both the immediate and extended family members. Yet they had hope, perseverance, patience, and persistence. These virtues were the Chadian people's only personal assets for improving their quality of life.

Although Betty and I were Peace Corps Volunteers and were rather frugal and conservative in our personal life style among the Chadians, we had so much more. We had nice clothes to wear (work clothes, that is), a short-wave radio, both a wristwatch and

eye glasses, had the capability to buy food, owned a kerosene refrigerator, used cheap dishes and silverware, could afford to purchase a bottled gas stove, had a Petromax, possessed a table and
chairs, had the capability to get medical attention if needed (Peace
Corps nurse) and much more. Villagers perceived us as being
very, very wealthy. When compared to their meager standard of
living, they were correct. We were certainly very wealthy.

How does one cope with this kind of wealth within such an
impoverished society? Betty and I made every attempt by showing compassion, being sociable, asking their opinions, supporting
them, helping them help themselves, smiling and saying "*Lapia*"
("hello" in their native tongue) reflecting a positive attitude, causing them to feel good when they achieved a goal, being responsive
to their requests, and above all, treating people with respect and
dignity. Putting together all these traits over time, our relationship with the people of the village and surrounding communities
became affectionate and trustworthy.

Yes, there were times when we had to draw the line and make
hard decisions not to fulfill unreasonable requests simply because
we did not have the means to do it. For example, we were constantly being asked by beggars to give them money for food or
school charges or a funeral or a sick mother. To see their eyes
of hope resort to eyes of disappointment was heartbreaking. We
hated that gut feeling of refusing to help someone in need. We had
been taught to not give to beggars because it encouraged people to
beg as opposed to earning money. Generally speaking, the populace was not very proud of having beggars within their midst and
they discouraged children and adults from the practice of begging.
There were times when one could not turn away a person who
was truly impoverished and in need. Often Betty and I assisted in
one way or another. Betty would sometimes simply give a person
some food if they were hungry. There was a middle-aged man who
was born with deformed legs and could walk only on his knees. I
always gave him a ride in my car when I saw him walking in the

village or along the road. These people were the same as you and me and were trying to survive. There we were, among starving people and poverty, yet we had so much. What a dichotomy!

There was one trait we tried to avoid. Even though Betty and I witnessed poverty at its lowest notch on a daily basis, we toiled not to let the suffering and impoverishment affect our psyches. We did not allow our personal feelings to get in the way of making decisions. It would have prevented us from achieving our many Peace Corps successes.

Seeing people without food to eat and children with yellow-ish orange hair were a sure indicator of under nutrition. Diseased people were dying with no hope of recovery. People with sores on their legs grew worse because there was no medical treatment. Women were having babies in a cotton field, and then walking back to the village (fifty percent of babies born died before age five). More than once we saw people with river blindness being led by a small child. We saw people being brought out of the bush lying in an ox-drawn cart to the village infirmary, only to discover that there was no medicine or nurse. People were pleading with us to take their injured husband or child to a hospital. Neither Betty nor I can find words to adequately describe the degree of suffer-ing we witnessed daily. Yes, Bessada was the President's home village, yet the people endured the many trials and tribulations of life like any other rural villagers in the region. This is the reason Betty and I tried not to allow these daily observations affect us emotionally and psychologically. Yet, as hard as we tried, it did! Do not ever let anyone say that you can completely block out such wretchedness. "It just ain't gonna happen!"

60

Departing Chad

Betty and I had extended our stay in Chad for three months to enable us to complete our respective projects. We did not want to leave anything undone for fear it would never get done. It was 2 May 1973, when our flight was scheduled and it was time to pack our suitcases and make preparations to begin our journey back to Pennsylvania. As we were packing, Betty and I looked back on two years as Peace Corps Volunteers in Chad, Africa and we said, "What an experience to have had in one's life!"

We moved to the Baptist Mid-Mission Station and lived there during our last three weeks in southern Chad. When the time came for us to depart for Fort-Lamy, we drove to Bessada one more time to say our goodbyes to our friends and to wish them all the very best and to have a good life. Betty and I truly hoped and prayed that in some small way we contributed something toward improving their quality of life. The last person we saw as we drove off toward Koumra was Papa John. He was standing under the mango tree in front of our house as we waved and blew our horn. Papa John enthusiastically waved back to us and that was our last view of a village to which we had grown attached. We certainly enjoyed, cherished, respected and appreciated our relationship, which evolved with the Sara Madjingaye people.

Our last night at Koumra was at the Baptist Mid-Missions. That evening we said our goodbyes to the missionaries, staff and our friends in Koumra. Betty and I departed Koumra at 3:30 the next morning for a long grueling eighteen-hour drive to Fort-Lamy on rough dirt roads.

When we arrived in Fort-Lamy we had five days to complete our Peace Corps departure protocol. After we finished all of our business with Peace Corps, we began repacking for our journey to

Pennsylvania via Europe. Our flight did not leave Fort-Lamy until mid-afternoon so we went to the Peace Corps office to wait until the Peace Corps driver would fetch us to the airport.

Chad at that time of the year was in the throes of their dry season and people were starving. The U.S. government sent in several cargo planes loaded with grain for distribution to the Chadian people and there was a need to safely store it in a secure facility until it could be dispersed. It was mid-morning when a newly employed USAID official came to the Peace Corps office and wanted to know where the grain bins funded by USAID were located. I knew where they were and he asked me if I would show him before we departed. He promised he would have me back at the Peace Corps Office by 1:00 P.M. Let it be said that Betty was not a happy Peace Corps Volunteer when I agreed to accompany him. She was so afraid I would not get back in time and we would miss our flight.

The two of us left about 10:15 and it was at least a forty-five-minute drive each way to and from the grain silos. Fortunately the road was good and we were able to make good time. When we arrived at the site of the Butler Grain Silos, my USAID friend was astounded that there was space to store enough grain to feed all of Chad for a month! All of these grain silos were empty. They had been built by USAID about three years prior to our arrival in 1971. Those Butler silos were virtually brand new and had never been used. There were long augers to move the grain from the bins to a truck or vice versa. In addition, there was a generator to make electricity for operating the facility. For all intents and purposes these grain silos had been built for storing grain to prevent starvation during times of drought. I do not have a clue as to why the Chadian government had not stored millet or sorghum in those silos as a grain reserve for droughts like the one they were experiencing in 1973.

After the site was located, the USAID official briefly examined the equipment. He decided that that facility was more than adequate to store American grain until it could be distributed. We began our return trip to Fort-Lamy so I could catch my flight. Betty was happy when I returned as promised.

Betty and I both had various emotions about leaving Chad. We had a concoction of both happy and sad feelings as we said our goodbyes. Many of the Peace Corps staff, volunteers, Chadian friends with whom we had warm relationships came to see us off. We knew that in all probability we would never see them again. At the same time we were anxious to continue on our journey to Europe where we would meet Betty's parents in Sweden. We planned to purchase a new car in Gothenberg and then travel throughout Europe for one month. We were also anxious to return to Ottsville, Pennsylvania to our farm, families, friends and Duchess the dog.

Helen Keller once said, "The world is so full of care and sorrow that it is a gracious debt we owe to one another to discover the bright crystals of delight hidden in somber circumstances and irksome tasks." Yes, the world is full of care and sorrow and those bright crystals of delight were certainly hidden as we said our goodbyes under such somber circumstances. Knowing the destiny for the people of Bessada and surrounding communities was bleak at best made us feel somber. Betty and I hoped and prayed that our endeavors one way or another improved the quality of life for people living in Bessada and surrounding communities. The only thing we took home with us was a trove of magnificent memories.

One half hour before we were to leave for the airport, a messenger from the U.S. Embassy arrived at the Peace Corps Office. He had a communiqué for Jim and Betty Diamond from the American ambassador. Betty and I were a bit perplexed for we did not know what this was about. The following is a copy of his communiqué:

American Embassy Seal

Embassy of the
United States of America
Fort-Lamy, Chad
May 2, 1973

Mr. and Mrs. James E. Diamond
c/o Peace Corps Headquarters
Fort-Lamy, Chad

Dear Betty and Jim:

Today is a date that I wish we could have somehow post-poned, for it marks the beginning of a period when Chad, the American Community in Chad, the Peace Corps in Chad and this Embassy must learn to get along without the Diamonds.

I cannot let you go, however, without putting into print the pride and satisfaction I personally feel in the achievements you both have accomplished during your years in Bessada. I know it will always be an equal and well-merited source of pride and satisfaction to you that your unflagging efforts to better the lot of thousands of Chadians who have already borne fruit. As I told you last evening, it is my firm intention to see that the great foundation you have laid will continue to be built upon. Just as soon as it is feasible the Embassy intends to arrange for the printing and distribution of the booklet through which we hope to keep spreading the Diamond gospel on better silage methods through this country. In this way we hope that your work can have a multiplier effect that will go on for generations.

From a personal point of view as well you will be missed by all of us in the American community in Chad. You have been the best sort of ambassadors our country can send out. Your professional attainments would never have been possible without the large addition of your warm, cheerful and generous natures. You have made the rest of us look good. You have given all of us, as Americans, real cause for pride in the friends you have made for the United States and for the boost you have given to the advancement of our objective in assisting this poor country in its development efforts. We know very well how uncomplainingly you have faced up to the many obstacles you found in your path. Your persistent but always tactful approach to people has impressed us all and has been an example for us.

On behalf of your fellow Americans in Chad I want to say how glad we have been to know you and how much we will all miss you. My wife joins me in wishing you, Betty and Jim, equal success and satisfaction in meeting the challenges you will face over your next horizon.

Sincerely,
Signature
Edward W. Mulcahy
Ambassador

61

Getting Readjusted

Both the Peace Corps Director and nurse advised us prior to our departure from Chad to begin preparing for a culture shock upon our return to the United States. We could not fathom how we could possibly have a culture shock going back to our home in Bucks County, Pennsylvania. We were away from our home for a total of twenty-seven months; it was not like we were gone for many years. Well, we were wrong! Yes, we certainly had a culture shock after we arrived home in June 1973, and it took six months for us to adjust to our own society and yet some of our sensitivities still exist today thirty-six years later.

One of the first things I wanted to do when I arrived home was to have a cold glass of whole milk and an ice cream cone. When we arrived at Doylestown, Pennsylvania from Philadelphia International Airport at 7:30 on a Saturday evening in June,

Betty's mother and father joyfully greeted us at their home. We would be staying there for the next couple of days. After visiting for a while, I said, "Let's call our dear friends Earle and Arlene Yerkes and go to the Milk House for a glass of milk and an ice cream cone." Earl and Arlene produced and processed milk on their dairy farm and sold it in their store called the "Milk House."

Earle was excited that we called and he said, "We're about to close, but you come on up, we'll be waiting for you." Betty and I drove to Pipersville to the Milk House. When we walked in we saw that Earle had already poured a cold glass of milk for each us. Oh my gosh! Did that cold glass of milk taste good! Then he scooped for each of us a huge ice cream cone and when I tasted that delicious ice cream, I thought I had died and gone to heaven. We truly had a wonderful time with the Yerkes family during those first few hours we were home and doing what I wanted to do first.

What a delight it was to once again be able to speak English. Although we were fluent in French, going into a store, visiting a friend, reading a newspaper, listening to the radio, watching and hearing television in English was such a relief to our psyche. Listening to the Sara Madjingaye or Arabic languages or poorly spoken French on a regular basis was a mental strain. We did not understand Sara Madjingaye or Arabic and we had to listen very keenly when the Chadians spoke French. French was not their first language and they generally were not very fluent in speaking it. It was such a relief for Betty and me to again hear our native language spoken!

We suddenly became very sensitive to how wasteful the American lifestyle is. It was incredible to realize how we waste our resources. Using paper cups, plastic plates, plastic forks, knives and spoons only once then throwing them away is inconceivable in a place like Chad. The items we throw away are such valuable possessions to Chadian villagers! We throw away paper bags, used furniture, clothing, buckets, newspapers, bottles, boxes, boards and so many other things. To this day when I look at the trash can in my home and office or what people place at the end of their driveways every week, I find the waste of our daily living appalling! I am very sensitive to what we throw away in a day's time, both at home, in the office and in the neighborhood.

One of our strongest impressions was the fact that nothing is wasted in Chad because there is nothing to waste. For example, we used to get the newspapers sent to us in Chad. I remember one morning when I was building a fire to boil our drinking water. Betty and I saw two young boys watching me start the fire with newspapers. We noticed a distressed look on their faces but they did not say anything. A couple hours later there was a clapping call at the door. Betty answered it and there stood the same two boys with two huge bundles of dried grass. As they handed them to Betty they said to her, "The next time you start the fire, use this grass and give us the newspaper." We abruptly learned from these two boys how important newspapers were for the people in the village. They were used for many things: for hats, wrapping food at the market and cutting out pictures to hang on their walls. They also hung newspapers in their doorways to keep out flies and they covered their children with newspapers at night to keep them warm. We knew a lady in Chad who was from England working on a sociological study of the Chadian people. She used to pay her houseboy with one page from a news magazine for drawing a bucket of water. The magazine cover was in color and a heavier paper and it was worth two buckets of water. We often would have empty tin cans. They were very useful to the Chadians. Betty knew the children would be waiting for them when she threw them away. Tin cans were used as cups, dishes and for making toys. We have pictures of children playing with toys made from old cans. One wastes nothing in a nation like Chad.

We remain disgusted at the amount of food that we see wasted in the United States in public school cafeterias, restaurants, hotels and homes. When we see food being wasted, we cannot help but think of all those people who yearned for a crumb or bite. We throw away so much! Shortly after we returned to Pennsylvania, we had dinner at a very exclusive restaurant with Betty's parents. When the waitress brought the check to our table, my father-in-law picked it up but only after I had accidentally seen the total. I was shocked! Later I said to Betty, "My God, we could have fed the whole village for a week for the $50.00 we paid for that one meal." Betty's mother replied, "Jim, you must quit thinking like that. You have to get used to our way of living again." She was correct but the guilt feelings still churned within me. As I went through the process of becoming accustomed to living within my own society, I realized over and over how much wealth we flaunt while Chadians scarcely can muster enough food for a day.

We have come to take for granted so many of what I now consider to be luxuries. It is wonderful to go to the sink and turn on the tap and have running water. It is so nice to be able to have a glass of drinking water from a spigot and not have to worry whether we would get amoebic dysentery. One cannot appreciate having a flush toilet until he or she must carry five-gallon buckets of water to flush a toilet for two years. The luxury of stepping into a hot shower each day to bathe is an extravagance that cannot be cherished until one bathes from a five-gallon bucket of cold water. We do not have to draw our water from a fifty-meter-deep, hand-dug well and boil it before we can drink it. Water in Pennsylvania is so plentiful most of the time and we need to be mindful of how privileged we are to have continual access to such an important resource.

As we began our life back in Bucks County, Betty certainly appreciated getting back to using her washing machine. Before she joined the Peace Corps, all she had to do was separate the clothes, place them into the machine with some detergent, push a couple buttons and let the work begin. In Chad Betty had to wash her clothes by hand in a medium-sized basin with water hand-drawn from the village well. She had to heat the water on a fire outside so she could do her wash in hot water. Then she would rinse the clothes and hang them on a clothesline to dry. The people in the village washed their clothes the same way except they did not use a clothesline. I had planted two wooden posts in the ground with a cross bar on top of each one and was able to attach three strands of rope for her to use. Women in the village used to walk by and watch Betty hang her clothes on her clothesline. They had never seen anyone hang clothes like that. The village women hung their wet clothes over bushes, a tree or on a hand-woven grass fence.

Life in Pennsylvania is so easy when compared to life in Chad. Flicking on a light and having electric light bulbs illuminating an entire room is such a spectacle that we take for granted! Now we realize what it is like to be without them. Each night in Chad we used kerosene-fueled Petromax lamps on a table when we ate our meals and to read. When we went to bed, we turned off the Petromax lamps and lighted lanterns to show us the way to the bedroom. In America electricity is used everywhere: to heat a home, operate an elevator, power electric stoves, operate stoplights at an intersection, run air conditioners, operate refrigerators and freezers, open a can with an electric can opener, operate electric tools, run milking machines on a dairy farm, operate trains— and the list of uses goes on and on. American life is so dependent on electricity. Without it over a large portion of the country for an extended period of time, the American people would find it difficult to muddle through daily living and working without electricity.

In our bedroom at Bessada, our mattress was filled with silk that had been removed from around the seeds of a kapok tree (*Ceiba pentandra*). The silk-filled mattress rested on top of wooden bed slats and was comfortable for the first six months. After that we felt the bed slats and our mattress of kapok silk was not as comfortable but we managed; we had no other choice. When we arrived back in Pennsylvania we truly appreciated our firm mattress and box spring.

The first time Betty went grocery shopping in Doylestown,

she was overwhelmed by the amount of food that was available on the shelves. She could purchase almost anything she wanted with the confidence that it was safe to eat. All of the food products were attractively displayed, some refrigerated or frozen, nicely wrapped, weighed, priced and placed in an organized fashion throughout a huge super market. She had a large grocery cart she could fill instead of having to carry her groceries. There was a cash register where everything she picked up was tallied; there was no bartering on prices. There were no flies covering the vegetables or fruits, especially the meats. There was no dust. There were no women sitting on the floor gossiping while waiting for a customer to purchase vegetables or fruit lying next to them. There were no goats, chickens, dogs or cows walking about in the grocery store. What a contrast to where she did her shopping in Chad.

When Betty went to the local village market, the women had their foodstuffs for sale in small lots on the ground. She had to barter the price for each small lot. There were no shopping bags or plastic bags; she always took her bag with her to the market. In a larger city like Fort Archambault, instead of the food being placed on the floor, there was a government-made sheltered building with shelved stalls in which women could place their food. In our village market some of the women sold peanut butter by the spoonful. Flies crawled all over the peanut butter display. Betty would pay one bartered amount for each spoonful, and she usually bought it all. Betty then took the peanut butter home and placed it into a pan and brought it to a boil to disinfect it from the fly contamination, dust, and handling. The peanut butter was actually quite good after the boiling. At a certain time of the year Betty was able to purchase shelled peas at the market. She bartered a price for each small pile (about a handful), and then she would buy several piles. She had to put the peas into her bag to carry them home.

Shortly before we returned home, the news media had reported a dire shortage of meat in the local stores throughout Eastern United States, including Doylestown, due to a butcher's strike. Betty walked to the meat section of the super market in Doylestown and found a large variety of meats. It was true that the beef and pork sections lacked the higher-priced cuts like steaks, chops and roasts. She did find ground meat, liver, heart, and some of the lower-priced cuts like shank meat and neck meat. There was plenty of poultry in the meat cases. People around her were complaining about having no meat readily available. Betty said to them, "This is more meat than I have seen in two years." Local beef in Chad was purchased early in the morning when a person butchered an older cow. One bartered a price for a hunk of meat, not a round roast or steak or hamburger. There were usually two prices, a lower price for the local people and a higher price for expatriates. We could only purchase a small piece of meat at a time because we had a very small kerosene refrigerator.

Each morning a man came through the village with a box tied to the back of his bicycle. The box was full of fresh fish covered with a wet burlap bag to keep them cool. The fish were caught early that morning in the Chari River. There was a fresh water fish called Capitaine (a.k.a. Nile perch), which was our favorite. Depending upon the size of the fish, we had to barter the price. Two or three times a week when this man passed by my cotton field, I negotiated a price for eleven fish, one for each of my workers. When it was time for their break, they would build a fire and placed their fish on it. The fish were not cleaned (scaled or gutted), as we would do here in America. After the fish were roasted, they ate everything except for the scales, including the heads and bones. My workers claimed the fish eyes were good for your health.

Chickens were always purchased alive because there was no refrigeration to keep them cool. They were brought to the market tied to the top of a bus or truck passing through the village or tied to the back of a bicycle or on the side of a donkey. Poultry was a favorite food for Chadian people.

Sheep and goats were bartered from farmers who had them

for sale. Mutton (aged sheep meat) and chevon (goat meat) was a favorite food for Muslims especially during celebrations at the end of Ramadan. They roasted a whole lamb or goat stuffed with couscous, tomatoes, onions, and lots of pili pili (very, very hot peppers) in a beehive oven. This was a very tasty meal if one liked highly spiced food. Personally I liked both the chevon and the mutton prepared this way.

Gasoline stations were very plentiful in Pennsylvania. When we returned home, we truly appreciated that we could drive up to a gasoline pump and find that the establishment was actually open for business. Furthermore it actually had gasoline to sell. I am being a bit cynical, since this was not the case in Chad. There were times when we traveled by dirt road 120 kilometers to Fort Archambault to buy supplies and we had to wait two or three days to go home because there was no gasoline in town. If there was gasoline, often there was no electricity for pumping the gasoline. One had to use a hand pump. In addition to filling my car, I filled a fifty-five-gallon drum and five jerry cans with gasoline. This would be enough to last about a month. There was no place within 120 kilometers where I could purchase it, so I had to keep a supply at home. If something would have happened to cause my little car to catch fire while transporting gasoline to Bessada, it would have blown us sky-high. We tried to not let people know we kept a supply of gasoline at our house because everyone would have wanted to purchase it from us or have it given to them. I selfishly would not sell it or give it away because it had been too risky and dangerous to carry it all the way to Bessada. Furthermore, I did not have the time to be running back and forth to Fort Archambault to fetch gasoline for someone else.

Riding on paved roads in Bucks County suddenly became a luxury. There were no paved roads in Chad. Driving on a smooth road was such a joy when one did not have to watch for cows, goats, sheep, donkeys or wild animals suddenly dashing in front of the car. In Chad animals were always on the road, especially at night. I felt safe driving on a road where everyone (well, almost everyone) obeyed the rules of the road. One does not have to give way to huge oncoming trucks whose drivers usually refuse to move their rig to their side of the road.

Walking on a sidewalk in Doylestown was suddenly converted into a special treat. There are no sidewalks in the Chadian towns. In Chad one walked on the side of the road and when it rained, the roads were muddy.

Calling friends and family on the telephone anywhere in the United States was just great! We had not talked on a telephone for more than two years. There were none in Chad except within Fort-Lamy, the capital city. The only way we could get a message through to Fort-Lamy from Koumra was by short-wave radio at the Baptist Mid-Mission Station if they could make contact at all. Every morning a missionary communicated at 8:00 with another missionary in Fort-Lamy. If we or another Peace Corps Volunteer had an emergency, the only way we could communicate with the Peace Corps Office was by way of a missionary using the radio. We could send letters by way of the post office to the Capitol but it would take two weeks for a letter to reach Fort-Lamy. Once I was able to send a telegram from Koumra to my parents in Pennsylvania to wish them a Merry Christmas. In Fort-Lamy those who had telephones in their homes or offices could talk only within Fort-Lamy. The government did not yet have the capability of making telephone calls to towns or villages within Chad or internationally at that time. Cell phones had not yet been invented.

Our most frustrating experience upon returning home was that we were bubbling over with the fantastic experiences we had had: not only living and working in Chad but going on a Chadian hunt, visiting the pygmies, crossing the Congo River, spending three days on the Congo River in Zaire and other exciting adventures. We wanted so badly to tell our story, but nobody in my home area in southwest Pennsylvania seemed to give a damn. They were more concerned about their arthritis, whether their car ran, their insurance rates and their own little menial problems within their little sphere of existence in Fayette County, Pennsylvania. When we visited my parents for the first time after returning home, the hot item in the news in the Fayette County region was a few instances of cattle rustling. My father and brother were more concerned about cattle rustling than about our return home and learning about our experiences in Chad. Betty and I had devoted much time to putting together a slide presentation reflecting our Peace Corps experiences for my family members. My mother invited my brother and his family and my aunts and uncles to come to their home to view the slides. While Betty and I showed and described the slides, they carried on their own conversations and paid no attention to what was being said. Betty finally said, "Jim, let's put these slides away. These people are not interested in what we have to say." They just did not seem to care about what went on outside their boundaries. This intolerant attitude was very frustrating and disheartening to us. We surmised that they could not relate to what we were saying. St. Augustine once said, "The world is a book, and those who do not travel, read only a page." The message in St. Augustine's quote is the reason we experienced frustrations when we tried to tell our story of Chad to family.

On the other hand, there were several groups of people in Eastern Pennsylvania who had a completely different attitude and wanted to hear our story. Betty and I were invited to present our slide program featuring our Peace Corps experience 117 times over a three-year period. We spoke to groups as small as ten and others as large as 450 from central to eastern Pennsylvania to Florida. We spoke to youth groups, garden clubs, banquets, annual meetings, senior citizens, service and farm organizations, college classes, radio, television and other innumerable groups. It was always so nice to be able to talk with people who had an interest in and appreciated what we had to say, what we observed, what we felt, and what we learned. Betty and I had an amazing experience and we needed to share it.

303

It is interesting that since having our international experiences, it seems that we now tend to surround ourselves with people who have also had international experiences. We seem to enjoy and appreciate discussing thoughts, beliefs, concepts, theories, comparisons, and knowledge that evolve from these experiences. They too have experienced similar disheartening frustrations upon their return among their own friends and families.

Our border collie dog Duchess was kept by our tenant Dave Nagorski at our farm during our absence. Once we sent a tape-recorded message to Betty's parents describing our activities. They took the tape to the farm and shared it with Dave and his wife. While Betty and I were talking, Duchess recognized our voices and excitedly ran all over the house looking for us! When we arrived at the farm in late June 1973, Duchess did not recognize the car we were driving and she ran across the lawn barking ferociously at our new car. When I stepped from the car I said, "What's the matter, girl?" She immediately recognized my voice and we thought she was going to turn herself inside out rolling around on the grass and jumping on us. Duchess was just as excited to see us as we were to see her. She was very, very good at working sheep. I could do more with Duchess while working a flock of sheep than if I had four or five people helping me. Talking to her was like talking to a human being while we worked the sheep. It did not matter how many were in the flock. Betty and I went for a walk down the road to look over the farm and of course Duchess accompanied us. On the way back I said, "Betty, let's see if she still remembers my command." I said to Duchess, "Go get-em girl!" Duchess took off like a bullet the way she always did. At the fence she stopped, looked back at me as if to say, "Look you dummy, there are no sheep in that field." She remembered her training! We truly appreciated having Dave Nagorski look after her during our twenty-seven-month absence.

Another thing we take for granted is being able to go to most restaurants and not have to worry about making sure the food, especially the meat, is well-cooked so you do not get tape worm or dysentery. It was so nice to go to a bar for a beer and not have to cover my glass to keep the flies out. Here in Pennsylvania we can be reasonably sure that foods are properly prepared and safe to eat.

It is the small things in life which we take for granted that count. Yes, we missed our comforts. We learned to appreciate a lifestyle that was certainly different from what we were accustomed. We found it easier to adapt to a lifestyle in Chad than it was to readapt to our lifestyle in Pennsylvania.

62

Modus Operandi

"Helping people help themselves" was the basic underlying philosophical foundation for carrying out my international projects and programs in Chad. People in Chad tended to have, in varying degrees, an interwoven ethnic and national pride, which was characterized by cultural dignity and personal integrity. Regardless of what stage of development this nation had reached, its people had their pride, dignity, and integrity. Constantly providing the populace in up-and-coming nations with charitable bounties from more affluent nations results in destroying these qualities and engenders a feeling of a welfare state. Donor nations that design projects and programs aimed at helping people help themselves can reinforce and instill this pride, dignity, and integrity.

To achieve this end, three essential functions must be addressed. First is identification of talents and skills that exist within a society. These talents and skills are already in place and are being passed on from one generation to another because they have helped the society survive for hundreds of years. These time-seasoned, inherent capabilities are an integral part of a culture and can often be incorporated into a well-planned development project. Innovative use of these abilities can promote the acceptance and effectiveness of introducing modern agricultural concepts. By identifying and fusing such talents and skills into a plan of work, modern concepts can become more palatable to the populace.

Second is identification of natural resources that exist and are readily available. Regardless of the resources, whether they are water, soil, trees, mud brick, people, tools, animals, grass, rocks, bamboo, or a combination of several resources, project goals should be aimed at using these reserves instead of relying on imported resources foreign to the populace. Such natural resources are already an integral part of the culture, are accepted by the populace, and will be available long after funded projects by donor nations have been phased down. Dependence upon non-manufactured or manufactured resources from outside the culture (e.g. Yugoslavian gift of a tractor and farm equipment) can seriously stifle or suppress the intended long-term effectiveness of a project.

The third function is to introduce modern agricultural concepts by using intrinsic talents and skills already in place and available natural resources. Such concepts should address the felt needs expressed by a nation's populace (e.g. making silage, trimming hooves on horses, baking bread).

This is where the agricultural technicians, specialists, and educators from donor nations might fit into a scenario. They should be capable of transferring modern technology and concepts to people in a way that would reflect relevancy to their expressed needs. The probability of having an impact should be greater when local skills, talents and natural resources are manipulated into development project goals of donor nations.

When a change occurs within a society, varying degrees of resistance can be expected. If the goals and objectives of a project

306

are to be achieved effectively within a reasonable time and with minimal cost, every attempt to keep the anticipated resistance to a minimum (e.g. keeping the village chief informed) could benefit the recipients.

Education cannot be forced upon people; they must have a felt need and look with trust and approval upon those who attempt to give it expression. It must address expressed needs and blend into cultural mores. It is crucial that modern concepts not compete with or replace traditional practices in a culture but should be added to the culture for consideration, acceptance, and ultimate implementation by those having the expressed need (e.g. using a long handled hoe).

63

So Do You Want To Do What You Have To Do?

Many times I have advised students who aspire to seek an overseas employment experience. To each one I would say, "To qualify for working with people in cultures different from their own, the student must in all honesty have these three qualifications:

1. **One must like people.** A goodhearted person must view people as human beings, without the influence of judgment or preconceived opinions or bias toward other human beings. One must not judge people based upon whether they are poor or rich, well-educated or not educated, poorly or nicely dressed, have a different skin color, speak a different language or any other variable.

People in other societies must be received, appreciated, respected, and cherished as they are.

2. **Be able to get along with all kinds of people.** When working with people in other cultures, one must be able to get along with all kinds of people. These people may be different in religious or philosophical viewpoints. They may be members of political parties or support governmental regimes that are different. Those who are less affluent will be envious of you because they perceive westerners as being wealthy. Compared to the economic standards of people in many countries around the world, you are perceived to be very wealthy simply because you have a wristwatch, eye glasses or wearing nice shoes, pants and shirt. Cultural differences are sensitivities that can jeopardize the image local citizens have toward their expatriate guests if cultural traits and traditions are not respected. These disparities are grounds for developing relationships with people in other lands. Thinking logically, being creative and diplomatic with words, deeds, actions, manners and respect are paramount.

3. **One must have a benevolent feeling of wanting to help people help themselves.** That feeling evolved within me while doing my undergraduate studies at Delaware Valley College. To grow a society's rural economic progress, one must possess a driving force from within to "want" to assist those who are less fortunate. As I began my career during the 1960s, that feeling grew stronger and stronger until it became a passion which I ultimately had to satisfy, and I did it. Before goodhearted expatriates can help people help themselves, they must first learn about the people who are to be helped and build upon the knowledge and skill base already in place. While implementing a project, I always felt that my duty and responsibility was to "plant" ideas within the leaders of the people and then remain in the background and cause "their" idea(s) or concept(s) to evolve successfully. It is always better to allow your colleagues to be perceived by peers as persons in charge and organizers. When project goals are achieved, it should

308

make no difference whose idea(s) it was or who gets credit. The mission is to help people help themselves. If the mission to help people were achieved without accolades, then the endeavor(s) came from the heart.

If a person can say "yes" without a shred of doubt, he or she possesses all three of these qualifications, then additionally they must also possess these three virtues:

1. **Patience.** The term patience can be defined as the ability to tolerate being hurt, provoked or annoyed. A patient person endures waiting for delays, without becoming annoyed, upset or losing one's temper when faced with difficulties. A Chinese proverb says, "Patience is power; with time and patience the mulberry leaf becomes silk." To make my point, so often after a long days work, one steps back and asks, "Just what did I achieve today?" Or after one year of endeavors to meet the perceived needs of villagers, one steps back and asks, "Just what did the people achieve this year?"

So often there is simply nothing tangible to observe to make one feel that something was accomplished. During one phase of my career, I was a professional sheep shearer. At the end of the day I could count how many sheep I sheared. That was something tangible. However, what educators usually achieve in the short term is intangible. Tangible results may not be seen until years later and more often, never. Hence, formal and non-formal expatriate educators are powerful in the sense that they can shape and mold their clientele to become contributing members of society. This in turn enhances the quality of rural lifestyles. With time and patience, educators can shape and change people by what was said, how it was said, when it was said, why it was said, how the expatriate dressed, their associates, behavior patterns, mode of transportation and where the expatriate educator is seen after working hours.

All of these variables and others influence clientele who look to expatriate educators with respect and as role models.

2. **Persistence.** The term persistence can be defined as the quality of continuing little by little despite tribulations or hindrances. When working in a society where resources are scarce or non-existent, expatriates must cope with people who have different customs and traditions. Completing a job within a reasonable time frame is not a priority. There is no money to pay salaries. There is no money for repairs or purchasing parts or replacing stolen equipment. One must continue to steadily make every attempt to be resourceful and creative to overcome such tribulations for the good of the people. This is an essential virtue because without it, these obstacles can certainly demoralize those who devote their time to help others.

3. **Perseverance.** This is how I define perseverance: "Never Give Up!" There are bound to be trials, tribulations and hindrances which one will endure when serving a long period of time in another country (e.g. Peace Corps Volunteers, missionaries, NGO Project Teams). Perseverance means being adamant, stable and continuing the endeavors that lead toward achieving goals. When one stands by what he or she believes over a long period despite difficulties or setbacks and never gives up, that is perseverance. Always remember, when working in or visiting another country, you are a guest of that country. One needs to learn to work within the parameters established by the host(s). To be effective, patience, persistence and perseverance are essential for expatriates living and working with people in different societies.

A hymn that is often sung in my church best summarizes the inner feeling which drove me to devote (after my two years in the Peace Corps) more than ten years of my career working overseas helping people help themselves. It is the refrain of E.W. Blandy's hymn entitled "Where He Leads Me":

Where He leads me I will follow,
Where He leads me I will follow,
Where He leads me I will follow,
I'll go with Him, with Him all the way.

These words seem to have put my inner desires into perspective as I look back on that formative time of my life and the years that followed.

If one can look within himself or herself and find these qualifications and virtues, then I say to them, "Go for it by following this formula: BS + WE + IE + LS + MD = IC." This formula was developed by the author and has been endorsed by the World Bank, United States Agency for International Development and Food and Agricultural Organization of the United Nations. The following describes the functions of the formula:

BS =   Bachelor of Science degree in one of the agricultural sciences. The greatest need on the international scene is agriculture. Finding Peace Corps Volunteers with an agricultural education and experience is difficult. There are many opportunities.

WE =   Work Experience. It is imperative that undergraduate students work part-time during their academic years and full-time during the summers to acquire agricultural experiences they can fall back on overseas. After graduation from college, the candidate should work full-time for one to three years to acquire work experience, life experience, maturity and pay a portion of their academic debt.

IE =   International Experience. Join the Peace Corps! This is the kind of experience that agencies and corporations prefer. Traveling to London and living in a four-star hotel, eating at upscale restaurants, riding on a bus touring London to see Big Ben and watching the changing of the Guard are all interesting and fun, but this is not considered an international experience that prepares one to live and work overseas. Living in a rural village with the people, having no special privileges, speaking the people's language, developing personal relationships with the people, sharing their happy times, sad times, successes, failures, participating in their traditional dances and ceremonies, these are the kinds of experiences which enables one to understand and appreciate the traits of another culture.

LS =   Language Skills. Allow Peace Corps to teach the language skills. They have a very effective system of teaching languages. If one has a choice, it will be to their professional advantage in the long run to learn one of the five official languages of the United Nations: English, French, Spanish, Chinese, Arabic.

MD =   Master's Degree. Another step in this process is to acquire a master's degree. If one is clever, an interested candidate will inquire about the opportunities that Peace Corps offers to volunteers, using part of the Peace Corps experiences for degree requirements. Otherwise one can select an institution of higher learning of choice to pursue the master's degree in an area of specific interest or need.

IC =   International Career. Now one is in his or her late twen-
            ties and is properly prepared to work overseas. A bach-
            elor's degree, work experience, international experi-
            ence, language skills and a master's degree plus being
            more mature and having life experiences are the kinds
            of credentials that international agencies and corpora-
            tions look for on applicant resumés. With these creden-
            tials one is well qualified to work effectively overseas.

Epilogue

I vividly remember when President John F. Kennedy was inaugurated as President of the United States of America in 1961 shortly after completing my studies at Delaware Valley College with a desire to enhance agriculture overseas. In his inaugural speech he issued a call to service to Americans with these words: "Ask not what your country can do for you, ask what you can do for your country." He revealed his vision by establishing the Peace Corps to promote peace and friendship throughout the world.

When JFK appointed Sergeant Shriver to organize the Peace Corps, there were three expressed goals that evolved:

1. To help country leaders in meeting their need for trained men and women.
2. To promote an understanding of Americans on the part of the peoples served.
3. To promote an understanding of other peoples on the part of Americans.

The men and women who serve as Peace Corps Volunteers reflect the rich diversity of the United States while at the same time sharing a common spirit of service, dedication, and commitment. They serve in their host countries for two or more years and often live in remote communities with the people. They generally are not given any out-of-the-ordinary privileges. Volunteers receive rigorous language and cross-cultural training to prepare them for becoming part of the communities where they live and serve. They learn to speak the local language and adapt to the

315

cultures and customs of the people with whom they work. Many volunteers work with teachers to improve the quality of education for children; they work with communities to protect the local environment; they create economic opportunities; work on health and nutrition projects to keep families healthy; they help people grow more food; they are there for instigating clean water programs in communities; they start new small businesses; they teach people how to curb the spread of AIDS; and they teach farmers approved agricultural practices. Their larger purpose is to work with people in other countries by helping them take charge of their own sustainability and futures. These exclusive programs and scores of others continue as I write this manuscript.

The Peace Corps fulfills its mission by sharing its citizens, our nation's most precious resource, with the world. Volunteer citizens have helped an immeasurable number of individuals who want to make progress by building a better life for themselves, their children and their communities. At the same time, Peace Corps Volunteers learn as much, if not more, from the people they get to know in their host countries. When they complete their service in the Peace Corps, thousands of returned Peace Corps Volunteers continue their good works by strengthening the American people's understanding of different cultural traits, customs, religious attributes, local traditions and physical characteristics of the countries they served.

We are ecstatic with what thousands upon thousands of Peace Corps Volunteers have accomplished since 1961 to improve upon the quality of life for humankind around the world. Paraphrasing President Kennedy, Betty and I are elated that we were able to "ask not what 'our' country 'could' do for us, but asked what 'we could' do for 'our' country." We are thrilled that we were two people among the thousands who have served our magnificent country by being Peace Corps Volunteers. I had this phenomenal journey because "**I did what I had to do.**"

As we look back at the incredible experience we had during our two years and three months in the Peace Corps, these lines are an attempt to put into perspective our first international encounter in a land far from home, Chad, Africa. While I had a strong, compelling desire to do agricultural work overseas, I simply cannot say why, but I do know that it truly existed. Nevertheless, that inner desire had to be fulfilled. Perhaps these lines can bring forward an explanation as to why those feelings existed for more than fifteen years.

The Toughest Job I Ever Loved

Why did you join the Peace Corps?
Don't ask me why I joined the Peace Corps, because I don't know why!
A deep intimate feeling that titillated a persuasive mandate to serve people less fortunate than I.
For what reason that feeling existed within, I simply don't know why.

The Peace Corps's *modus operandi* was extraordinarily apropos.
Helping people to help themselves blended tolerably with personal axioms of thought.
The Peace Corps's *modus operandi* was extraordinarily apropos.

Life in the bush was a humbling experience where one quickly learned to adapt and endure.
Living two years in the bush, yearning for running water and electricity, was a humbling encounter.
Boiling drinking water twenty minutes before filtering it was a necessary daily chore.
Life in the bush was a humbling experience.

Every day was chock full of opportunities to serve.
To serve people who struggled daily to overcome trials and
tribulations to survive.
Living in the bush was challenging, educational and eventful.
Every day was chucked full of opportunities to serve.

Surviving with the Sara Madjingaye, one of Chad's many tribes,
was the toughest job I ever loved.
Each day was a struggle, yet the Sara Madjingaye endured with
pride, dignity and integrity.
Surviving with the Sara Madjingaye people in Chad was the
toughest job I ever loved.

Why did I join the Peace Corps?
The Peace Corps's *modus operandi* was extraordinarily apropos.
Life in the bush was a humbling experience.
Every day was chock full of opportunities to serve.
Surviving with the Sara Madjingaye people in Chad was the
toughest job I ever loved.
That's why I joined the Peace Corps.
—James E. Diamond

318

References

Anderson, D. Craig. 1984. Agricultural Education: Definitions and Implications for International Development. *NACTA Journal*. Urbana, IL: National Association of Colleges and Teachers of Agriculture, Volume IIVIII, Number 2, June, pp. 34–36.

Ascroft, Joseph. 1978. Functional Education Programme, *ADAB NEWS*. Dharmondi, Bangladesh: Agricultural Development Agencies, Volume V, Number 3, pp. 6–7.

Diamond, James E. 1986. An Overview: Short-term Educational Consultants In International Agriculture. *NACTA Journal*. Huntsville, Texas: Sam Houston State University. Volume XXX, Number 2, June, pp. 53–55.

Diamond, James E. 1983. *Observation Training Tours*. Chapel Hill, NC: South-East Consortium for International Development, a final report, May, p. 1.

Diamond, James E. 1971–1973. Personal letters sent to author's parents and father- and mother-in-law: Mr. and Mrs. Earl F. Diamond and Mr. and Mrs. William J. Rohrman.

Riggan, John. 1973. Peace Corps Director, N'djamena, Chad: Peace Corps Office, a quote during a meeting with a cadre of newly arrived Peace Corps Volunteers, 29 April.

USAID. *Additional General Provisions*. 1981. Washington, DC: State Department, Form N, 1420–230, item IM, 10/81, p. 1.

USAID. *Additional General Provisions*. 1981. Washington, DC: State Department, Form N, 1420–23c, item ID, 10/81, p. 1.

Ngong-Massah, Edward N. (1982). *Communication Skills for Development Professionals*. Brookings, SD: South Dakota State University, unpublished paper submitted to the Department of Rural Sociology, March, pp. 35–41.

Notes

"Ensilage? What's That?" According to American missionaries at Baptist Mid-Missions in Koumra, the silage that was stored in pit silos survived much of the destruction in Bessada during a horrifying civil war in 1979. The silage was not destroyed because the rebels could not get to the buried silage quickly or easily. When the villagers ultimately returned to the village after the civil war, they were able to access their stored silage to feed their oxen.

President François Tombalbaye's National Arbor Week: According to Peace Corps officials and American missionaries at Baptist Mid-Missions in Koumra, Chad the President was able to get the Chadian Government to pass a bill in May 1973 declaring the second week of June as "National Arbor Week" for all of Chad.

Glossary

ablution block	a building housing both showers and toilets
Ag-Bag	trade name for long plastic disposable bags that are filled with chopped forage
Animation Rurale	French Extension System (Rural Training)
Animist	a religious belief that has little or no influence from modern day religions (e.g. Christianity, Judaism, Buddhism, Islam)
barrière de pluie	rain barriers that protect dirt roads by stopping traffic during rainstorms
BBC	British Broadcasting Company
BDPA	Bureau for Production Agriculture Development
beaucoup	many
beignet	deep fried dough dunked in sugar
bienvenue	welcome
bili-bili	a form of local beer made from sorghum
bonjour	good morning
bonne anné	happy new year

boule	Cooked millet that is dipped into vegetable or meat sauce
Bureau de Eau et Forêts	Department of Waters and Forests
Bureau de Transport	Department of Transportation
Boite Postal	post office box
browse	tender sprouts of grass that are consumed by livestock three to four weeks after the bush is burned
buck	male rabbit
café au lait	coffee with milk and sugar
calabash	a dried round gourd cut in half and used as a bowl for cooked or dry foods
cambium layer	a thin formative layer of cells between the xylem and phloem located under the bark of a tree and is where new cells originate
capitaine	(a.k.a. Nile perch) large fresh water fish
case	rectangular or round mud brick house
castrating a bull	the destruction or removal of the testicles causing male traits to diminish
case de passage	guesthouse
Quest-ce que c'est?	What's that?
CFA	Money used in Chad. It means Central French Speaking Africa (*Central Francophone Afrique*) and between 1971-1973 its value fluctuated around 12 CFA = US$1.00.

chef de village	(village chief) equivalent to a town mayor in USA
chefs d'quartier	villages are divided into quarters and each quarter has a chief who answers to the *chef de village*
chevon	goat meat
Cinva Ram Press	trade name for a steel box with a steel lid and false bottom plate attached to a long pipe-like lever and is used to press mud to make bricks
clapping call	when a person went to their neighbors hut, they clapped their hands because there was no door to knock on
combien	How much?
comby	pickup truck
cord	one-half hectare
counseleur diplomatique	diplomatic counselor
croup	rump of a horse
demi-john	wine bottle that holds four liters
directeur de	director of
Directeur de la Veterinaire, Region de Mopti	Veterinarian Director for Mopti Region
d'accord	okay
desertification	Harmattan Winds blow from the Atlantic Ocean across the Sahara Desert repositioning sand in a southerly direction toward where people live and produce their meager sustainable food crops

Director de lÉlevage	director of government sponsored livestock programs
doe	female rabbit
Donnez l'argent	give me the money
donnez-moi un cadeau	give me a gift
douane	customs at an international airport
DUMC	Doylestown United Methodist Church
eucalyptus tree	eucalyptus trees are fast growing trees that have a deep root system
Encarta® World English Dictionary	©1999 Microsoft Corporation. All rights reserved. Developed for Microsoft by Bloomsbury Publishing Plc.
faire la chasse	go hunting
farrier	a skilled person who trims feet on horses, makes, fits and attaches horseshoes on the feet of horses
Ferme d'état Samanko	Samanko State Farm
gee	horse command to go right
gendarme	a police officer in French-speaking countries
gestation	period of time a fetus is in the uterus of a female animal (conception to birth)
Gehl Chopper	trade name for a piece of equipment that is either pulled by a tractor or self-propelled to chop forages
giddy-up	horse command to go forward

Governor de Mopti Region	Governor of Mopti Region, equivalent to a state in USA.
grand marché	great market in Bamako, Mali
hectare	2.47 acres
Ingenieur des Institute Économique Rural	Coordinator of Rural Economics Institute
JFK	John Fitzgerald Kennedy, former President of the United States
kilometer (km)	.6 mile
kilogram (kilo)	2.2046 pounds
kindle	act of giving birth (rabbits)
Kob de Buffon	kob (*Kobus kob*) is an antelope that eats grasses in groups on or around wetlands found on Chad's savanna lands
lapin	French for rabbit
lapia ea-tow-cari wah	"Hello, how are you" in Sara Madjingaye language
litter	several offspring born at the same time from the same female rabbit
Madjingaye	(mud-gen-guy) the best or great in their local language
Mali Lait	Mali Milk
Malian Franc	money used in The Republic of Mali and in 1973 its value was US$1.00 = MF 50)
Marietta Silo	trade name for upright concrete slab silos seen near barns to store silage
merci beacoup	thank you
mutton	aged sheep meat

New Zealand White	breed of rabbits with white hair coat
NGO	Non-Government Organization
on doit avoir une raison d'être	one must have a reason to be
ONDR	*Office Nationale du Development Rural*, Office for National Rural Development
patron	boss
parturition	generalized term for the act of giving birth to offspring
petit déjeuner	breakfast
petrol	gasoline
Petromax	a kerosene fueled lantern that had netting over a lit flame that glowed white and gave off much light in a darkened room
pirogue	hand hewn canoe from a log
polder	manmade dams to stop water flowing from Lake Chad into inlets during the rainy season
Préfecture	equivalent to a state in USA
Présidence	equivalent to the White House in Washington, DC
san du riz	by-product of cleaning process of rice
Sara Madjingaye	the largest of the sara sub-groups (tribe) of people in southern Chad
secca fence	woven grass that is used as a fence around huts
seedlings	young trees less than one year old

shaman	a person who works with magic to cure sickness, cast spells upon people or animals, and for a fee can remove spells cast upon people
silage	forages converted into a succulent feed through the process of fermentation to preserve nutrients and the fodder for ruminants
singletree	a sturdy wooden bar that has a ring on each side attached by a short chain to each side of the harness on a horse and a ring in the center that is attached to a horse drawn implement (i.e. cultivator)
soirée	reception or party
Sous-Préfet	equivalent to a county commissioner in Pennsylvania
town crier	person designated to go into the village to shout out messages people need to know.
transhumance	seasonal movement of livestock under the care of herders.
travaux agricole	agricultural workers
UNESCO	United Nations Educational, Scientific and Cultural Organization
USAID	United States Agency for International Development
USIS	Untied States Information Services
VITA	Volunteers for International Technical Assistance
VOA	Voice of America

Vraiment	really
whoa	horse command to stop
whoa-haw	horse command to go left.
withers	ridge between the shoulder bones of a horse.
yellowish orange hair	sure indicator of under nutrition
Zaire	money used in The Democratic Republic of Congo (a.k.a. Zaire) and in 1972 its value was one Zaire = US$2.00